DATE DUE

JE 6 '07			
FE 1 2 09			

DEMCO 38-296

Francis Poulenc

Francis Poulenc. Collection Francis Poulenc. Authorization to reproduce this photograph granted by Rosine Seringe.

FRANCIS POULENC

A Bio-Bibliography

Compiled by
GEORGE R. KECK

Bio-Bibliographies in Music, Number 28
DONALD L. HIXON, Series Adviser

GREENWOOD PRESS
New York • Westport, Connecticut • London

Library of Congress Cataloging-in-Publication Data

Keck, George Russell.
    Francis Poulenc : a bio-bibliography / compiled by George R. Keck.
      p. cm.—(Bio-bibliographies in music, ISSN 0742-6968 ; no.
  28)
    Includes bibliographical references and index.
    Includes discography.
    ISBN 0-313-25562-8 (lib. bdg. : alk. paper)
    1. Poulenc, Francis, 1899-1963—Bibliography. 2. Poulenc,
  Francis, 1899-1963—Discography. I. Title. II. Series.
  ML134.P87K3 1990
  016.78'092—dc20   90-40200

British Library Cataloguing in Publication Data is available.

Library of Congress Catalog Card Number: 90-40200
ISBN: 0-313-25562-8
ISSN: 0742-6968

First published in 1990

Greenwood Press, 88 Post Road West, Westport, CT   06881
An imprint of Greenwood Publishing Group, Inc.

Printed in the United States of America

∞

The paper used in this book complies with the
Permanent Paper Standard issued by the National
Information Standards Organization (Z39.48-1984).

10 9 8 7 6 5 4 3 2 1

Contents

Preface

Francis Poulenc ranks among the most important composers of this century. Coming to prominence in 1920s Paris during a period of great social and cultural changes, he quickly established himself as one of the leaders of the avant garde. But he continued to compose long after the ."jazz age" twenties gave way to more serious concerns. Virtually all of his compositions were performed in public during his lifetime, most to critical acclaim, and nearly all have been recorded again and again by the best interpreters. His music continues to be performed in concert halls and on recordings.

Much has been written about this popular composer. One volume could not begin to cover all the material published about Poulenc and his music. I have, therefore, been forced to be selective. While the book does not include a complete annotated bibliography on the subject, material covering every development in the life and compositional career of Poulenc is included.

This book includes four main sections. The brief biography gives the pertinent facts of Poulenc's life and some analysis of his musical style. The works and performances section, classified by genre and then by title of composition, includes composition date, publisher, performance time, the person to whom the work is dedicated, and information about the premiere of each work.

Section three is a list of recordings that is highly selective, because an excellent Poulenc discography is available. (See the Introduction to the Discography section of this work for a complete citation and discussion of Francine Bloch's work.) I listed those recordings that are significant and for which there are reviews that add substantially to the literature on Poulenc. In addition, I updated Bloch's work by listing recordings issued after 1982. References are made to the reviews annotated in the bibliography section of this volume.

The annotated bibliography makes up a major portion of this book. The writings by and about Poulenc cover every phase of his career--biographical, musical, and stylistic. The annotations often quote from the published sources, especially in the cases of record reviews and reviews of live performances. Because there is so much published material, I presented only a selection in the annotated bibliography. But I included additional references in the works and performances and discography sections that the interested reader may consult.

Titles of all compositions are listed alphabetically in Appendix I and chronologically in Appendix II. A thorough index completes the volume.

Many individuals and institutions contributed to the preparation of this book. I express my deepest gratitude to the following: to Ouachita Baptist University for a Research Grant that allowed me to complete much of the research; to Sherrill Martin, Professor of Music, University of North Carolina, Wilmington, for reading the manuscript and for all her excellent suggestions and advice in the preparation of the final copy; to Mike Gray, Discography Editor, Greenwood Press, and Edwin M. Matthias, Recorded Sound Reference Center of the Library of Congress, for their help in the preparation of the discography; to the entire staff of the Performing Arts Division of the Library of Congress, Washington, D. C.; and to the staff of the New York Public Library. I am greatly indebted to Caroline Cagle, Assistant Professor of Computer Science, Ouachita Baptist University, for her help in preparing the computer-generated manuscript.

No words can express my gratitude for the help, advice, and support that I received from the staff of Riley-Hickingbotham Library, Ouachita Baptist University. I can merely state my thanks and list the names of those to whom I am indebted: Jean Raybon, Emerita; Ray Granade, Director of Library Services; Janice Cockerham, Assistant Librarian; Jean Rick, Inter-Library Loan; Jenny Petty, Periodicals Librarian; and Schelley Childress, Cataloger.

Above all I wish to thank Don Hixon for his advice and encouragement at every stage of the preparation of this volume. His contributions are so numerous that the work would never have been completed without his help.

Abbreviations

This list is arranged alphabetically by full title of the periodical.

AbH	*About the House*
ACR	*American Choral Review*
AMT	*American Music Teacher*
ARG	*American Record Guide*
AM	*Atlantic Monthly*
Au	*Audio*
BMI	*BMI, The Many Worlds of Music*
BP	*Boston Post*
BAM	*Buenas Aires Musical*
CMJ	*Canadian Music Journal*
Ch	*Chesterian*
ChJ	*Choral Journal*
CSM	*Christian Science Monitor*
Cl	*Clavier*
CRB	*Consumer's Research Bulletin*
Dia	*Diapason*
Emp	*Empreintes*
Fa	*Fanfare*
FeuM	*Feuilles musical*
GaM	*Gazeta Musica*
Gram	*Gramophone*
GC	*Guide du Concert*

HF/SR *HIFI/Stereo Review*
HF   *High Fidelity*
HF/MA *High Fidelity/Musical America*
HT   *New York Herald Tribune*

IM   *International Musician*

JMF   *Journal music française*

LJ   *Library Journal*
List   *Listener*

MensM *Mens en Melodie*
MM   *Modern Music*
MEJ   *Music Educators Journal*
MusE   *Music Events*
MusJ   *Music Journal*
MusL   *Music Leader*
ML   *Music and Letters*
MusM   *Music and Musicians*
MR   *Music Review*
Mus   *Musica*
Mu(Ch) *Musica (Chaix)*
MusO   *Musica d'Oggi*
MA   *Musical America*
MusC   *Musical Courier*
MusN   *Musical Newsletter*
MusOp *Musical Opinion*
MQ   *Musical Quarterly*
MT   *Musical Times*
MusB   *Musik und Bildung*
MusG   *Musik und Geschichte*

NATS   *NATS Bulletin*
NZM   *Neue Zeitschrift für Musik*
NYPN   *New York Philharmonic Program Notes*
NYP   *New York Post*
NYT   *New York Times*
NY   *New Yorker*
News   *Newsweek*

Ob   *Observer*
OpK   *Oper und Konzert*
Op   *Opera (England)*
OpC   *Opera Canada*
OpJ   *Opera Journal*
OpN   *Opera News*
OpW   *Opernwelt*

OeMZ   *Österreichische Musikzeitschrift*

RasM   *Rassegna Musicale*
Revue   *Revue des lettres modernes*
RM   *Revue musicale*
RMSM   *Revue Musicale de Suisse Romande*

SR   *Saturday Review*
SchM   *Schweizerische Musikzeitung*
SM   *Sovetskaya Muzyka*
StR   *Stereo Review*

TLS   *Times Literary Supplement* (London)

VV   *Village Voice*

WSJ   *Wall Street Journal*

Francis Poulenc

Biography

On January 23, 1920, an article by the French critic, Henri Collet, appeared in the journal *Comoedia*. Entitled "Les Cinq russes et les six français," the article brought wide public attention to a group of six young French composers that had begun to form in 1917 under the leadership of Erik Satie. Georges Auric, Louis Durey, and Arthur Honegger had been the first to join with Satie for performances of their music at the Salle Huygens. Soon after, Germaine Tailleferre became a member of the group; Poulenc returned in 1918 (His early association in 1917 was interrupted when he was drafted into the army.); and in 1919 Darius Milhaud completed the group, when he returned to Paris from Rio de Janeiro where he had been an attaché in the French Legation. Collet's article gave these young musicians not only public recognition but also a name--Les Six. They were quick to take advantage of the publicity and notoriety that followed.

The time was right for the formation of such an alliance in Paris. Stravinsky's *Le Sacre du printemps* had, almost literally, exploded upon pre-war Paris in 1913; dominance by the Impressionistic style of Debussy and Ravel was at an end; Satie was prepared to lend a guiding hand; and Jean Cocteau, literary spokesman for the band of musicians, was ready to create a public for their music.

The six young composers shared the spirit of a generation facing a new mechanistic world of machines and motion, of experimentation, of music hall and American jazz. They also shared an irreverence for the artistic conventions of the time. These forces shaped their music and gave them validity as a group. But they could not help but be influenced by their own cultural heritage as well. Each composer sought his own interpretation of that cultural heritage and his own understanding of the compositional process. These facts gave individuality to the accomplishments of each member of this loose federation. While each sought the common goal of a simpler, clearer, more direct means of musical expression, each pursued that goal in his own way.

The musical goals of Les Six and the friendship that existed among its members were ideal for nurturing the talents of the young Poulenc. Poulenc would undoubtedly have achieved success on his own merits as a composer, but his association with the poets, artists, intellectuals, performers, and members of the nobility who made up the circle gathered around Satie was an important influence on his early works, and Poulenc gained musical, intellectual, and social support from them. Poulenc's earliest pieces were performed on the concerts devoted to compositions by Les Six. The reviews gave him both publicity and a reputation as an "enfant terrible" of French music, a reputation that he enjoyed enormously.

While the group lasted for only a brief period of time, Poulenc maintained life-long friendships with its original members. When the composers went their separate ways, several continued to make important contributions to music--none more significant than those of Poulenc.

THE MAN

Francis Jean Marcel Poulenc was born in Paris on January 7, 1899. His mother, Jenny Royer Poulenc, was descended from several generations of Parisian craftsmen. She was well educated, an excellent pianist, a woman of sophistication, and thoroughly Parisian in her tastes and outlook. Poulenc's father, Emile, was also well educated, but shy and middle class in background and attitudes. The Poulenc family members, originally from Espalion, were devout Catholics. One of the composer's great-uncles, the Abbé Joseph Poulenc, was the curé of Ivry-sur-Seine. The Poulenc family was wealthy, its fortune secured when the composer's grandfather founded a pharmaceutical company still in existence today under the name Rhône-Poulenc.

Poulenc was educated in the best Catholic schools of Paris, principally at the Lycée Condorcet. From his mother he received his earliest musical training, when he began to study piano under her instruction at the age of five. Describing his mother's musical abilities, Poulenc remembered that she "had faultless musical taste and a most lovely touch."[1] At the age of eight Poulenc continued his piano study with Boutet de Monvel, a niece of César Franck. During this period he started to discover and explore the works of a wide range of composers, including the compositions of Debussy and Schubert. In 1915 Poulenc met the pianist Ricardo Viñes through a family friend. Viñes recognized Poulenc's great musical gifts and taught him piano, theory, composition, and music literature. Poulenc gave his teacher credit for forming his musical taste and critical judgment, and it was Viñes who introduced the young Poulenc to Satie, Georges Auric, and Jane Bathori, who had first sung the songs of Fauré, Debussy, Ravel, and Satie. Bathori proved to be one of the most ardent supporters of the young composers of Les Six.

In January 1918 Poulenc was drafted into the military. While he spent a brief period at the front, the war soon ended, and Poulenc served the majority of his military duty as a typist at the Ministry of Aviation, where he remained until his discharge in 1921.[2] During this period of military service, Poulenc continued to compose and from 1919 was able to participate in the musical life of Paris.

Hélène Jourdan-Morhange described the young Poulenc of this era as a "young boy who seemed--nose in the air, crew-cut hair, absent-minded and roving eyes--a schoolboy grown-up too fast." "How gifted he is, provided that he works," Ravel said of him.[3]

Even though Poulenc had already achieved modest success as a composer by 1921, he still felt that he needed additional study in composition. On the recommendation of Milhaud, Poulenc became a private student of Charles Koechlin with whom he worked until 1924. Also in 1921 Poulenc traveled to Austria with Milhaud. In Vienna they visited at the home of Mahler's widow, Alma Mahler, where they met Alban Berg and Anton Webern. They later visited Schoenberg at his home, where they performed their own works for him. The following year the two went to Italy for visits with Alfredo Casella and the young Italian composers, Malipiero, Labrocca, and Rieti.[4]

During the decade of the 1920s the reputation of Poulenc spread beyond the city of Paris, culminating in 1929 in the production of the ballet *Aubade* and the premiere of the *Concert champêtre*. For Poulenc the decade ended much as it had begun, when on December 11, 1929, Les Six met to celebrate their tenth anniversary. But for Poulenc, as for many others, the closing of the 1920s and the ushering in of a new decade would bring troubled times that would last until after the war.

Three decisive events influenced Poulenc during the 1930s. Although the crash of the American stock market in 1929 was not a severe financial blow to Poulenc, the lifestyle he and his circle had enjoyed during the 1920s changed drastically. The remaining two events greatly affected Poulenc's compositional career. The first of these was the beginning in 1935 of the composer's lifelong friendship with the singer Pierre Bernac, whom he had met several years before. Poulenc composed many of his songs for Bernac, and the two performed and recorded the songs of Poulenc and other composers on their extensive concert tours throughout Europe and in America.

In 1936 Poulenc's close friend, the composer and critic Pierre-Octave Ferroud, was killed in a particularly gruesome automobile accident. Poulenc received word of the accident while in the vicinity of the shrine of Rocamadour which housed a black wooden statue of the Virgin. Following a visit to the shrine, Poulenc's faith in his Roman Catholic heritage was restored, and he began work on the first of many religious choral works.

Poulenc enlisted at the beginning of the Second World War and was stationed at Bordeaux when the French signed an armistice with Germany. He spent the years of the German occupation from 1940 to 1945 in Paris and at his country house at Noizay, where he carried on his personal "resistance" through concerts given with Bernac devoted exclusively to performances of music by French composers. He kept the outside world informed about conditions in war-time Paris through Milhaud to whom he sent letters posted in Spain by those who escaped from France.[5] Poulenc also remained active as a composer during the war.

The years following the war remained a period of intense activity for Poulenc. He continued to compose, gave recitals with Bernac, and recorded his compositions and those of others, especially Satie and Chabrier. He often traveled abroad for concert tours and granted interviews for publication or for radio broadcasts. In addition, he wrote articles about his own works and about those of composers whom he admired.

Poulenc achieved a new level of success in 1947 with the performance of his first opera, *Les Mamelles de Tirésias*, starring the young and still unknown Denise Duval in one of the principal roles. This opera marked the beginning of Duval's professional association with the composer. She performed leading roles in each of Poulenc's operas, and the singer and Poulenc gave numerous song recitals together in Europe and in America.

In November 1948 the composer and Bernac were in America for their first concert tour outside Europe. They performed recitals of French songs in several cities, and Poulenc played the piano version of his *Concert champêtre* in New York. By the time he arrived in the United States, Poulenc was already well known as a composer and as a performer, and he was popular with both audiences and music critics. While in Boston Poulenc received a commission to compose a piano concerto for the Boston Symphony.

This first concert tour was such a success that Poulenc made several trips to America between 1948 and his death in 1963. He and Bernac returned in 1950 for a second American tour, and Poulenc played the first performance of the Piano Concerto in Boston.   The performers made their first recordings together for American record companies during this visit. From January through March 1952, they were again in America for a third tour, this time including South America.   Poulenc and Bernac did not again return together to America but continued to tour in Europe as a duo until their retirement in 1959.

This was, however, not the end of Poulenc's visits to America. He returned again in 1960 to accompany Denise Duval in a series of concerts. Their American debut occurred at Town Hall on March 10, 1960. His final visit to America was for the world premiere of *Gloria* by the Boston Symphony conducted by Charles Münch in January 1961. At this time he received a commission to compose a sacred work for the inaugural season of Lincoln Center.

In January 1963 Poulenc and Duval gave a recital in Holland. The composer returned to Paris on January 28.   On the twenty-ninth he phoned Duval to arrange a date for lunch but phoned again on the thirtieth to cancel the appointment. That afternoon, alone in his apartment, Poulenc suffered a sudden heart attack and died almost instantly. He left his affairs in complete order and no compositions unfinished. Following the performance with Duval in Holland, Poulenc had sent flowers to her room with a note:

> My Denise
> I owe to you my last joy.
> Your poor Francis[6]

Poulenc never married but, instead, devoted himself to a wide circle of friends, many of whom have written about the composer. Ned Rorem and others have pointed out the contradictions in his personality and appearance: dapper and ungainly; elegant clothes from Lanvin that were often unpressed; scrubbed hands with bitten fingernails; his physiognomy a cross between weasel and trumpet "with a large nose through which he wittily spoke." He is "witty and bright and religious and knows it," Rorem remembered.[7] The composer was tall and heavy with rugged features and enormous hands. Bernac stated that he had a complex, often contradictory personality, "a disconcerting mixture of cheerfulness and melancholy, seriousness and futility, triviality and nobility. . . . His mood could vary from one day to the next, even from one moment to another, for he was extremely sensitive and emotional, actually an anxious person."[8]

Poulenc belonged to the highest social circles in Paris but was acquainted with people from tradesmen to the nobility. He loved company and feared being alone. Corresponding with his friends constantly, he left many letters and often telephoned and wrote to one person in the same day. He loved art and knew personally most of the Parisian artists. His collection included works by Matisse (his favorite artist), Dufy, Picasso, Mantegna, and Zurbaran.

Poulenc was thoroughly Parisian. "Paris is the only place in the world where I can withstand deep sorrow, anguish or melancholy," he confessed.[9] He spent most of his life in the Paris apartment that his uncle, a brother of Poulenc's mother, had first occupied. Rorem described the quarters as a "sunny high apartment on the Luxembourg, with chairs of orange plush and squeaking floors."[10] The rooms were filled with vases of flowers that Poulenc loved and that he arranged himself.

And yet Poulenc could not work in Paris. He bought a country house at Noizay in the Loire Valley, where he composed and entertained his friends. At Noizay he awoke early in the morning and composed until noon, and then enjoyed himself for the remainder of the day. A gourmet cook, Poulenc did his own shopping, riding around the countryside on a motor scooter.

Was Poulenc homosexual? Sources are scant and information circumstantial. He did not marry and his many friends filled for Poulenc the place of the family he never had. Many of his friends mention that underneath Poulenc's apparent gaiety there lay depths of sadness, but the composer kept his inner life strictly private. One of the few documented references to Poulenc's sexuality is Rorem's remark, "As he's always been rather *le cher maître* in my eyes, I was chilled by his talk of sexual success."[11] Many of those with whom Poulenc socialized were openly homosexual. For almost thirty years he and Bernac were devoted friends, spending much of their time together (often in professional activities) and vacationing together for about a month each summer. But none of this answers the question.

James Harding finds in *Aubade* the revelation of Poulenc's sexuality:

The inspiration, that of Diana condemned to a life of chastity, leads Poulenc to write passages suggestive of a longing that will never be assuaged. This, in turn, may well reflect his own experience of life. We know that even Cocteau, the prince of love à la grecque, had one or two flirtations with women that verged on reality. There are no such events recorded in Poulenc's history. He was aware that his emotional make-up precluded marriage and a family. Like Diana, he sublimated his great reserves of warmth and affection. . . . If Aubade purports to be the story of Diana, it also tells us something about Poulenc.[12]

This question is important to ask, because Poulenc himself stated, "My music is my portrait."[13] Poulenc is one of those composers whose music faithfully reflects both the personality of the composer and the events of his life. For that reason it is necessary to understand the inner life of the composer and to what extent his compositions were influenced by his sexual nature. At this time it appears that that part of Poulenc's inner life had little if any affect on his musical life. Certainly the question lessens in importance in comparison with the influence of his association with Satie and Les Six on his early works, his religious experience at Rocamadour, and the influences of his associations with Bernac and Duval on his vocal compositions.

THE MUSIC

If the music of Poulenc is a reflection of the man, it is, like the man, full of contradictions and difficult to categorize. But Poulenc was lucky as a composer in that he found his style early in his career and never really changed. His style was formed under the influence of Satie and the other members of Les Six who professed antagonism to Romanticism and Impressionism and sought simplicity, clarity, and brevity of expression in music. Poulenc was influenced by music of the circus and music-hall with its breezy charm and easygoing rhythms. These characteristics, however, were balanced by a concept of lyric melody unequaled in the twentieth century.

He was acutely aware of the musical movements of his day and genuinely admired the music of many of his contemporaries. But he firmly believed that an artist must speak his own language. In reply to the question of whether music's future lay in a tonal or atonal direction, Poulenc wrote:

> There were one time three great cubist painters: Picasso, Braque, Juan Gris. About the same time there were likewise three great atonal musicians: Schoenberg, Berg and Webern. Cubism and atonality were for them a means of expression as natural as breathing. To make from cubism or atonality a system, is to make the whole world breath with an iron lung. For my part I refuse to submit to it.[14]

His first pieces were composed for the piano and were, Poulenc later admitted, inferior imitations of Debussy and Stravinsky. His first success came with the *Rapsodie nègre* in 1917. This piece exhibits several traits that are typical. Scored for baritone, piano, string quartet, flute, and clarinet, the work reveals Poulenc's early interest in unusual combinations of instruments and his lifelong interest in vocal music. Sequences of ninth chords, alternation of extremely fast and slow tempi, contrasts of musical character, clarity of texture, and emphasis on humor opposed to lyric beauty are standard characteristics in this composer's works. The successful premiere of the work attracted the attention of Diaghilev, Ravel, and Stravinsky, and the piece was published by Chester in London.

In a succession of short works, Poulenc refined his style following the premiere of the Rapsodie. Piano pieces, songs, a choral work for male voices, incidental music, and several sonatas were completed before 1924. "Music, it seems, flows from him like a natural river with a delicious ingenuity," wrote one critic.[15]

The first songs on poems by Apollinaire were set to music at Pont-sur-Seine in February 1919. Adrienne Monnier, Poulenc's friend and neighbor, sent to the composer a copy of the new edition of *Le Bestiaire* recently published with illustrations by Raoul Dufy. Poulenc was immediately taken with the poems and illustrations. In his musical settings Poulenc captured the mood of the miniature poems by simple direct means, exhibiting at this early stage of his career a melodic genius that he continued to explore in the more than one hundred songs he composed.

These six songs were the first of thirty-four poems by Apollinaire, one of the composer's favorite poets, that he set to music. Obviously the poems of Apollinaire spoke to Poulenc, and he found in this poet's works a tone that he described as both melancholy and gay, precisely the same contrasting qualities so often found in Poulenc's compositions.

Poulenc began composition of his first large-scale work in 1923. The ballet *Les Biches* is a suite of dances, each complete in itself, without a plot or scenario. Instead, sixteen female and three male dancers perform on the stage designed as a drawing-room containing a large sofa as the single piece of furniture. The work was commissioned for the Ballet Russe by Diaghilev and received its first performance in January 1924 with choreography by Nijinska and scenery and costumes by Marie Laurencin. Although the critics were not unanimous in praising the work, the ballet was an immediate success with audiences and remains one of the composer's most popular works.

In 1924 Poulenc began work on the *Poèmes de Ronsard*, five songs on texts by the sixteenth-century French poet. The next year he began composition of a second group of songs that were much more successful, the *Chansons gaillardes,* with texts on anonymous eighteenth-century poems. With their distinctive melodic lines, perfectly matched piano accompaniments, and precise setting of text to music, the *Chansons gaillardes* mark Poulenc's first mastery of the art song. In addition, the first performance of these songs marks the beginning of Poulenc's association with Pierre Bernac, who premiered the works in 1926. Poulenc's final efforts in this medium during the 1920s were the four songs comprising the *Airs chantés*. Although these songs have achieved critical and popular success, Poulenc himself severely condemned them in his *Journal de mes mélodies*, explaining that he had no gift for the paradox that he tried to achieve in this group.

During the 1920s Poulenc continued to compose piano pieces and chamber music. Reductions for piano solo of the Sonata for clarinet and bassoon and the Sonata for horn, trumpet, and trombone were completed in 1925. *Deux novelettes* was completed in 1928 and *Trois pièces* in 1929. For the latter work Poulenc reworked a "Pastorale" completed ten years earlier, wrote a "Toccata," and added a final piece entitled "Hymne," Poulenc's favorite of the three pieces. Also in 1929 Poulenc arranged the "Pastourelle" from *L'Éventail de Jeanne* for piano solo, composed the first of eight Nocturnes for piano solo, and completed the *Pièce brève sur le nom d'Albert Roussel*.

The Trio for Oboe, Bassoon, and Piano is the most successful of Poulenc's chamber works composed during this period. The two outer movements contain the typical grace, charm, and youthful high spirits of his early style coupled with great skill in dealing with the unusual combination of instruments.   The middle-movement Andante exhibits a new level of maturity in that it is melancholy in spirit and serious throughout.   The movement contains some of the most deeply moving music in Poulenc's compositions to that time.

Poulenc wrote that a turning point in his career came with his acquaintance with Wanda Landowska, who inspired him to write one of his most significant works.   Poulenc was introduced to the great harpsichordist in 1923, and she immediately suggested that the composer write something for her.   But it was not until October of 1927 that Poulenc began the *Concert champêtre*.   By the following August the piece was virtually complete, and Poulenc went to Landowska's country house at Saint-Leu to work with her on the final version, "measure by measure, note by note," not to change a single note of the melodic line "but to clarify the writing, to simplify the voicing."[16]

The work was influenced by the galant style of eighteenth-century French harpsichord composers.   Form in the three movements is free with little musical development but with several thematic links between the two outer movements. One of the most striking characteristics of the piece is the sudden alternations between hectic gaiety and deep melancholy.   This successful work is the first of five concertos all of which were influenced by the concerto of the French "concert" tradition rather than that of the symphonic and virtuoso Romantic concerto.

Poulenc's final large-scale work of the 1920s was the ballet *Aubade*, commissioned by the Vicomte and Vicomtesse de Noailles.   Poulenc conceived this work to serve as both a ballet or *Concerto choréographique* and as a concerto for piano and chamber orchestra of eighteen instruments. As is the case with the other ballets, the scenario was written by the composer.   And it is a scenario rather than a plot, for there is little development of a story line in the traditional sense.   The subject is Diana, condemned to eternal chastity.   The ballet opens in early morning as Diana, surrounded by her companions, rebels against her fate.   The companions present her with the bow that is her symbol as patroness of the hunt.   At first she rebels against this fate also, but eventually accepts her lot.   At the premiere Nijinska devised the choreography, and Poulenc himself performed the piano part.

The first year of the new decade was a meager one for composition.   The song *Epitaphe* on a text by Malherbe was completed, and *Les Soirées de Nazelles*, not finished until 1936, was begun.   The following year was as productive as 1930 was lean.   Poulenc turned again to the composition of songs on poems by Apollinaire, completing two cycles, *Quatre poèmes* and *Trois poèmes de Louise Lalanne*, a pen name devised by Apollinaire, who wrote the second of these poems while the other two are by his mistress Marie Laurencin.

In 1931 Poulenc also completed the *Cinq poèmes* on texts by Max Jacob, another poet for whose works he discovered an affinity.   Poulenc met Jacob in 1917 through their mutual friend Raymond Radiguet.   They immediately became close friends, but it was not until 1931 that Poulenc set to music the poems of Jacob.

Jacob's poems have been described as containing ingenuity and artifice, skill and a deliberate clumsiness, irresponsible high spirits and gravity, proseyness and sheer fantasy.[17] Apparently these same qualities applied equally to the personality of the poet, which may account for Poulenc's friendship with Jacob and his interest in setting his works to music. But the *Cinq poèmes* were considered by the composer to be essentially descriptive, and he treated them in that manner in setting them to music.

Poulenc turned again to the poetry of Jacob for texts for the secular cantata *Le Bal masqué* completed in 1932. The work is filled with wit and humor contrasted with lyric moments typical of Poulenc. The composer said that the "Finale" of this work is a portrait of Max Jacob as the composer knew him in 1920.[18] The "Finale" was immediately arranged for piano solo, and in 1952 Poulenc created a "Capriccio" for two pianos on selected themes from the work.

Poulenc composed a Sextet for piano and wind instruments in 1932 but re-wrote it in 1939, a year in which several other early works were revised. The Sextet follows the usual order of movements in Poulenc's chamber music, fast-slow-fast, and the piano dominates throughout. In this work Poulenc continued the stylistic approach of the Trio for oboe, bassoon, and piano coupled with the energy and wit of *Le Bal masqué*.

During the five years from 1930 to 1935, Poulenc composed much of his output for solo piano. Among these works are many of his finest compositions for piano, including ten of the Improvisations, six of the Nocturnes, and *Les Soirées de Nazelles* (a piece for which Poulenc had an intense dislike). But the composer himself has admitted that his works for piano solo are not always up to the level of his other compositions: "My compositions for piano solo are, alas, the weakest. . . . My piano compositions are perhaps too facile."[19] The best of the piano works, however, contain writing that is fresh, appealing, and inspired.

The compositions of the early 1930s mark the end of Poulenc's youthful period and reveal his search for new approaches and new directions. The beginnings of the stylistic characteristics of the mature songs can be heard in *Cinq poèmes* on texts by Paul Eluard. Poulenc stated that in these songs "the key begins to creak in the lock," that would open to him the door to the poetry of Eluard.[20] Poulenc met the poet at the end of the war through their mutual friend, Adrienne Monnier, and had admired Eluard's poetry since their first meeting. It was not until 1935, however, that the composer attempted to set this poet's words to music. In all, Poulenc set thirty-four of Eluard's poems, the same as the number of poems by Apollinaire that he gave musical treatment. The first performance of this cycle was given in 1935 by the composer and Bernac, to whom the work is dedicated.

The following year Poulenc began work on a new cycle, *Tel jour, telle nuit*. The cycle, completed in 1937, is a setting of nine poems by Eluard that continued to explore the new stylistic traits introduced in *Cinq poèmes*. Emphasis on lyric melody and on maximum expression in the piano accompaniment with the minimum of means characterize this style. The nine songs form a true cycle with numbers three, five, and eight serving as transitions between the more important songs. Poulenc was never more successful in bringing to life the imagery of the poetry nor in expressively uniting words, melody, and accompaniment. This cycle is one of Poulenc's masterpieces and, in addition, one of the masterpieces of song literature.

In 1935 Poulenc also composed incidental music for the play *La Reine Margot*. The music, based on sixteenth-century French dances, is scored for a small ensemble of instruments. In an arrangement under the title *Suite française*, this work became one of the composer's most popular compositions. In addition, Poulenc provided the song *A sa guitare* for Yvonne Printemps, who played the part of Marguerite Valois in the original production. Printemps sang the song with harp accompaniment.

In 1936 Poulenc began composing *Litanies à la vierge noire*, his first sacred choral work following the recovery of his religious faith. The text, set for women's or children's voices, was chosen from one of the recitations by a pilgrim to the shrine of the Black Virgin of Rocamadour. Harmonically the choral writing is dissonant, and the organ is used to punctuate the choral litanies in an antiphonal manner. The treatment is sophisticated and dramatic in character, and the work is intense but deeply pious.

More choral works followed--*Sept chansons* and *Petites voix* in 1936 and *Sécheresses* and the Mass in 1937. The *Sept chansons* were commissioned by the Lyons Choir and utilize five texts by Eluard and two by Apollinaire. This composition was begun after Poulenc had made a thorough study of motets by Monteverdi. Thus it was influenced by the a capella choral style of the French and Italian Renaissance.

The Mass was completed in 1937 at Anost, where Poulenc was on a summer vacation. The Mass is serene and simple in comparison with the extravagance of nineteenth-century religious music. The five sections of the Mass Ordinary are treated as five unified movements for a capella choir and soloists, and the music is conceived to illustrate the text rather than to glorify it.

Another major work of 1937 was *Trois poèmes*, three songs set to the poetry of Louise de Vilmorin. Introduced to the poetry of Vilmorin in 1936 by Marie-Blanche de Polignac, Poulenc wrote to the poet and asked her for additional poems. The two he received in reply were combined with the poem given to him by Marie-Blanche to form this cycle. According to the composer, "The poems of Louise de Vilmorin provide material for truly feminine songs. This is what delights me."[21] The poems inspired Poulenc to write music that is "romantic," almost constantly diatonic, with regular phrasing and meter.

Poulenc completed the Organ Concerto in 1938. The work is one of his most serious and significant compositions. Poulenc himself explained the nature of this concerto:

> The *Concerto pour orgue* occupies an important place in my work, alongside my religious music. It is not a "concerto da chiesa," properly speaking, but in limiting the orchestra to strings alone and three timpani, I made performance in a church possible. If one wants an exact idea of the serious side of my music, he must look here, as well as in my religious works.[22]

For inspiration Poulenc turned to the Baroque style of a Buxtehude fantasia, creating a one-movement form divided into several sections. There is little flashy, virtuosic writing for the solo instrument. There is, instead, an equal partnership between the organ and the strings. The work successfully juxtaposes diverse elements ranging from intimate lyricism to romantic drama. The Organ Concerto remains one of Poulenc's most popular compositions.

The year 1938 was again a productive one for writing songs, as Poulenc continued to compose songs for the increasingly frequent and successful Bernac-Poulenc recitals. Two songs on poems by Apollinaire, *La Grenouillère* and *Le Portrait*, and *Priez pour paix* were all completed in 1938. In addition, *Tu vois le feu du soir*, one of the two songs of the cycle *Miroirs brûlants*, was completed. During 1939 Poulenc revised and completed earlier works (*Les Biches* and *Sextuor*), completed the *Quatre motets pour un temps de pénitence* begun the previous year, and finished several new songs.

In spite of the difficulties endured by Poulenc during the war years, he continued to compose throughout the period 1940 to 1945. Each year he completed at least one major work and numerous smaller compositions. Several of the pieces composed during this period reveal Poulenc's reactions to events of the war. During the summer of 1940 while France suffered several tragedies, Poulenc began work on a new ballet completed in 1941, *Les Animaux modèles*. Poulenc wrote the scenario himself, choosing six fables from those of La Fontaine. The score, like that of *Les Biches*, is in the form of a suite of dances. Unlike *Les Biches* the mood of this ballet is totally serious. In order to heighten the symbolism, Poulenc portrayed the animal characters of the fables as humans in human situations. In "The Grasshopper and the Ant," for example, one character is a famous dancer past her hour of success who seeks help from a childhood friend, now old and wealthy. Poulenc himself supervised the production at the premiere of the work at the Opéra in August 1942.

The most important songs composed during this period are the five songs of the cycle *Banalités* on poems by Apollinaire composed in 1940 for Bernac. The songs contrast beautiful, lyric melody in three of the songs with popular song styles in the remaining two. The songs do not form a true cycle, as the poems have no connection with each other and neither does the music. Poulenc's settings show his ability to adopt varied musical styles to express the sentiments of each text.

The composition of *Banalités* brought to a close the intense interest in song writing brought on by Poulenc's association with Bernac. In 1941 Poulenc composed no songs (he started work on *Montparnasse* but did not complete it until 1945), and in 1942 he finished only the six settings of poems by Maurice Fombeure called *Chansons villageoises*. In 1943 Poulenc turned again to song composition, completing settings of two poems by Louis Aragon and three songs in the cycle *Métamorphoses*. No solo songs were composed in 1944, perhaps because Poulenc was involved in a new project that required all his attention.

During the summer of 1944 Poulenc stayed at Noizay, where he began work on the two-act opera, *Les Mamelles de Tirésias*, using as a libretto Apollinaire's surrealist play of the same title. Poulenc considered setting the work in the late 1930s but postponed beginning the composition. Anticipating the end of the war and a return to his normal activities, Poulenc composed this joyful and tuneful score in only six short months from May to October, but the premiere of the opera did not take place until 1947.

Les Mamelles de Tirésias was composed after Poulenc had mastered the art of song writing and at the beginning of his compositional maturity. The opera is, therefore, one of his most successful works for the stage. Stylistically, the work is in the French comic opera tradition with influences from Chabrier and Ravel and with additional influences from popular music. Poulenc gives structure to the scenes through a series of songs strung together with spoken dialogue and occasional recitative. Each act ends with a large ensemble finale. While there are comic elements, the opera never descends to slap-stick and succeeds in being both funny and beautiful. The music contains elements of Poulenc's earlier style, but it also contains new ideas that become standard in his later works. Poulenc confessed a particular fondness for this opera. And, indeed, it is one of his most important works, occurring at the juncture between the early compositions and his mature period.

During the war years Poulenc composed several choral works, including *Exultate Deo* and *Salve Regina* (1941), *Figure humaine* (1943), *Un Soir de neige* (1944), and *Chansons françaises* (begun in 1945 and completed in 1946). *Figure humaine* is certainly the choral masterpiece of this period, and Poulenc himself believed that the piece was one of his most successful compositions. Written during some of the darkest days of the war, it is an imposing and difficult work with the pessimism of the first two-thirds of the work leading to a powerful and optimistic conclusion. The piece is a cantata in eight sections on texts by Paul Eluard and is scored for double mixed chorus a capella. *Un Soir de neige*, although on a much smaller scale, is an equally successful work and recalls in style and treatment of text its antecedent, *Figure humaine*.

Between 1945 and 1950 Poulenc composed over one-fourth of his songs, completing twenty-six songs during this period. These include the two cycles *Calligrammes* (1948) and *La Fraîcheur et le feu* (1950). The seven songs of *Calligrammes*, set to texts by Apollinaire, are Poulenc's farewell tribute to the poet:

> For me it represents the culmination of a whole range of experiments in setting Apollinaire to music. The more I turn the pages of his volumes, the more I feel that I shall no longer find what I need. Not that I like the poetry of Apollinaire any less (indeed I have never liked it more), but I feel that I have drawn from it all that is suitable for my purposes.[23]

Nevertheless, Poulenc set two additional Apollinaire texts, *Rosemonde* (1954) and *La Souris* (1956).

Calligrammes is a true song cycle with an overall plan of tonal relationships, alternation of moods, and a piano postlude. In addition, the piano accompaniments exhibit a new degree of subtlety. *La Fraîcheur et le feu* is an even more closely integrated cycle with the same characteristics of *Calligrammes* but with the additional device of repetition of the opening piano motive at the end of the last song. The seventh song of the set recalls the opening in key, mood, and tempo. This cycle is a complex, difficult work and a fitting close to a period of intense song composition.

During this period Poulenc completed his only symphonic work, the Sinfonietta (1947). Some of the themes for this piece were taken from the String Quartet completed in 1945 and discarded in disgust after only one performance. The Sinfonietta is one of Poulenc's more Romantic scores. It contains the usual contrasts of character with moments reminiscent of *Les Biches* on the one hand, and on the other, long, lyric lines influenced by the vocal works of the period.

Other works completed during this era include *Quatre petites prières de Saint François d'Assise* (1948), a Sonata for cello and piano (1948), the Piano Concerto (1949), and the *Stabat Mater* (1950).   The Piano Concerto was commissioned by the Boston Symphony Orchestra and received its premiere in Boston in January of 1950 with Poulenc as piano soloist.   The piano is not treated as a virtuosic solo instrument in the Romantic manner, but there is great beauty and interest in the thematic material, particularly in the first two movements.   The final movement quotes Foster's "Old Folks at Home," the composer's tribute to America, the country that Poulenc believed "at present, contains my greatest and most loyal audience."[24]

The *Stabat Mater* is Poulenc's first religious choral work with orchestra. The styles and techniques that he developed here serve as a model for the later choral works and for sections of *Dialogues des Carmélites*. The twelve sections contrast with each other in mood and tempi, but the slow movements, in which lyric and harmonic beauty are emphasized, carry most of the musical interest in the piece. The *Stabat Mater* received the New York Critics' Circle award for the best choral work of the year and remains one of Poulenc's most popular compositions.

The most important works of 1951-53 are *Quatre motets pour le temps de Noël*, begun in 1951 and completed the following year, *Ave verum corpus*, and the Sonata for two pianos. In contrast to the drama of the Easter motets, the four a capella motets for Christmas are joyful, serene, and filled with a quiet intensity. The *Ave verum corpus* is Poulenc's final effort in the motet genre. Scored for three part women's choir, the motet contains in twenty-eight brief measures some of this composer's most beautiful and masterful choral writing.

The Sonata for two pianos, completed in 1953, was commissioned by the American duo-piano team of Arthur Gold and Robert Fizdale. The work is one of Poulenc's masterpieces and certainly his finest piece for piano. It is a powerful composition--serious, difficult, complex, and unusually dissonant for this composer. The work lacks the popular tunes, the Romantic harmonies, and the helter-skelter, scurrying virtuosity of the earlier piano compositions.

After this monumental work, Poulenc composed only two additional pieces for piano. Both the *Novelette sur un thème de Manuel de Falla* and the *Élégie* for two pianos were completed in 1959. Neither effort is the equal of the Sonata, but each of these pieces exhibits the lyric, serene style of much of Poulenc's later music.

From 1953 to 1956 Poulenc was so occupied by the composition of his first serious opera, *Dialogues des Carmélites*, that he finished only four other short works. In 1954 he completed *Bucolique* for orchestra, the two songs of *Parisiana*, and the song *Rosemonde*. Poulenc professed that he had wanted to write an opera since he began as a composer.[25] While in Rome on a concert tour with Pierre Fournier in March 1953, Poulenc visited the offices of Ricordi to discuss a ballet that the publishing company had commissioned. The proposed project did not interest Poulenc. Mr. Valcaranghi, the director of Ricordi, suggested instead setting Georges Bernanos' *Dialogues des Carmélites* as an opera. Poulenc immediately bought a copy of the play adapted from Bernanos' film script and settled at the café "Tre Scallini" on the Piazza Navone, where he remained from ten in the morning until two in the afternoon reading. He then sent Valcaranghi a telegram accepting a commission to write the opera.

Poulenc immediately immersed himself in the project, reading further about the Carmelite order of nuns and even visiting their convents. A letter to a friend reveals his obsession with his work:

> I am working like a madman, don't go out, see no one. . . . I am composing a tableau each week. I no longer recognize myself. I am so obsessed with my subject that I am beginning to believe that I knew these women.[26]

The intensity with which he worked was both a physical and a mental strain, and Poulenc was depressed much of the time while composing this opera. In addition, there were legal problems over the performing rights to the text that added to the composer's anxiety. The result was a nervous breakdown and a period of convalescence in a clinic in Switzerland.

Recovering a degree of physical and mental stability, Poulenc completed the piano-vocal score in August 1955 and the orchestration in June of the following year. The premiere, in Italian, took place at La Scala on January 26, 1957, followed by the French premiere in Paris four months later. Productions were quickly mounted throughout the world--in German in Cologne, in English in San Francisco, and soon after in Rome, Lisbon, Vienna, and even on television from New York. *Dialogues* has become a staple of the operatic repertory, performed every season somewhere in the world. The creation of this masterpiece was a significant episode in Poulenc's life. The compositions of the eight years remaining until his death would be greatly affected by his achievement.

The first work following the opera, *Le Travail du peintre* completed in August 1956, shares both the spirit of the music of the opera and a motive derived from the music: "Its initial theme, likewise found a long time ago, served as *rootstock* for the theme of Mother Marie in the *Dialogues des Carmélites*."[27] In addition, in these songs Poulenc continued the trend toward greater emphasis on the piano accompaniment: "It is more than ever a duo where the material for voice and piano is closely integrated. There is no question of an accompaniment."[28] The texts for the seven songs of this cycle were chosen from poems by Eluard honoring modern painters. Poulenc had hoped that Eluard would provide two additional poems for the painters Dufy and Matisse who were his favorites, but that hope was never realized.

With the Sonata for flute and piano Poulenc turned again in 1956 to the composition of chamber music, having written nothing in this genre since 1948. But the Sonata follows the structure and pattern of moods of the early works--a moderate tempo first movement in ternary form, a lyric slow movement, and a vibrant, driving finale. Again in this work several motives have much in common with themes from *Dialogues*.

Between 1957 and 1961 he completed three sacred works: *Laudes de Saint Antoine de Padoue* (1957-59), *Gloria* (1959), and *Sept répons des ténèbres* (1961). *Laudes de Saint Antoine de Padoue*, for male chorus a cappella, is one of Poulenc's most original choral works with dramatic melodic lines, uneven phrases, complex harmonies, and frequent meter changes.

Gloria, for chorus, soprano soloist, and orchestra, was commissioned by the Koussevitzky Foundation and received its world premiere in Boston on January 20, 1961, with Poulenc present as a member of the audience. While the chorus is the dominant force in this work, the soprano soloist appears in three of the six sections, and the orchestra is far more colorful and important than in earlier sacred compositions such as the *Stabat Mater*. Each of the sections has its own distinct character with a great deal of contrast of mood between sections, ranging from the gaiety of the "Laudamus te" to the lyric solemnity of the "Domine Deus." Following the successful premiere of *Gloria*, Poulenc's popularity in America was at its high point.

Poulenc received a commission to write a piece for the opening season of Lincoln Center while he was in the country for the premiere of *Gloria*. This commission turned out to be the composer's final choral work. *Sept répons des ténèbres* is set for boy soprano, male chorus, and orchestra. The work is a kind of miniature Passion based on liturgical texts for Maundy Thursday, Good Friday, and the Saturday before Easter. The musical style of this piece is somewhat experimental with angular and chromatic melodic lines, harsh dissonances, a cappella choral passages, and the use of twelve-tone rows. Poulenc had previously used tone rows in the *Élégie* for horn and piano (1957), three rows that were merely monophonically stated and then abandoned. In the third movement of *Sept répons* Poulenc presented two tone rows that are stated without harmonization. Here, as in the other work where tone rows are introduced, the rows are not used as the basis for serial composition. This work was not completed in time for the opening of Lincoln Center and received its posthumous premiere by the New York Philharmonic in Carnegie Hall on April 11, 1963.

Following the success of *Dialogues des Carmélites*, Poulenc completed two additional dramatic works, *La Voix humaine* in 1958 and *La Dame de Monte Carlo* in 1961. It was Hervé Dugardin, director of the Paris office of Ricordi, who suggested to Poulenc that he set Jean Cocteau's 1930 monologue, *La Voix humaine*, to music. Poulenc immediately began work, completing the score between February and June 1958. The drama is concentrated in one forty-minute act with a single female character, "Elle," on stage. The woman moves through a variety of emotions, restlessly pacing about her bedroom and speaking to her lover on the telephone as she realizes that their relationship is at an end. The score reveals several new compositional ideas for Poulenc. The vocal line is most often traditional recitative that closely follows the inflections of natural speech, but the usual lyricism of the solo vocal music rarely appears. The harmonic style is tonally ambiguous, often nonfunctional, and dissonant. It is the orchestra that holds the work together by presenting several recurring motives and by providing much of the lyricism that occurs in the work.

La Dame de Monte Carlo resembles *La Voix humaine* in several respects. This work was also conceived for Poulenc's favorite female singer, Denise Duval. It also used a text by Cocteau. And the musical style of this work is similar to that of its predecessor. The text is the story of a degenerated, old woman who tries her luck a final time at the gambling tables of Monte Carlo and who ends by throwing herself into the Mediterranean.

In the final year of his life Poulenc completed two chamber works, a Sonata for clarinet and piano and a Sonata for oboe and piano. The Clarinet Sonata follows the formal structure and contrast of moods of the early chamber works, but the Oboe Sonata, Poulenc's last work, reveals significant departures from his earlier practices. The sonata opens with a slow movement, "Élégie," followed by a scherzo that contrasts a lighthearted opening section typical of Poulenc's early style with a slow section filled with lyric sentimentality. The third movement is a "Déploration" in Poulenc's most religious style. The harmonies recall those of his earlier religious works and the melody resembles plainchant. Indeed, Poulenc described this movement as "a sort of liturgical chant."[29] The music is soft, gentle, serene. The movement is a fitting conclusion to this sonata and to the compositions of Poulenc.

STYLE

"Music should humbly seek to please," Debussy succinctly stated. This observation captures the traditional French attitude about music, an attitude that Poulenc could hardly resist expressing in his own music. This statement also describes one of the most obvious reasons for Poulenc's popular success, as several generations of music lovers have found pleasure in the beauty of this composer's music. The best of his works contain genuine depth of feeling, mastery of technique, and musical interest that attracts listeners again and again.

Melody was the most important musical element for Poulenc. His melodies are simple, pleasing, easily remembered, and most often emotionally expressive. While there is wide variety in Poulenc's melodic style, characteristics commonly found include diatonic motion, lyricism, and regular phrase structure. Poulenc was greatly influenced by popular music, and his melodies frequently exhibit the characteristics of popular French music of the Parisian café and music hall.

Poulenc stated that he was not particularly inventive in his harmonic language. Yet his harmonic language is equally as beautiful, interesting, and personal as the melodic writing. He preferred clear, simple harmonies moving in obviously defined tonal areas with chromaticism that is rarely more than passing. Chords are almost without exception traditionally tertian, but he favored seventh chords, including the added seventh on the tonic triad. True harmonic innovation lies in the way in which Poulenc borrowed chord structures and progressions from a wide variety of composers and combined them in a manner that is uniquely his own. In addition, the music is filled with rapid and frequent modulations to colorful and unexpected tonal areas.

Poulenc composed for the standard instruments of the late nineteenth century, except for works that include harpsichord, and he requires only the traditional performing techniques for these instruments. His use of the orchestra is conservative for the twentieth century in both size and make-up.

The genres and forms in which Poulenc composed are traditional. He derived inspiration from earlier composers and revived forms of earlier French music. In company with many twentieth century composers, Poulenc's compositions tend to be short. While the piano pieces are generally not his best compositions, Poulenc's chamber music is of uniformly high quality and performed both for its technical expertise and great beauty.

He composed the finest songs in the French language since Debussy. With his extensive knowledge about literature, his mastery of piano technique and composition for the piano, his sensitive melodic and harmonic style, and his alliance with soloists such as Denise Duval and Pierre Bernac, Poulenc was ideally suited to song composition. Aside from the other compositions, the songs alone would assure his future reputation as a composer.

His other compositions with texts, the choral music and the operas, are equally important. Poulenc is one of the few composers of this century who was interested in composing sacred music, especially Catholic choral music. The three operas are all highly original approaches to the treatment of dramatic works, and each succeeds on its own merits. His other stage works, the ballets, were all successful and have remained popular, if not on the stage, then in instrumental versions.

Poulenc was fortunate in forming his style early in his career, and, although he continued to develop and to refine that style to the last composition, he never really changed his basic approach. He had the rare privilege of doing what he wished and only what he wished for much of his life. As much as any composer in the twentieth century, Poulenc's compositions reflect his personality, the personalities of those with whom he associated, and the culture that spawned the music. Poulenc fulfilled the promise of his musical talent noted by Ravel, and he spoke beautifully and eloquently for his generation.

NOTES

1. Henri Hell, *Francis Poulenc*, translated and introduced by Edward Lockspeiser (New York: Grove Press, 1959), 2.

2. Hell, 8.

3. Hélène Jourdan-Morhange, *Mes amis musiciens* (Paris: Éditeurs français réunis, 1955), 127, 141.

4. Hell, 23-24.

5. Darius Milhaud, "Music and Politics," *Modern Music*, 22:6.

6. Quoted by James Harding in *The Ox on the Roof* (London: Macdonald, 1972), 239-40.

7. Ned Rorem, *Music From Inside Out* (New York: George Braziller, 1967), 121-23; Ned Rorem, *The Paris Diary of Ned Rorem* (New York: George Braziller, 1966), 109.

8. Pierre Bernac, "A Certain Grace," *Opera News* (February 5, 1977), 29.

9. Bernac, 30.

10. Rorem, *The Paris Diary*, 129.

11. Rorem, *The Paris Diary*, 211.

12. Harding, 223-24.

13. Bernac, 30.

14. Reprinted in *Music Today*, ed. Rollo Myers (London: Dennis Dobson, 1949).

15. Jean Marnold, "Musique," *Mercure de France*, 165:200.

16. Lucien Chevaillier, "Un entretien avec Francis Poulenc," *Le Guide du concert et du théâtre lyriques*, April 26, 1929, 855.

17. Hell, 39.

18. Hell, 42.

19. John Gruen, "Poulenc," *Musical America* (April 1960), 6.

20. Hell, 47-48.

21. Francis Poulenc, *Diary of My Songs*. Translated by Winifred Radford (London: Victor Gollancz, 1985), 39.

22. Francis Poulenc, *Entretiens avec Claude Rostand*. (Paris: R. Juilliard, 1954), 115-16.

23. Poulenc, *Diary*, 93.

24. Poulenc, *Entretiens*, 133.

25. Francis Poulenc, "Comment j'ai composé les 'Dialogues des Carmélites'," *L'Opéra de Paris* 14:15.

26. Francis Poulenc, *Francis Poulenc Correspondance, 1915-1963*. Ed. Hélène de Wendel (Paris: Éditions du Seuil, 1967), 212.

27. Poulenc, *Diary*, 101.

28. Poulenc, *Diary*, 105.

29. Keith Daniel, *Francis Poulenc: His Artistic Development and Musical Style* (Ann Arbor, Michigan: UMI Research Press, 1982), 131.

Works and Performances

The compositions listed here are classified by genre and arranged alphabetically by title. "See" references, e.g., See: B1, identify citations in the "Bibliography" section. In addition, "See" and "See Also" citations refer to articles that might be of interest to some researchers but that did not warrant full annotation. Instrumentation is given in the order woodwinds, brass, percussion, and strings with the number of each instrument included in the score. The list 2.2.3.2./2.2.1.1./timp/perc/hp/strings, for example, indicates 2 flutes, 2 oboes, 3 clarinets, 2 bassoons, 2 French horns, 2 trumpets, 1 trombone, 1 tuba, timpani, additional percussion, harp, and strings.

OPERAS

W1   *Dialogues des Carmélites* (1953-56; Ricordi; 150')

Opera in three acts.
Libretto by Georges Bernanos.
Dedicated to the memory of the composer's mother, Claude Debussy, Claudio Monteverdi, Giuseppe Verdi, and Modeste Moussorgski.
7 female roles; 2 male roles; 3.1.3.4/4.3.3.1/timp/perc/pf/2 hp/strings
Premieres: 26 Jan 1957:   Milan; La Scala; Nino Sanzogno, cond.; Virginia Zeani (Blanche de la Force), Gianna Pederzini (La Prieure), Leila Genger (La Nouvelle Prieure), Gigliola Frazzoni (Mère Marie), Eugénia Ratti (Soeur Constance), Vittoria Palombini (Mère Jeanne), Fiorenza Cossoto (Soeur Mathilde), Scipio Colombo (Le Marquis de la Force), Nicola Filacuridi (Le Chevalier de la Force); Margherite Wallmann, producer; Georges Wakhévitch, scenery and costumes.
21 June 1957:   Paris; Opéra; Pierre Dervaux, cond.; Denise Duval (Blanche de la Force), Denise Scharley (La Prieure), Régine Crespin (La Nouvelle prieure), Rita Gorr (Mère Marie), Liliane Berton (Soeur

Constance); Maurice Jaquemont, director; Suzanne Lalique, scenery and costumes.

See: B12; B109; B123; B141; B153; B161; B180; B198; B199; B222; B234; B245; B261; B274; B289; B291; B330; B336; B337; B356; B358; B365; B406; B423; B437; B439; B457; B492; B494; B498; B504; B508; B515; B531; B542; B545; B546; B551; B559; B560; B561; B577.

Also See: AbH 2/12:50; ARG 40/6:62; BAM 20/325:1; BMI May 1966:4; Canon 11:282; Carrefour 6 Feb 1957; Ch 31/190:120; CSM 3-9-77:17; Figaro littéraire 22 June 1957; HF 16/5:128; HF/MA 27/6:MA21; HT 2-2-64; List 1-16-58; London Music Mar 1958:22; Melos 24:84; Melos 24:332; Melos 25:135; MensM 12:40; MensM 12:351; MensM Aug 1983:326; MusJ 37/2:46; MusJ March 1981:43; MusL 98/4:16; ML 39:197; MusM Dec 1963:33; MusM Sept 1968:40; Mus 11:147; Mus 11:560; Mu(Ch) Nov 1959:12; MuO 6/1:22; MuO 81:371; MuO n.s. 2/4:162; MusC 3-1-57:28; MusOp Mar 1958:371; MusOp Nov 1963:73; MusOp June 1983:274; MT 118:329; MT 118:580; MT 99:139; MT 99:144; MT 99:205; MT 99:262; MT 100:433; MT 104:877; MusG April 1959:43; News 50/14:93; NY 42/3:163; NYT 1-15-64:28; NYT 1-30-77,VI:15; NZM 118:232; NZM 118:434; NZM 118:507; Ob 1-12-58; OpK 15/4:19; Op 8:767; Op 9:9; Op 9:194; Op 10:233; Op 14:840; Op 17:360; Op 28:352; Op 30:618; Op 32:741; Op 33:654; Op 34:179; Op 34:868; Op 35:1359; Op 36:647; Op 37:944; Op 37:1067; Op 37:1180; Op 38:29; Op 38:467; OpC 14/1:34; OpC 18/2:34; OpC 20/2:27; OpN 22/8:25; OpN 22/10:28; OpN 28/14:33; OpN 30/22:34; OpN 31/1:24; OpN 31/4:25; OpN 41/13:20; OpN 41/13:43; OpN 41/19:30; OpN 42/22:44; OpN 43/10:9; OpN 43/10:16; OpN 43/10:24; OpN 43/15:50; OpN 45/9:12; OpN 45/9:18; OpN 46/3:40; OpN 47/10:34; OpN 48/6:46; OpN 49/1:43; OpW 1/1:27; OpW 4/4:32; OpW 18/5:48; OpW 18/6:34; OpW 18/8:34; OpW 22/6:20; OpW 22/6:29; OpW 22/12:28; OpW 24/5:27; OpW 25/2:32; OeMZ 14:4; OeMZ 14:126; RasM 27/1:58; San Francisco Opera 6 (entire issue); SchM Sept 1957:369; TLS 1-28-57:30, 5c, 12d; TLS 1-12-58; TLS 2-26-58:3b; Variety 2-16-77:75; Variety 1-10-79:111; VV 28/50:105.

W2   *Les Mamelles de Tirésias* (1944; Heugel: vocal score; 57')

Comic opera in two acts and a prologue.
Libretto by Guillaume Apollinaire.
Ded. to Darius Milhaud.
4 female roles; 8 male roles.
Premiere: 3 June 1947: Paris; Opéra-Comique; Albert Wolff, cond.; Denise Duval (Thérèse and La Cartomancienne), Jane Atty (La Marchande de journaux), Irène Gromova (La Dame élégante), Yvonne Girard-Ducy (La Grosse dame), Paul Payen (Le Mari), Emile Rousseau (Le Gendarme), Robert Jeantet (Le Directeur), Marcel Enot (Presto), Alban Derroja (Lacouf), Serge Rallier (Le Journaliste), Jacques Hivert

(Le Fils), Gabriel Jullia (Le Monsieur barbu); Max de Rieux, producer; Erté, scenery and costumes.

See: B3; B28; B35; B74; B126; B140; B159; B244; B255; B281; B290; B321; B342; B384; B429; B431; B443; B448; B487; B495; B518.

Also See: BP 6-7-53:42; CSM 3-12-81:19; Disques 62:81; HF/MA 24/8:32; HF/MA 31/6:MA18; HT 7-17-65; MM 27/6:45; MM 27/8:50; MusE Aug 1970:18; MusO n.s. 3/6:281; MA 77/4:34; MusC July 1953:6; MusOp Apr 1979:294; MusOp Jan 1982:148; MT 106:528; MT 120:61; MT 1; 20:327; News 41/25:61; NY 33/3:119; NZM 118:434; NZM 124:303; NZM 124:304; NZM 135:563; OpK 12/9:9; OpK 19/4:21; OpK 22/5:21; Op 14:386; Op 16:879; Op 19:338; Op 21:682; Op 25/Autumn:66; Op 29:977; Op 30:82; Op 30:388; Op 32:185; Op 33:187; Op 37/Festival Issue:37; OpC 15/4:32; OpC 22/2:30; OpN 24/20:28; OpN 30/4:26; OpN 38/26:28; OpN 39/4:52; OpN 39/20:34; OpN 43/21:48; OpN 44/11:33; OpN 45/13:21; OpN 45/13:24; OpN 47/6:30; OpN 48/4:92; OpN 48/6:32; OpW 9/9:12; OpW 22/8-9:59; OpW 22/6:46; RasM 18:58; Revue nos. 123-26, 1965, p. 28; SchM May 1957:205; Time 52/20:58; Variety 2-25-81:106; VV 3-11-81:70; WSJ 2-27-81:17.

W3   *Recits for Gounod: La Colombe* (1923; unpublished)

Recitatives for the one act opera by Gounod.
Libretto by Barbier and Carré, after La Fontaine.
Composed for a lyric spectacle of Serge Diaghilev.
See: MM 7:1; RM 5/4:163.

W4   *La Voix humaine* (1958; Ricordi; 40')

Lyric tragedy in one act.
Solo soprano with orchestra: 2.2.3.2./2.2.1.1./timp/perc/hp/strings.
Ded. to Daisy and Hervé Dugardin.
Libretto by Jean Cocteau.
Premiere: 6 Feb 1959: Paris; Opéra-Comique; Georges Prêtre, cond.; Denise Duval; Jean Cocteau, producer and designer.
See: B33; B51; B89; B103; B117; B118; B126; B142; B154; B162; B184; B206; B207; B233; B259; B319; B328; B369; B429; B445; B456; B495; B532; B536; B556.
Also See: GaM 9:336; HF/MA 19/7:MA21; HF/MA 27/8:MA16; HF/MA 27/10:MA38; HT 2-21-60; Melos 26:156; MensM Apr 1959:118; MM26/5:43; MEJ Nov 1972:10; MusE Oct 1960:9: Mus 18/1:73; Mus 18/2:73; MusO 2:162; MusO 3:281; MusO n. s. 3/6:281; MusC Apr 1959:18; MusC Mar 1960:19; MusOp 100:573; MusOp Nov 1983:52; MT 101:644; MT 118:661; MT 118:828; NYT 4-17-69:56; NYT 5-4-69,II:15; NYT 11-4-71:57; NYT 11-28-71,II:15; NYT 6-11-76,C:12; OpK 18/4:20; Op 10:309; Op 10:316; Op 11:471; Op 21:682; Op 25:820; Op 28/Autumn:28; Op 29:977; Op 30:903; Op 34:159; Op 36:552; Op

37:446; Op 37:813; Op 37:895; Op 37:1144; OpC 16/5:37; OpJ 2:5; OpJ 2:6; OpN 24/20:28; OpN 33/27:22; OpN 37/12:22; OpN 41/25:30; OpN 43/6:60; OpN 47/12:38; OpN 44/7:29; OpW 18/10:26; OpW 20/3:36; OpW 20/3:38; OeMZ Feb 1971:97; RasM Mar 1959:64; SR 52/18:41; SchM 99:117; SoM 29/6:93; VV 12-7-73;VV 7-20-82:77.

BALLETS

W5   *Les Animaux modèles* (1940-41; Eschig: piano score)

Ballet in one act.
After the Fables of La Fontaine.
Ded. to the memory of Raymonde Linossier.
Premiere: 8 Aug 1942: Paris; Opéra; Roger Désormière, cond.; Maurice Brianchon, scenery and costumes after Le Nain; Serge Lifar, choreography; with Mlle Lorcia, Solange Schwarz, Yvette Chauviré, Serge Peretti, Serge Lifar, Efimov.
See: B265; B315; B417.

W5A   *Les Animaux modèles: Ballet Suite* (1942; Eschig; 20')

Premiere: 7 March 1943:   Paris; Salle du Conservatoire; Paris Conservatoire Orchestra; Roger Désormière, cond.
See: RasM 17:75; Time 52/20:58.

W6   *Aubade* (1929; Lerolle: incl. min. score, reductions by the composer for piano solo or two pianos; 21')

Choréographic concerto for piano and 18 instruments: 2.3.2.2./ 2.1.0.0./ timp/strings (0-0-2-2-2).
Ded. to Vicomte and Vicomtesse de Noailles.
Premiere: 18 June 1929: Paris; home of Vicomte and Vicomtesse de Noailles; Poulenc, piano; Nijinska, choreography; Jean-Michel Franck, scenery.
See: B167; B376; B501; B519; B544.
Also See: MM 15:55; MM 20:121; RasM 3:160; RasM 3:493.

W7   *Les Biches* (1923; Heugel; 25')

Ballet in one act with chorus.
Text anonymous, 17th century.
Ded. to Misia Sert.

Premier: 6 Jan 1924: Monte Carlo; Théâtre de Monte Carlo; Edouard Flament, cond.; Fouquet, tenor; Cérésol, baritone; Romanitza; Marie Laurencin, scenery and costumes; Nijinska, choreography; with principal dancers Vera Nemtchinova, Lydia Sokolova, Nijinska, Lubov Tchernicheva, Léon Woizikovsky, Anatole Vilzak.
See: B96; B98; B110; B194; B210; B310; B311; B335; B368; B427; B535.
Also See: MM 2:2; MM 3:1; MM 4:3; MM 5:1; MM 7:1; MM 10:41; MM 20:73; RasM 18:142.

W7A   *Les Biches* (1923; Heugel)

Transcribed for piano solo by the composer.
The four movements are: *Ouverture; Rondeau; Adagietto; Andantino*.
See: Disques 6:28; Emp nos. 7-8, 1950:62-67; MusC 10-1-49:30.

W7B   *Les Biches: Suite* (1939-40; Heugel; 15' 30")

Suite for orchestra: 3.2.3.3./4.3.3.1./timp/perc/hp/celesta/strings.
Re-orchestrated.
Ded. to Misia Sert.
The five movements are: *Rondeau; Adagietto; Rag-Mazurka; Andantino; Final*.

W8   *L'Éventail de Jeanne: Pastourelle* (1927; Heugel; 2')

Piece for the ballet in one act: 2.2.2.2./2.1.0.0./perc/strings.
Additional music by Maurice Ravel, Pierre Octave Ferroud, Jacques Ibert, Roland-Manuel, Marcel Delannoy, Albert Roussel, Georges Auric, Darius Milhaud, Florent Schmitt.
Premiers: 16 June 1927: Paris; private performance given by René and Jeanne Dubost; Roger Désormière, cond.; Yvonne Franck and Alice Bourgat, choreography; Marie Laurencin, costumes; Pierre Legrain and René Moulaët, scenery and lighting; with Alice Bourgat.
4 Mar 1929: First public performance; Paris; Opéra; J. E. Szyfer, cond.; Yvonne Franck and Alice Bourgat; with Tamara Toumanova, Mlle Storms, Marcelle Bourgat, Odette Joyeux.
See: RM 1 Oct 1927:251.

W8A   *L'Éventail de Jeanne: Pastourelle* (Copyright by Heugel in 1929; Chester)

Version for piano solo.

W9   *Les Mariés de la Tour Eiffel: La Baigneuse de Tourville* and *Discours du général* (1921; unpublished; 47')

Ballet in one act by Jean Cocteau.
For orchestra: *La Baigneuse . . .*: 3.2.2.2./4.2.2.1./timp/perc/strings.
Discours . . .: 2.2.2.2./0.0.+2 cornets.2.1./perc/strings.
Additional music by Georges Auric, Arthur Honegger, Darius Milhaud, and Germaine Tailleferre.
Premiere: 18 June 1921: Paris; Théâtre des Champs-Elysées; Ballets Suédois; Jean Börlin, choreography; Irène Lagut, scenery; Jean Hugo, costumes.
See: B11; B24; B36; B210; B284; B344. Also See: Mus 26/4:355.

INCIDENTAL MUSIC

W10   *Amphitryon* (1947; unpublished)

Incidental music for a play by Molière.
Premiere: 5 Dec 1947: Paris; Compagnie Madeleine Renaud--Jean-Louis Barrault; Christian Bérard, scenery and costumes; Jean-Louis Barrault, director.

W11   *Esquisse d'un fanfare* (1921; Published 15 Oct 1921, in *Fanfare*, No. 2)

Overture to Act 5 of Romeo and Juliet by Shakespeare.

W12   *La Fille du jardinier* (1941; unpublished)

Incidental music for a play by Charles Exbrayat.

W13   *Le Gendarme incompris* (1921; unpublished)

Incidental music for a play by Jean Cocteau and Raymond Radiguet.
For violin, cello, bass, clarinet, trumpet, trombone.
Premiere: 23 May 1921: Paris; Théâtre des Mathurins.

W13A   *Le Gendarme incompris: Suite* (1921; unpublished)

For orchestra.
The three movements are: *Overture; Madrigal; Finale.*
Premiere?: 11 July 1921: London; Prince's Theatre.

W14   *Intermezzo* (1933; unpublished)

Incidental music for a play by Jean Giraudoux.
Premiere: March 1933: Paris; Comédie des Champs-Elysées; with Valentine Tessier, Louis Jouvet, Pierre Renoir, Roman Bouquet, and Robert Le Vigan.

W15   *L'Invitation au château* (1947; unpublished)

Incidental music for a play by Jean Cocteau.

W16   *Léocadia* (1940; unpublished except for song *Les Chemins de l'amour*: Eschig)

Incidental music for a play by Jean Anouilh.
See: W68.

W17   *La Nuit de la Saint-Jean* (1944; unpublished)

Incidental music for a play by James Barrie.

W18   *La Reine Margot* (1935; unpublished)

Incidental music for a play by Edouard Bourdet.
Later published as *Suite française* (See W120) and *A sa guitar* (See W58).
Composed in collaboration with Georges Auric.
Premiere: 1935: Paris; Yvonne Printemps as Marguerite de Navarre.
See: B327; B502. Also See: MM 13:4.

W19   *Renaud et Armide* (1962; unpublished)

Incidental music for a play by Jean Cocteau.

W20   *Le Soldat et la sorcière* (1945; unpublished)

Incidental music for a play by Armand Salacrou.

W21   *Le Voyageur sans bagages* (1944; unpublished)

Incidental music for a play by Jean Anouilh.

FILM SCORES

W22   *La Belle au bois dormant* (1935)

    Music for a film by Alexandre Alexeieff.

W23   *Ce siècle a 50 ans* (1950)

    Collaboration with Georges Auric.

W24   *La Duchesse de Langeais* (1942; Salabert)

    Production of Films Orange; Jacques de Baroncelli, director; with Edwige Feuillère.

W25   *Le Voyage en Amérique* (1951; unpublished)

    For two pianos.
    Production of Le Monde en Images; Henri Lavorelle, director; with Pierre Fresnay and Yvonne Printemps.
    Premiere: 14 Aug 1951: Cannes; Cinéma aux Étoiles.

W26   *Le Voyageur sans bagages* (1944)

    Production of Eclair-Journal; Jean Anouilh, director; with Pierre Fresnay.

ORCHESTRAL MUSIC

W27   *Bucolique*: contribution to *Variations sur le nom de Marguerite Long* (1954; Salabert; 2')

    For orchestra: 3.3.3.3./4.3.3.1./perc/pf/celesta/hp/strings.
    Additional music by Henri Dutilleux, Darius Milhaud, François Lesur, Jean Rivier, Henri Sauguet, Georges Auric, Jean Françaix.
    Premiere: 1956: Paris; Sorbonne; Charles Münch, cond.

W28   *Concert champêtre* (1927-28; Rouart Lerolle, reduction by the composer and miniature score; 27')

For harpsichord and orchestra: 3.3.2.2./4.2.1.1./timp/perc/strings (8.8.4.4.4.).
Ded. to Wanda Landowska.
Premiere: 3 May 1929:   Paris; Salle Pleyel; Wanda Landowska; l'Orchestre symphonique de Paris; Pierre Monteux, cond.
See: B26; B92; B152; B389; B499; B535.
Also See: AMT 22/4:25; Diap 70/7:9; GC 4-26-29; IM 12-1948:14; MM 17:172; MM 18:262; MM 23:56; MM 23:274; MT 108:824; NYP 11-12-48:60; NYPN 11-14-48; NYPN 11-20-49; RasM 2:279; RasM 3:65; Time 52/20:58.

W28A   *Concert champêtre*: Version for piano and orchestra

Premiere: 10 March 1934: Paris; Salle Pleyel; Mme Durand-Texte; R. Siohan, cond.

W29   *Concerto in D Minor for Two Pianos and Orchestra* (1932;   Rouart Lerolle; 20')

3.2.2.2./2.2.2.1./perc/strings.
Ded. to Princesse Edmond de Polignac.
Premiere: 5 Sept 1932: Venice; ISCM Festival; Francis Poulenc and Jacques Février; Orchestra of La Scala Milan; Desiré Defauw, cond.
See: B55; B88; B146; B496.
Also See: MM 17:105; MM 19:174; MM 20:46; MT 86:60; MT 96:153; RasM 12:357; RasM 17:244.

W30   *Concerto in G Minor for Organ, Strings, and Timpani* (1938; Deiss; 17')

Ded. to Princesse Edmond de Polignac.
Premiere: 21 June 1939:   Paris; Salle Gaveau; Maurice Duruflé; l'Orchestre symphonique de Paris; Roger Désormière, cond.
See: B57; B314; B506; B507. Also See: Diap 54/4:26; HT 4-12-63; MM 19:181; MM 21:41; MM21:223; MM 22:256; MM 23:204; MM23:211; MR 1/3:286; Mus 18/1:73; MT 79:284; MT 81:263; MT 121:260; Music (AGO Magazine) July 1974:22; Muzsika Dec 1967:15; RM 20/193:107.

W31   *Concerto for Piano and Orchestra* (1949; Salabert; 21')

For 2.2.2.2./4.2.3.1./timp/strings.
Ded. to Denise Duval and Raymond Destouches.
Premiere: 6 Jan 1950: Boston; Francis Poulenc; Boston Symphony Orchestra; Charles Münch, cond.
See: B219; B467.

Also See: Ch 25/163:23; List 11-2-50:474; MensM 5:273; MA 70/1:59; MusC 141/2:18; MQ 36/4:595; MT 91:47; MT 91:355; MT 91:482; NYT 3-19-39, II:7; RasM 20:342.

W32   *Deux marches et un intermède* (1937; Rouart Lerolle; 6')

For chamber orchestra: fl, ob, cl, bsn; tpt; strings.
Composed for an entertainment at the Paris Exhibition.
Additional music by Georges Auric.
Ded. to Antoinette d'Harcourt.
Premiere: 24 June 1937: Paris; Exposition Universelle; at a party given by Duke François d'Harcourt.

W33   *Deux prèludes posthumes et une Gnossienne* (1939; Rouart Lerolle)

Orchestration of three piano pieces by Satie.
The three pieces are: *Fête donnée par des chevaliers normands en l'honneur d'une jeune demoiselle*: 2.2.0.2./2.1.2.0./ strings; *Ier Prélude du Nazaréen*: 0.2.2.2./2.2.2.0./hp/strings; *3ème Gnossienne*: 1.1.1.2./ 2.0.0.0./strings.

W34   *Matelote provençale* (1952; Salabert)

Contribution to *La Guirlande de Campra: Sept variations ou meditations sur un thème de son opéra Camille.*
For 2.2.2.2./2.2.0.0./timp/strings.
Additional music by François Lesur, Roland-Manuel, Germaine Tailleferre, Henri Sauguet, Georges Auric, Arthur Honegger.
Ded. to Roger Bigonnet.
Premiere: 31 July 1952: Aix-en-Provence Festival; Paris Conservatoire Orchestra; Hans Rosebaud, cond.

W35   *Sinfonietta* (1947; Chester; 24')

For 2.2.2.2./2.2.0.0./timp/hp/strings.
Ded. to Georges Auric.
Premiere: 24 Oct 1948:   England; BBC broadcast; Philharmonia Orchestra; Roger Désormière, cond.
See: Ch 25/163:23; Ch 25/165:57; MR 13:246; MusOp 71:591.

CHORAL MUSIC

W36   *Ave Verum Corpus* (1952; Rouart Lerolle; 3')

Motet for three female voices (SMezA).
Ded. to La Chorale féminine de Pittsburgh.
See: B147. Also See: MT 116:550.

W37   *Chanson à boire* (1922; Rouart Lerolle; 3'30")

Anonymous text, 17th century.
For male choir (TTBB) a cappella.
Ded. to the Harvard Glee Club.
See: B316. Also See: ChJ 15/3:10.

W38   *Chansons françaises* (1945-46; Rouart Lerolle; 18' 30")

For mixed choir a cappella.
Ded. to Henri Screpel.
The eight pieces are: *Margoton va t'a l'iau* (SATB, 1945); *La Belle se
    siet au pied de la tour* (SATBarB, 1945); *Pilons l'orge* (SATBarB, 1945);
    Clic, clac, dansez sabots (TBB, 1945); *C'est la petit'fille du prince*
    (SATBarB, 1946); *La Belle si nous étions* (TTBB, 1946); *Ah! Mon beau
    laboureur* (SATB, 1945); *Les Tisserands* (SATBarB, 1946).
See: B391. Also See: MT 116:1076.

W39   *Exultate Deo* (1941; Rouart Lerolle; 2' 35")

For 4-part mixed choir a cappella.
Ded. to Georges Salles.
See: B147.

W40   *Figure humaine* (1943; Rouart Lerolle; 25')

Cantata for double 6-part mixed choir a cappella.
Ded. to Pablo Picasso.
Text by Paul Eluard; English version by Rollo H. Myers.
Premiere: Jan 1945: England; BBC Choir; Leslie Woodgate, cond.
See: B67. Also See: RasM 18:59.

W41   *Gloria* (1959; Salabert; 28')

For soprano, mixed choir and orchestra: 3.3.3.3./4.3.3.1./timp/hp/strings.
Commissioned by the Koussevitzky Music Foundation.
Ded. to the memory of Serge and Nathalie Koussevitzky.
Premiere: 20 Jan 1961: Boston; Adela Addison, soprano; Chorus Pro
   Musica; Boston Symphony Orchestra; Charles Münch, cond.
See: B89; B146; B208; B292; B390; B465; B553.
Also See: AbH 5/12:16; ACR 19/2:11; CMJ 6/1:49; FeuM 14/4-5:75; HT
   2-19-61; MA 81/3:24; MA 81/5:44; MUsC Mar 1961:16; MusC May
   1961:6; MusC May 1961:17.

W42   *Laudes de Saint Antoine de Padoue* (1957-59; Salabert; 6'30")

For male choir (TBB) a cappella.
The four pieces are: *O Jésu* (1957); *O Proles* (1958); *Laus Regi* (1959);
   Si quaeris (1959).

W43   *Litanies à la vierge noire* (1936; Durand; 7')

For women's or children's voices (SSA) and organ; also version for choir
   and orchestra: SSA/timp/strings.
Premiere: 17 Nov 1936: England; BBC broadcast; Ensemble conducted
   by Nadia Boulanger.
See: B535. Also See: MM 23:202.

W44   *Messe en sol majeur* (1937; Rouart Lerolle; 14'25")

For 4-part mixed choir a cappella.
Ded. to the memory of the composer's father.
Premiere: May 1938: Paris; Dominican Chapel; Chanteurs de Lyons.
See: B108; B181; B388; B554.
Also See: Caecilia 80:247; Diap 60/4:18; Disques 63-64:225; MM 16:247;
   MM 17:42; MR 2/4:265; MT 79:352; RasM 11:429; Sacred Music
   95/4:33.

W45   *Petites voix* (1936; Rouart Lerolle; 6')

Five easy choruses for 3-part children's choir (SSA) a cappella.
Text by Madeleine Ley.
The five pieces are: *La Petite fille sage* (Ded. to Martine Paul Rouart);
   Le Chien perdu (Ded. to Claude Lerolle); *En rentrant de l'école* (Ded.
   to Emmanuel Hepp); *Le Petit garçon malade* (Ded. to Daniel Milhaud);
   Le Hérisson (Ded. to Jean Destouches).

See: B316. Also See: ChJ 15/5:11; MM 23:202.

W46   *Quatre motets pour le temps de Noël* (1951-52; Rouart Lerolle; 11')

For mixed choir a cappella.
The four pieces are: *O magnum mysterium* (1942, Ded. to Félix de Nobel); *Quem vidistis pastores* (1951, Ded. to Simone Gerard); *Videntes stellam* (1951; Ded. to Madeleine Bataille); *Hodie Christus natus est* (1952, Ded. to Marcel Couraud).
See: B147; B273.

W47   *Quatre motets pour un temps de pénitence* (1938-39; Rouart Lerolle; 13')

For 4-part mixed choir a cappella.
The four pieces are: *Timor et tremor* (1939, Ded. to M. L'Abbé Maillet); *Vinea mea electa* (1938, Ded. to Yvonne Gouverné); *Tenebrae factae sunt* (1938, Ded. to Nadia Boulanger); *Tristis est anima mea* (1938, Ded. to E. Bourmauck).
Premiere: Feb 1939: Les Petits Chanteurs à la Croix de Bois.
See: B147; B273.

W48   *Quatre petites prières de Saint François d'Assise* 1948; Rouart Lerolle; 5'45")

For male choir a cappella.
Ded. "Aux Frères mineurs de Champfleury et spécialement à Frère Jérôme en souvenir de son grand-père: mon oncle, Camille Poulenc."
The four pieces are: *Salut, dame sainte* (TBB); *Tout puissant, très saint* (TTBB); *Seigneur, je vous en prie* (TBB); *O mes très chers frères* (TTBB, T solo).
Premiere: 1948 or 1949: Paris; Plaisir de la musique concert; Chorale Gouverné.
See: B316. Also See: Caecilia May 1957:84.

W49   *Salve Regina* (1941; Rouart Lerolle; 3' 45")

For 4-part mixed choir a cappella.
Ded. to Hélène [Salles].
See: B182.

W50   *Sécheresses* (1937; Durand; 18')

Cantata for mixed choir and orchestra: 3.3.2.2./4.2.3.1./timp/perc/ celesta/hp/strings.

Text by Edward James.
Ded. to Yvonne de Casa Fuerte.
The four pieces are: *Les Sauterelles; Le Village abandonné; Le Faux avenir; Le Squelette de la mer.*
Premiere: May 1938: Paris; Concerts Colonne; Chanteurs de Lyons; Paul Paray, cond.
See: B115; B160. Also See: MusC July 1959:9.

W51   *Sept chansons* (1936; Durand; 14')

For mixed choir a cappella.
Ded. to André and Suzanne Latarget, and to the Chanteurs de Lyon.
The seven pieces are: *Blanche neige* (text by Apollinaire); *A peine défigurée* (Eluard); *Pour une nuit nouvelle* (Eluard); *Tous les droits* (Eluard); *Belle et ressemblante* (Eluard); *Marie* (Apollinaire); *Luire* (Eluard). *La Reine de Saba* (Jean Legrand) was originally included but was replaced by *Blanche neige* after the first performance.
Premieres: 15 Nov 1936:   England; BBC broadcast; *Belle et ressemblante* only; Ensemble conducted by Nadia Boulanger.
21 May 1937: La Sérénade concert; Chanteurs de Lyons.
See: B88; B182; B316. Also See: ChJ 15/4:13; RasM 10:389.

W52   *Sept répons des ténèbres* (1961; Salabert; 25')

For child soprano, mixed choir of boys' and men's voices, and orchestra: 3.3.3.3./4.3.3.1./timp/hp/strings.
Commissioned by the New York Philharmonic in celebration of its opening season in the Lincoln Center for the Performing Arts.
Premiere: 11 April 1963:   New York; Carnegie Hall; New York Philharmonic; Thomas Schippers, cond.
See: B59; B314; B454; B506; B507.
Also See: HT 4-12-63; Melos Apr 1964:136; MensM Feb 1964:55; Mu(Ch) Feb 1964:22; SR 46/17:53.

W53   *Un Soir de neige* (1944; Rouart Lerolle; 6')

Chamber cantata for six mixed voices or a cappella choir.
Text by Paul Eluard.
Ded. to Marie-Blanche [de Polignac].
See: B67; B391. Also See: MT 116:1076.

W54   *Stabat Mater* (1950; Rouart Lerolle: vocal score; 35')

For soprano, mixed choir (SATBarB), and orchestra: 3.3.3.3./4.3.3.1./
timp/2 hp/strings.
Ded. to the memory of Christian Bérard.
Premiere: 13 June 1951: Strasbourg Festival; Geneviève Moizan; Les
Choeurs de Saint-Guillaume; Orchestre municipal de Strasbourg; Fritz
Münch, cond.
See: B28; B29; B147; B424.
Also See: Ch 25/165:57; Disques 77:92; RasM 22:266.

VOCAL SOLO WITH ENSEMBLE OR ORCHESTRA

W55   *Le Bal masqué* (1932; Rouart Lerolle; 18')

Cantata for baritone or mezzo-soprano; ob, cl, bn, pf, perc, vn, vc.
Text by Max Jacob.
Ded. to Vicomte and Vicomtesse de Noailles.
The six pieces are: *Préambule et air de bravoure; Intermède; Malvina;*
Bagatelle; La Dame aveugle; Finale.
Premiere: 20 April 1932: Hyères, home of Vicomte de Noailles; Gilbert
Moryn, baritone; Francis Poulenc, piano; Roger Désormière, cond.
See: B466. Also See: Disques 5:665; Mus 24/1:50; MT 90:121; MT
122:840; RasM 6:124.

W55A   *Caprice: d'après le final du Bal masqué* (1932; Rouart Lerolle)

For solo piano.

W55B   *Capriccio: d'après Le Bal masqué* (1952; Rouart Lerolle; 5')

For two pianos.
Ded. to Samuel Barber.
See: B19; B539.

W56   *La Dame de Monte Carlo* (1961; Ricordi; 6' 30")

Monologue for soprano and orchestra: 2.2.2.2./2.2.0.0./timp/perc/vib/
hp/strings.
Text by Jean Cocteau.
Ded. to Denise Duval.
Premiere: Nov 1961: Monte Carlo; Denise Duval; Georges Prêtre, cond.

See: Mu(Ch) Feb 1962:9; Music Magazine Feb 1962:38; Nouvelle littéraires 14 Dec 1961.

W57   *Rapsodie nègre* (1917; Chester; rev 1933; 11')

For baritone, fl, cl, str qt, pf.
Text by "Makoko Kangourou."
Ded. to Erik Satie.
The five pieces are: *Prélude; Ronde; Honoloulou; Pastorale; Final.*
Premiere: 11 Dec 1917:   Paris; Théâtre du Vieux-Colombier; Jane Bathori concert with Francis Poulenc singing.
See: RM 8/2:171.

VOCAL SOLO WITH PIANO

W58   *A sa guitare* (1935; Durand; 2' 45")

Alternately with harp; also orchestrated.
Ded. to Yvonne Printemps.
Text by Ronsard.
Composed as incidental music for *La Reine Margot* (See W18).

W59   *Airs chantés* (1927-28; Rouart Lerolle; 8')

Text by Jean Moréas.
The four pieces are: *Air romantique* (Ded. to François Hepp); *Air champêtre* (Ded. to Suzanne Peignot); *Air grave* (Ded. to Jacques Lerolle); *Air vif* (Ded. to Jane Bathori).
Premieres: 3 Mar 1928: Incomplete performance; Paris; Théâtre du Vieux-Colombier; Jane Bathori.
    10 June 1928: Complete performance; Paris; Salle Chopin; Suzanne Peignot; Auric-Poulenc concert.
See: B290; B384; B431. Also See: MM 21:36; RM 9/6:268.

W59A   *Airs chantés* (?; Salabert)

Soprano and orchestra: 2.3.2.2./2.0.0.0./timp/hp/strings.

W60   *Banalités* (1940; Eschig; 10')

Text by Guillame Apollinaire.

The five pieces are: *Chanson d'Orkenise* (Ded. to Claude Rostand);
Hôtel (Ded. to Marthe Bosredon); *Fagnes de Wallonie* (Ded. to Mme
Henri Fredericq); *Voyage à Paris* (Ded. to Paul Eluard); *Sanglots* (Ded.
to Suzette).
Premiere: 14 Dec 1940: Paris; Salle Gaveau; Pierre Bernac and Francis
Poulenc.
See: B273; B466; B535. Also See: NATSB 35/3:12.

W61   *Le Bestiaire* (1919; Eschig; 6')

Text by Guillaume Apollinaire.
Ded. to Louis Durey.
The six pieces are: *Le Dromadaire; La Chèvre du Thibet; La Sauterelle;
Le Dauphin; L'Écrevisse; La Carpe.*
Premiere: 1919: Suzanne Peignot and Francis Poulenc.
See: B4; B466. Also See: MM 15:46; RM 9/3:270.

W61A *Le Bestiaire* (1919)

For voice, fl, cl, bn, str qt.

W61B *Le Bestiaire* (before 1922)

For voice and orchestra.
Premiere: 17 Mar 1922: Paris; Salle du Conservatoire; Concerts Marthe
Martine; Roger Désormière, cond.

W62   *Bleuet* (1939; Durand)

Text by Guillaume Apollinaire.
Ded. to André Bonnélie.

W63   *Calligrammes* (1948; Heugel; 9' 20")

Text by Guillaume Apollinaire.
The seven pieces are: *L'Espionne* (Ded. to Simone Tilliard); *Mutation*
(Ded. to Pierre Lelong); *Vers le sud* (Ded. to Jacqueline Apollinaire);
Il pleut (Ded. to the memory of Emmanuel Fäy); *La Grâce exilée* (Ded.
to the composer's sister Jeanne); *Aussi bien que les cigales* (Ded. to
Jacques Soulé); *Voyage* (Ded. to the memory of Raymonde Linossier).
Premiere: 20 Nov 1948: New York City; Pierre Bernac and Francis
Poulenc.
See: IM Dec 1948:14.

W64   *Ce doux petit visage* (1939; Rouart Lerolle; 1' 45")

Text by Paul Eluard.
Ded. to the memory of Raymonde Linossier.
Premiere: Feb 1941: Pierre Bernac and Francis Poulenc.

W65   *Une Chanson de porcelaine* (1958; Eschig; 1' 30")

Text by Paul Eluard.
Composed in honor of and ded. to Jane Bathori on her 80th birthday.

W66   *Chansons gaillardes* (1925-26; Heugel; 11')

Anonymous text, 17th century.
Ded. to Mme Fernand Allard.
The eight pieces are: *La Maîtresse volage; Chanson à boire; Madrigal; Invocation aux Parques; Couplets bachiques; L'Offrande; La Belle jeunesse; Sérénade.*
Premiere: 2 May 1926: Paris; Salle des Agriculteurs; Auric-Poulenc Concert; Pierre Bernac.
See: B503. Also See: HF 17/6:20; MM 4:1; MM 18:40; MR 5:141; MT 85:339.

W67   *Chansons villageoises* (1942; Eschig; 11')

Text by Maurice Fombeure.
The six pieces are: *Chanson du clair tamis* (Ded. to Louis Beydts); *Les Gars qui vont à la fête* (Ded. to Jean de Polignac); *C'est le joli printemps* (Ded. to Roger Bourdin); *Le Mendiant* (Ded. to André Schaeffner); *Chanson de la fille frivole* (Ded. to André Lecoeur); *Le Retour du sergent* (Ded. to André Dubois).
Premiere: 28 June 1943: Paris; Salle Gaveau; La Pléîde Concert; Roger Bourdin and Francis Poulenc.
See: B538. Also See: IM Dec 1948:14; RasM 18:135.

W67A *Chansons villageoises* (1943; Eschig)

Version for voice and chamber orchestra: 2.2.2.2./2.1.0.0./hp/perc/celesta/string quartet.

W68   *Les Chemins de l'amour* (1940; Eschig; 3' 35")

Valse chantée from *Léocadia*: Text by Jean Anouilh.

Ded. to Yvonne Printemps.
See: W16.

W68A *Les Chemins de l'amour* (1940?)

Version for voice and orchestra.

W69 *Cinq poèmes* (1931; Rouart Lerolle; 7' 35")

Text by Max Jacob.
The five pieces are: *Chanson* (Ded. to Marie-Blanche [de Polignac]);
Cimetière (Ded. to Madeleine Vhita); *La Petite servante* (Ded. to
Suzanne Peignot); *Berceuse* (Ded. to Suzanne Balguerie); *Souric et
Mouric* (Ded. to Eva Curie).
Premiere: 24 May 1932: Nos 4 & 5; Paris; Salle du Conservatoire;
Suzanne Peignot and Francis Poulenc.
See: RasM 7:147.

W70 *Cinq poèmes* (1935; Durand; 7')

Text by Paul Eluard.
The five pieces are: *Peut-il se reposer?* (Ded. to the Vicomtesse de
Noailles); *Il la prend dans ses bras* (Ded. to Valentine Hugo); *Plume
d'eau claire* (Ded. to Suzanne Nivard); *Rôdeuse au front de verre*
(Ded. to Pierre Bernac); *Amoureuses* (Ded. to Nora Auric).
Premiere: 3 April 1935: Paris; École Normale; Pierre Bernac and Francis
Poulenc.

W71 *Cocardes* (1919; Éditions de la Sirène; 6' 20")

Text by Jean Cocteau.
Ded. to Georges Auric.
The three pieces are: *Miel de Narbonne; Bonne d'enfant; Enfant de
troupe.*
Premiere: 21 Feb 1920: Paris; Théâtre des Champs-Elysées; S.
Koubitzky.
See: B4.

W71A *Cocardes* (1919)

Version for voice, violin, cornet à piston, trombone, bass drum and
triangle.

W72   *La Courte paille* (1960; Eschig; 9' 15")

    Text by Maurice Carême.
    Ded. to Denise Duval and Richard Schilling
    The seven pieces are: *Le Sommeil; Quelle aventure!; La Reine de coeur; Ba, be, bi, bo, bu; Les Anges musiciens; Le Carafon; Lune d'avril.*
    Premiere: Festival de Royaumont; Colette Herzog.
    See: B80.

W73   *Dernier poème* (1956; Eschig; 1' 50")

    Text by Robert Desnos.
    Ded. to Youki Desnos.
    See: B80.

W74   *Deux mélodies* (1946; Eschig; 2' 45")

    Text by Guillaume Apollinaire.
    The two pieces are: *Le Pont* (Ded. to the memory of Raymond Radiguet); *Un Poème* (Ded. to Luigi Dallapiccola).
    Premiere: 6 Nov 1946: Pierre Bernac and Francis Poulenc.

W75   *Deux mélodies 1956* (1956; Eschig; 3')

    The two pieces are: *La Souris* (text by Guillaume Apollinaire, Ded. to Marya Freund); *Nuage* (text by Mme Laurence de Beylié, Ded. to Rose Plaut-Dercourt).

W76   *Deux poèmes* (1938; Rouart Lerolle; 6')

    Text by Guillaume Apollinaire.
    The two pieces are: *Dans le jardin d'Anna* (Ded. to Reine Bénard); *Allons plus vite* (Ded. to Georges Auric).
    Premiere: 19 Dec 1938: Paris; Salle Gaveau; Pierre Bernac and Francis Poulenc.

W77   *Deux poèmes* (1943; Rouart Lerolle; 4')

    Text by Louis Aragon.
    The two pieces are: *"C"* (Ded. to Papoum); *Fêtes galantes* (Ded. to Jean de Polignac).

Premiere: 8 Dec 1943: Paris; Salle Gaveau; Pierre Bernac and Francis Poulenc.
See: B273.

W78   *Le Disparu* (1947; Rouart Lerolle; 1' 25")

Text by Robert Desnos.
Ded. to Henri Sauguet.

W79   *Epitaphe* (1930; Rouart Lerolle; 1')

Text by Malherbe.
Ded. to Raymonde Linossier.

W80   *Fancy* (1962?; Anthony Blond; 1' 35")

Text by Shakespeare.
Ded. to Miles and Floria.
Commissioned for "Classical Songs for Children," ed. by The Countess of Harewood and Ronald Duncan.

W81   *Fiançailles pour rire* (1939; Rouart Lerolle; 11' 30")

Text by Louise de Vilmorin.
The six pieces are: *La Dame d'André* (Ded. to Marie Blanche [de Polignac]); *Dans l'herbe* (Ded. to Freddy); *Il vole* (Ded. to Suzanne Peignot); *Mon cadavre est doux comme un gant* (Ded. to Ninon Vallin); *Violon* (Ded. to Denise Bourdet); *Fleurs* (Ded. to Solange d'Ayen).
Premiere: 21 May 1942: Geneviéve Touraine and Francis Poulenc.
See: B80; B273.

W82   *La Fraîcheur et le feu* (1950; Eschig; 8')

Text by Paul Eluard.
Ded. to Igor Stravinsky.
The seven pieces are: *Rayon des yeux; Le Matin les branches attisent; Tout disparut; Dans les ténèbres du jardin; Unis la fraîcheur et le feu; Homme au sourir tendre; La Grande rivière qui va.*
Premieres: 1 Nov 1950: Birmingham, England; Pierre Bernac and Francis Poulenc.
16 Nov 1950: England; BBC broadcast; Pierre Bernac and Francis Poulenc.
See: B80.

W83   *La Grenouillère* (1938; Deiss; 1' 40")

Text by Guillaume Apollinaire.
Ded. to Marie-Blanche [de Polignac].
Premieres: ?19 Dec 1938:   Paris; Salle Gaveau; Pierre Bernac and
Francis Poulenc.
16 Feb 1939: Paris; Salle Gaveau; Pierre Bernac and Francis Poulenc.

W84   *Huit chansons polonaises* (1934; Rouart Lerolle; 10' 45")

The eight pieces are: *La Couronne* (text by Wianek, Ded. to Ida
Godebska); *Le Départ* (Odjazd, Ded. to Misia Sert); *Les Gars polonais*
(Polish melody, Ded. to Mme la Comtesse Elisabeth Potocka); *Le
Dernier mazour* (Ostatni Mazur, Ded. to Marya Freund); *L'adieu*
(Pozegnanie, Ded. to Mme Kochanska); *Le Drapeau blanc* (Biala
Choragiewka, Ded. to Mme Artur Rubinstein); *La Vistule* (Wisla, Ded.
to Wanda Landowska); *Le Lac* (Jezioro, Ded. to Maria Modrakowska).
See: B273; B316. Also See: MM 21:98.

W85   *Hyde Park* (1945; Eschig; 1' 30")

Text by Guillaume Apollinaire.
Ded. to the memory of Audrey Norman Colville.
Premiere: 27 April 1945: Pierre Bernac and Francis Poulenc.

W86   *Hymne* (1947; Salabert; 3' 35")

Text by Jean Racine.
Ded. to Doda Conrad.
Premiere: 1949: New York City; Doda Conrad and David Garvey.
See: MusN Feb 1949:4.

W87   *Main dominée par le coeur* (1947; Rouart Lerolle; 1' 10")

Text by Paul Eluard.
Ded. to Marie-Blanche [de Polignac].

W88   *. . . mais mourir* (1947; Heugel; 1' 20")

Text by Paul Eluard.
Ded. to "the memory of Nush" [Nusch Eluard].

W89   *Mazurka* (1949; Heugel; 3' 10")

Text by Louise de Vilmorin.
To the memory of Chopin for the centenary of his death.
Contribution to *Mouvements du coeur.*
Additional music by Henri Sauguet, Georges Auric, Jean Françaix, Leo
    Preger, Darius Milhaud.
Commissioned by the Polish Bass, Doda Conrad.
Premiere: 1949: New York City; Doda Conrad and David Garvey.
See: MusC 149/4:38.

W90   *Métamorphoses* (1943; Rouart Lerolle; 4' 15")

Text by Louise de Vilmorin.
The three pieces are: *Reine des mouettes* (Ded. to Marie-Blanche [de
    Polignac]); *C'est ainsi que tu es* (Ded. to Marthe Bosredon); *Paganini*
    (Ded. to Jeanne Ritcher).
Premiere: 8 Dec 1943: Paris; Salle Gaveau; Pierre Bernac and Francis
    Poulenc.

W91   *Miroirs brûlants* (1938-39; Salabert; 5' 30")

Text by Paul Eluard.
The two pieces are: *Tu vois le feu du soir* (Ded. to Pierre Bernac); *Je
    nominerai ton front* (Ded. to Marie-Laure).
Premieres: 19 Dec 1938: Paris; Salle Gaveau; Pierre Bernac and
    Francis Poulenc; number one only.
    16 Feb 1939: Paris; Salle Gaveau; Pierre Bernac and Francis Poulenc;
    complete performance.
See: B577.

W92   *Montparnasse* (1941-45; Eschig; 3' 35")

Text by Guillaume Apollinaire.
Ded. to Pierre Souvtchinsky.
Premiere: 27 April 1945: Pierre Bernac and Francis Poulenc.

W93   *Parisiana* (1954; Salabert; 2' 30")

Text by Max Jacob.
The two pieces are: *Jouer du bugle* (Ded. to the memory of Pierre
    Colle); *Vous n'écrivez plus?* (Ded. to Paul Chadourne).
Premiere: 12 Oct 1954: Amsterdam; Pierre Bernac and Francis Poulenc.

W94   *Paul et Virginie* (1946; Eschig; 1')

Text by Raymond Radiguet.
Ded. to Lucien Daudet.

W95   *Poèmes de Ronsard* (1924-25; Heugel; 10')

The five pieces are: *Attributs* (Ded. to Mme Charles [Suzanne] Peignot); *Le Tombeau* (Ded. to Marya Freund); *Ballet* (Ded. to Vera Janacopoulos); *Je n'ai plus que les os* (Ded. to Mme Croiza); *A son page* (Ded. to Jane Bathori).
Premiere: 10 Mar 1925: Paris; Salle des Agriculteurs; Marcelle Meyer concert; Suzanne Peignot and Francis Poulenc.
See: B242; B503. Also See: RM 6/7:180.

W95A   *Poèmes de Ronsard* (before 1934; unpublished)

Version with orchestra: 2.3.3.2./4.2.3.0./timp/perc/hp/strings.
Premiere: 16 Dec 1934: Paris; Salle Gaveau; Suzanne Peignot and l'Orchestre Lamoureux; Jean Morel, cond.

W96   *Le Portrait* (1938; Deiss; 1' 40")

Text by Colette.
Ded. to Hélène Jourdan-Morhange.
Premiere: 19 Dec 1938: Paris; Salle Gaveau; Pierre Bernac and Francis Poulenc.

W97   *Priez pour paix* (1938; Rouart Lerolle; 2' 30")

Text by Charles d'Orléans.
Premiere?: 19 Dec 1938: Paris; Salle Gaveau; Pierre Bernac and Francis Poulenc.

W98   *Quatre chansons pour enfants* (1934; Enoch; 10')

The four pieces are: *Nous voulons une petite soeur* (text by Jean Nohain, Ded. to Marie-Blanche [de Polignac]); *La Tragique histoire du petit René* (Jaboune [Jean Nohain], Ded. to Mme H. Ledoux); *Le Petit garçon trop bien portant* (Jaboune [Jean Nohain], Ded. to Mario Beaugnies de St. Marceaux); *Monsieur sans souci* (Jaboune [Jean Nohain], Ded. to Jean de Polignac).

W99   *Quatre poèmes* (1931; Rouart Lerolle; 4' 20")

Text by Guillaume Apollinaire.
The four pieces are: *L'Anguille* (Ded. to Marie Laurencin); *Carte postale* (Ded. to Mme Cole Porter); *Avant le cinéma* (Ded. to Mme Picasso); *1904* (Ded. to Mme Jean-Arthur Fontaine).
Premiere: 1 June 1931: Festival Poulenc; Suzanne Peignot.
See: RasM 7:147.

W100   *Rosemonde* (1954; Eschig; 2')

Text by Guillaume Apollinaire.
Ded. to Comtesse Pastré.
Premiere: 12 Oct 1954: Amsterdam; Pierre Bernac and Francis Poulenc.

W101   *Tel jour, telle nuit* (1936-37; Durand; 14' 50")

Text by Paul Eluard.
The nine pieces are: *Bonne journée* (Ded. to Pablo Picasso); *Une ruine coquille vide* (Ded. to Freddy); *Le Front comme un drapeau perdu* (Ded. to Nush [Nusch Eluard); *Une roulotte couverte en tuiles* (Ded. to Valentine Hugo); *A toutes brides* (Ded. to Marie-Blanche [de Polignac]); *Une herbe pauvre* (Ded. to Marie-Blanche); *Je n'ai envie que de t'aimer* (Ded. to Denise Bourdet); *Figure de force brûlante et farouche* (Ded. to Pierre Bernac); *Nous avons fait la nuit* (Ded. to Yvonne Gouverné).
Premiere: 3 Feb 1937: Paris; Salle Gaveau; Pierre Bernac and Francis Poulenc.
See: B182; B224; B538. Also See: HF 17/6:20; IM Dec 1948:14; NATSB 35/2:2; NYT 10-23-38,IX:7; RasM 11:388.

W102   *Toréador* (1918; rev. 1932; Deiss; 5' 20")

Text by Jean Cocteau.
Ded. to Pierre Bertin.

W103   *Le Travail du peintre* (1956; Eschig; 11' 30")

Text by Paul Eluard.
Ded. to Alice Esty.
The seven pieces are: *Pablo Picasso; Marc Chagall; Georges Braque; Juan Gris; Paul Klee; Joan Miró; Jacques Villon.*
Premiere: 5 Sept 1957: Edinburgh; Pierre Bernac and Francis Poulenc.

W104   *Trois chansons de F. Garcia Lorca* (1947; Heugel; 4' 20")

The three pieces are: *L'Enfant muet* (Ded. to Mme Geneviéve Touraine);
Adelina à la promenade (Ded. to Mme Auguste Lambiotte); *Chansons
de l'oranger sec* (Ded. to Gérard Souzay).
Premiere: 12 Nov 1947: Pierre Bernac and Francis Poulenc.

W105   *Trois poèmes* (1937; Durand; 5' 50")

Text by Louise de Vilmorin.
Ded. to Marie-Blanche de Polignac.
The three pieces are: *Le Garçon de Liége; Au-delà; Aux officiers de
la garde blanche.*
Premieres: 28 Nov 1938: Paris; Salle Gaveau; La Sérénade Concert;
Francis Poulenc, piano.
See: B290; B384; B431.

W106   *Trois poèmes de Louise Lalanne* (1931; Rouart Lerolle; 3')

Ded. to Comtesse Jean de Polignac.
The three pieces are: *Le Présent* (text by Guillaume Apollinaire, under
the pseudonym Louise Lalanne; *Chanson* (text by Marie Laurencin);
Hier (text by Marie Laurencin).
Premieres: ?1 June 1931: Festival Poulenc; Suzanne Peignot.
1932: Paris; Salle du Conservatoire; Concerts de la Sérénade; Roger
Bourdin.
See: B290; B384; B431. Also See: RasM 7:147.

W107   *Vocalise* (1927; Leduc)

Ded. to the memory of Evelyne Brélia.
Premiere: 3 Mar 1928: Paris; Théâtre du Vieux-Colombier; Jane Bathori.

VOCAL DUET WITH PIANO

W108   *Colloque* (1940; published by Salabert in 1978; 3')

For soprano and baritone voices and piano.
Text by Paul Valéry.
Ded. to Solange Lemaître.
See: MT 121:507.

MELODRAMA

W109   *L'Histoire de Babar* (1940-45; Chester; 22')

> For piano and reciter.
> Story by Jean de Brunhoff.
> Ded.: "For my little cousins Sophie, Sylvie, Benoit, Florence & Delphine Périer; Yvan, Alain, Marie-Christine & Margueritte-Marie Villotte; and my little friends Marthe Bosredon & André Lecoeur, in memory of Brive."
> Premiere: First public performance 8 Feb 1949: London; London Contemporary Music Centre Concert; Bruce Belfrage, narrator; Francis Poulenc, piano.
> See: B1. Also See: MensM Jan 1966:24; MR 10/2:130; OpN 44/12:8; RasM 22:274.

W109A *L'Histoire de Babar* (1962; Chester; 22')

> Version for orchestra by Jean Françaix: 2.3.3.3./2.2.+cornet.1.1./timp/ perc/hp/strings.

CHAMBER AND INSTRUMENTAL MUSIC

W110   *Élégie*: For horn and piano (1957; Chester; 8')

> Ded. to the memory of Dennis Brain.
> Premiere: 17 Feb 1958: England; BBC broadcast; Neill Sanders and Francis Poulenc.
> See: TLS 2-8-58:3c.

W111   *Sarabande*: For guitar (1960; Ricordi; 2' 30")

> Ded. to Ida Presti.

W112   *Sextuor*: For piano, flute, oboe, clarinet, bassoon and horn (1932-39; Hansen and Chester; 20')

> Ded. to Georges Salles.
> Premieres: 5 July 1933: England; BBC broadcast; Francis Poulenc, Robert Murchie, Leon Goossens, Haydn Draper, Fred Wood, Edmund Chapman.

9 Dec 1940:   rev. version; Paris; Salle Chopin; Association Musicale Contemporaine concert; Quintette à Vent de Paris.

W113   *Sonata for Cello and Piano* (1948; Heugel; 21' 25")

Ded. to Marthe Bosredon and Pierre Fournier.
Premiere: 18 May 1949: Paris; Pierre Fournier and Marthe Bosredon.
See: MR 10:211; MusC 5-15-50:30; NOTES 7:451; RasM 20:62; STRAD 60:69; STRAD 60:338.

W114   *Sonata for Clarinet and Bassoon* (1922; rev. 1945; Chester; 9')

Ded. to Audrey Parr.
Premiere?: 7 Jan 1923: Concert Wiéner.
See: B311. Also See: MM 1:3; MM1:25; RM 4/4:66; RM 8/2:171.

W114A *Sonata* (1925; Chester)

Reduction for piano solo by the composer.

W115   *Sonata for Clarinet and Piano* (1962; Chester; 13')

Ded. to the memory of Arthur Honegger.
Premiere: 10 April 1963: New York City; Benny Goodman and Leonard Bernstein.
See: B273. Also See: MT 105:835; SR 46/17:53.

W116   *Sonata for Flute and Piano* (1956; Chester; 11')

Ded. to the memory of Elizabeth Sprague Coolidge.
Premiere: 18 June 1957: Strasbourg Festival; Jean-Pierre Rampal and Francis Poulenc.
See: B453. Also See: Mus 11:569; MusC Aug 1957:18.

W117   *Sonata for Horn, Trumpet and Trombone* (1922; rev. 1945; Chester; 8' 30")

Ded. to Mlle Raymonde Linossier.
Premiere?: 7 Jan 1923: Concert Wiéner.
See: B311. Also See: MT 55:911; NYPN 1-29-38; RM 4/4:66.

W117A *Sonata* (1925; Chester)

Reduction for piano solo by the composer.

W118   *Sonata for Oboe and Piano* (1962; Chester; 13')

Ded. to the memory of Serge Prokofiev.
Premiere: 8 June 1963: Strasbourg Festival; Pierre Pierlot and Jacques Février.
See: MT 105:835.

W119   *Sonata for Two Clarinets* (1918; rev. 1945; Chester; 6' 20"; also reduction for piano solo by the composer)

Ded. to Edouard Souberbielle.
Premiere: 1919: Paris; Salle Huyghens; Lyre et Palette Concert.
See: B25; B311; B333. Also See: RM 8/2:171.

W120   *Sonata for Violin and Piano* (1942-43; rev. 1949; Eschig; 18')

Ded. to the memory of Federico Garcia Lorca.
Premiere: 21 June 1943: Paris; La Pléaide concert; Ginette Neveu and Francis Poulenc.
See: B14; B38. Also See: MT 87:339; RasM 17:86; Violins Mar 1954:89.

W121   *Suite française: d'après Claude Gervaise* (1935; Durand; 14')

For 2 ob, 2 bsn; 2 tpt, 3 tmb; tambour, cym, GC; harpsichord.
Originally composed as incidental music for *La Reine Margot* (See W18).
See: Diap Mar 1976:4.

W121A *Suite française: d'après Claude Gervaise* (1935; Durand; 12')

Version for piano solo.
Ded. to Édouard Bourdet.
See: MR 1/3:286.

W122   *Trio for Oboe, Bassoon and Piano* (1926; Hansen; 14')

Ded. to Manuel de Falla.

Premiere: 2 May 1926:   Paris; Salle des Agriculteurs; Auric-Poulenc
concert.
See: B466; B501; B535. Also See: MM 4:1; MM 4:37.

W123   *Villanelle*: For pipe and piano (1934; Éditions de l'Oiseau Lyre; 2')

Ded. to Mrs. Louise Dyre.

PIANO SOLO

W124   *Badinage* (1934; Deiss)

Ded. to Christiane.

W125   *Bourrée au Pavillon d'Auvergne* (1937; Deiss: in *A l'Exposition*; Salabert;
1' 20")

Ded. to Marguerite Long.

W126   *Deux novelettes* (1927-28; rev. 1939; Chester; 4' 50")

The two pieces are: C major (Ded. to Aunt Liénard); B̄ flat minor (Ded.
to Louis Laloy).
Premiere: 10 June 1928: Paris; Salle Chopin; Auric-Poulenc concert;
Francis Poulenc.
See: MM 14:231; MR 1/3:286; MT 71:517; RasM 3:167.

W127   *Feuillets d'album* (1933; Rouart Lerolle)

The three pieces are: *Ariette* (Ded. to Yvonne Martin); *Rêve* (Ded. to
Mme A.Bassan); *Gigue* (Ded. to Marcelle Meyer).
See: RasM 8:278.

W128   *Humoresque* (1934; Rouart Lerolle; 1' 40")

Ded. to Walter Gieseking.
See: MT 77:1005.

W129 *Impromptus* (1920-21; rev. 1939; Chester)

Ded. to Marcelle Meyer.
The six pieces are: Vite--Con fuoco; Lent; Allegro vivace; Violent;
Andante; Brusque.
See: MT 64:479.

W130 *Improvisations* (1932-59; Nos. 1-12 Rouart Lerolle, Nos. 13-15 Salabert;
18')

The fifteen pieces are: No. 1, B minor, 1932, Presto ritmico (Ded. to
Mme Long de Marliave).
No. 2, A flat major, 1932, Assez animé (Ded. to Louis Duffey).
No. 3, B minor, 1932, Presto très sec (Ded. to Brigitte Manceaux).
No. 4, A flat major, 1932, Presto con fuoco (Ded. to Claude Popelin).
No. 5, A minor, 1932, Modéré mais sans lenteur (Ded. to Georges Auric).
No. 6, B flat major, 1932, A toute vitesse (Ded. to Jacques Février).
No. 7, C major, 1933 (Ded. to Comtesse de Noailles).
No. 8, A minor, 1934 (Ded. to Nora & Georges Auric).
No. 9, D major, 1934 (Ded. to Thérèse Dorny).
No. 10 F major, 1934, Eloge des gammes (Ded. to Jacques Lerolle).
No. 11, G minor, 1941 (Ded. to Claude Delvincourt).
No. 12, E flat major, 1941, *Hommage à Schubert* (Ded. to Edwige
Feuillère).
No. 13, A minor, 1958, Allegretto commodo (Ded. to Mme Auguste
Lambiotte).
No. 14, D flat major, 1958 (Ded. to Henri Hell).
No. 15, C minor, 1959, *Hommage à Edith Piaf.*

W131 *Intermezzi* (1934; Rouart Lerolle; 5')

The two pieces are: C major (Ded. to Raymond Mallet); D flat major
(Ded. to Comtesse Jean de Polignac).
See: RasM 8:278.

W132 *Intermezzo in A flat major* (1943; Eschig; 4')

Ded. to Mme Manty Rostand.

W133 *Mélancolie* (1940; Eschig; 5' 40")

Ded. to Raymond Destouches.
Premiere: 23 May 1941: Paris; Salle Gaveau; Marcelle Meyer.

W134   *Napoli: Suite for piano* (1922-25; Rouart Lerolle; 9' 30")

Ded. to the memory of Juliette Meerovich.
The three pieces are: *Barcarolle; Nocturne; Caprice italien.*
Premieres: 17 Mar 1924: Nos. 1 and 2; Paris; Marcelle Meyer.
  2 May 1926: Salle des Agriculteurs; Auric-Poulenc Concert; Marcelle
  Meyer.
See: MM 4:1; MM 4:37.

W135   *Nocturnes* (1929-38; Heugel)

The eight pieces are: No. 1, C major, 1929 (Ded. to Suzette).
No. 2 *Bal de jeunes filles*, A major, 1933 (Ded. to Janine Salles).
No. 3, F major, 1934 (Ded. to Paul Collaer).
No. 4, C minor, 1934 (Ded. to Julien Green).
No. 5, D minor, 1934 (Ded. to Jean Michel Frank).
No. 6, G major, 1934 (Ded. to Waldemar Strenger).
No. 7, E flat major, 1935 (Ded. to Fred Timar).
No. 8 *Pour servir de coda au cycle*, B major, 1938.
See: MM 13:2; MM 13:46.

W136   *Novelette sur un thème de Manuel de Falla* (1959; Chester; 2' 15")

In E minor.
Theme from *El Amor Brujo.*
Ded. to [R. Douglas] Gibson.

W137   *Pièce brève sur le nom d'Albert Roussel* (1929; Leduc; 1' 50")

See: RasM 3:73.

W137A *Pièce brève sur le nom d'Albert Roussel* (1949)

Version for orchestra: 2.2.2.2./2.1.0.0./timp/hp/strings.

W138   *Préludes* (1916; unpublished)

W139   *Presto* (1934; Deiss; 1' 30")

In B flat major.
Ded. to Vladimir Horowitz.
See: RasM 8:278.

W140 *Promenades* (1921; revised 1952; Chester)

Ded. to Artur Rubinstein.
The ten pieces are: *A pied; En auto; A cheval; En bateau; En avion;
En autobus; En voiture; En chemin de fer; A bicyclette; En diligence.*
See: B334; B426. Also See: MR 1/3:286.

W141 *Les Soirées de Nazelles* (Sketched, 1930; dated 1936; Durand; 18')

Ded. to the composer's aunt Liénard.
The four sections are: Préambule; Variations; Cadence; Final
Premiere: 1 Dec 1936: England; BBC broadcast; Francis Poulenc.
See: RasM 10:389.

W142 *Suite in C* (1920; Chester; 4' 30")

Ded. to Ricardo Viñes.
Premiere: 11 April 1920: Paris; Société Nationale de Musique; Ricardo
Viñes.
See: MR 1/3:286.

W143 *Thème varié* (1951; Eschig; 10')

Ded. to Geneviève Sienkewicz.

W144 *Trois mouvements perpétuels* (1918; revised 1962; Chester; 5')

Ded. to Valentine Gross.
The three pieces are: Balancé--Modéré; Modéré; Alerte.
Premiere: 9 Feb 1919: Paris; Salle Huygens; Lyre et Palette Concert;
Ricardo Viñes.
See: B4. Also See: CI 9/3:36; MR 1/3:286; Music Teacher and Piano
Student (England) Dec 1971:13; RM 8/2:171.

W144A *Trois mouvements perpétuels* (before 1927; unpublished)

Version for orchestra: 1.1.2.1./2.1.1.0./perc/celesta/organ/strings.
Premiere: 7 April 1927: Paris; Concerts Straram; Walter Straram, cond.

W145 *Trois pastorales* (1918; unpublished)

No. 1 revised 1928 as No. 1 of *Trois pièces.*

See: W146.

W146   *Trois pièces* (1928; Heugel)

Ded. to Ricardo Viñes.
The three pieces are: *Pastorale; Toccata; Hymne.*
Premiere: 10 June 1928; Paris; Salle Chopin; Auric-Poulenc Concert.
See: B312.

W147   *Valse* (1919; Demets in *Album des six*; Eschig; 1' 30")

Ded. to Micheline Soulé.
Premiere?: 1919: Paris; Lyre et Palette Concert; Ricardo Viñes.
See: RasM 8:278.

W147A *Valse*

Version for orchestra: 1.1.1.1./1.1.1.0./timp/perc/strings.

W148   *Valse-improvisation sur le nom de Bach* (1932; first appeared in *La Revue musicale*; Rouart Lerolle)

Ded. to Vladimir Horowitz.

W149   *Villageoises* (1933; Rouart Lerolle; 4' 25")

Children's pieces for piano.
Ded. to Jean Giraudeux and Louis Jouvet.
The six pieces are: *Valse Tyrolienne; Staccato; Rustique; Polka; Petite ronde; Coda.*
See: RasM 8:147; RasM 8:281.

PIANO DUET

W150   *Sonata* (1918; revised 1939; Chester; 6')

Ded. to Mlle Simone Tilliard.
Premiere?: 24 July 1933: England; BBC broadcast; Vronsky and Babin.
See: MM 22:266; MR 1/2:155.

TWO PIANOS

W151   *Élégie* (1959; Eschig; 6')

Ded. to the memory of Marie-Blanche [de Polignac].
See: B19; B539.

W152   *L'Embarquement pour Cythère* (1951; Eschig; 2'30")

"Valse-musette" from the music for the film *Le Voyage en Amérique*.
Ded. to Henri Lavorelle.

W153   *Sonata* (1952-53; Eschig; 19')

Commissioned by and ded. to Arthur Gold and Robert Fizdale.
Premiere: 2 Nov 1953: England; BBC broadcast; Gold and Fizdale.
See: B273; B539. Also See: MusC 3-15-54:4; MT 94:577.

Discography

Virtually all the compositions of Poulenc have been recorded, most of them many times. Discographies of the recordings are available. The most complete is that by Francine Bloch, *Francis Poulenc, 1928-1982*, (Paris: Bibliothèque nationale, Départment de la phonothèque nationale et de l'audiovisuel, 1984). This list of commercial recordings issued between 1928 and 1982 is a virtually complete discography based on the collections of the Bibliothèque nationale: Départment de la phonothèque nationale, Discothèque centrale de Radio-France, Phonothèque de l'institut national de l'audiovisuel, and the British Institute of Recorded Sound. Bloch also included recordings located through discographies in periodicals and indexes.

Bloch's discography is arranged alphabetically by title of composition and performers with complete discographical information for each entry. Recordings by Poulenc of his own compositions and those of other composers are listed in a separate section. Also listed separately are spoken recordings by Poulenc and by others discussing the works of Poulenc intended primarily for radio broadcast. A list of compositions by Poulenc and an index to performers complete the work.

Because Bloch's discography is recent and virtually complete, I believe it would be redundant to repeat the information here. Instead, I include in the present discography only recordings also appearing in Bloch for which I located reviews that contribute substantial information about Poulenc and his compositions. Also listed are recordings issued after 1982 not included in Bloch and several noncommercial items of historical interest, such as tape recordings prepared for radio broadcasts, included in a separate list at the end of the Discography.

For recordings listed here and in Bloch, only the record label and number are given. The reader is referred to Bloch for complete discographical information. Complete information is given for recordings not in Bloch. "See" references, e.g., See: B100 or See: D1, identify citations in the "Bibliography" or "Discography" sections. Additional "See" and "See Also" references identify reviews in periodicals that include some information that might prove useful to scholars but that are not annotated in the Bibliography of the present work.

A sa guitare

D1   Calliope CAL 1885 digital. 1985.
      Jacques Herbillon, baritone; Jeffrey Grice, piano.
      In: Le Tombeau de Ronsard.
      See: B433. Also See: Gram 63:1450.

D2   EMI 2C-165.16231-35. See: B121; B493; B533.

D3   EMI EL 270296-1 digital. Compact disc CDC7 47550-2. 1987.
      Mady Mesplé, soprano; Gabriel Tacchino, piano.
      With: *Airs chantés. Ce doux petit visage. Les Chemins de l'amour. La*
        Courte paille. La Dame de Monte-Carlo. Deux poèmes (Aragon): "C".
        Fiançailles pour rire. Métamorphoses. Quatre chansons pour enfants:
        Nous voulons une petite soeur. Trois poèmes.
      See: B484.

D4   Fanfare FL 6005 stereo. 1984.
      Rosemarie Landry, soprano; Dalton Baldwin, piano.
      In: Chansons d'Acadie et de France.
      With: *Les Chemins de l'amour.*
      See: B282.

D5   Hyperion A 66147. 1984.
      Ann Murray, mezzo-soprano: *A sa guitare. Toréador.*
      Felicity Lott, soprano: *Banalités: Hôtel; Voyage à Paris. Bleuet. Hyde*
        Park. Montparnasse.
      Anthony Rolfe Johnson, tenor: *Calligrammes: Voyage. Deux poèmes*
        (Aragon). Métamorphoses. Miroirs brûlants: Tu vois le feu du soir.
        Priez pour paix. Tel jour, telle nuit. Trois poèmes de Louise Lalanne.
      Richard Jackson, baritone: *Les Chemins de l'amour. Colloque* (duet with
        Johnson). *Quatre chansons pour enfants: Nous voulons une petite*
        soeur.
      Graham Johnson, piano.
      See: B7; B482; B574.

D6   Nimbus 2118 stereo. Re-issued on compact disc Nimbus NI 5027.
      See: B105; B573.

D7   Spectrum SR147 stereo. 1982.
      Maria Logios, soprano; Elizabeth Buccheri, piano.
      In: Songs of "Les Six."

With: *Airs chantés: Air romantique; Air vif. Cinq poèmes* (Jacob):
Souric et Mouric. Fiançailles pour rire: Il vole.
See: B113; B346.

Airs chantés

D8   EMI 2C-165.16231-35. See: B121; B493; B533.

D9   EMI EL 270296-1 digital. Compact disc CDC7 47550-2. 1987.
Mady Mesplé, soprano; Gabriel Tacchino, piano.
With: See D3.
See: B484.

D10   Musical Heritage Society MHS 3948 stereo.
See: Fa 2/5:113.

Airs chantés: Air champêtre

D11   Cambridge CRS 2777 stereo.
See: B113; B128. Also See: ARG 46/2:42; HF/MA 31/10:88; NR
50/6:11; StR 46/8:100.

Airs chantés: Air champêtre; Air vif

D12   Westminster WST 17146 stereo. See: B361; B549.
Also See: ARG 35/10:996; NYT 5-4-69,D:26.

Airs chantés: Air romantique

D13   RCA LSC 3018 stereo. LM 3018 mono. See: B124; B217.
Also See: NR 36/7:11.

D14   Turnabout TV 4489 mono. See: B119.

Airs chantés: Air romantique; Air vif

D15   Spectrum SR 147 stereo. 1982.
Maria Logios, soprano; Elizabeth Buccheri, piano.
In: Songs of "Les Six."
With: See D7.

See: B113; B346.

Air chantés: Air vif

D16   Columbia ML 4158 mono. 1949. See: ARG 15/11:350; LJ 74:1340; SR
        32/26:54; SR 32/27:39.

D17   Philips PHM 500132 mono. PHS 900132 stereo.
        See: B254; B377; B246. Also See: HF/SR 18/6:83.

Les Animaux modèles

D18   Angel 36421 mono. S 36421 stereo. See: B525.

D19   Golden Crest CR 4042 mono. See: B101; B131; B174.

Aubade

D20   Angel 36426 mono. S 36426 stereo. Also released as HMV ALP2306.
        Gabriel Tacchino, piano; Orchestre de Société des Concerts du
            Conservatoire de Paris; Georges Prêtre, cond.
        With: *Concerto for Piano and Orchestra.*
        Re-issued on compact disc Angel CDC 47369.
        See: B229; B271; B295. Also See: NR 35/6:5.

D21   Columbia C LF 33-35. See: B107; B530.

D22   Erato ECD 88140. Compact disc. 1986. Also stereo disc NUM 75203.
        François-René Duchable, piano; Rotterdam Philharmonic; James Conlon,
            cond.
        With: *Concerto for Piano and Orchestra. Concerto in D minor for Two
            Pianos.*
        See: B136; B478.

D23   Gallo 30.169 stereo. 197?.
        Francesco Zaza, piano; Camerata de Genève; Marcello Viotti, cond.
        See: B266. Also See: Fa 8/3:219.

D24   MGM E 3069 mono.

See: B298. Also See: MA 73/16:16; NYT 12-27-53,X:11.

D25   MGM E 3415 mono. See: Disques n 79/5:381

D26   Nonesuch H 1033 mono. H 71033 stereo.
       See: B15; B176; B271; B296. Also See: ARG 31/9:868.

D27   Orion ORS 74139 stereo.
       See: B72. Also See: NR 42/3:12.

D28   Supraphon 1410.2705 quadraphonic. 1981.
       See: Fa 5/1:244; Gram 59:552; StR 47/1:95.

Badinage

D29   EMI 173196-1. 1985?
       Gabriel Tacchino, piano.
       With: *Bourée au pavillon d'Auvergne; Feuillets d'album; Impromptus;
         Napoli; Promenades.*
       See: B179.

Le Bal masqué

D30   Adès 14052-2. 2 compact discs. 1987.
       Pierre Bernac, baritone; Francis Poulenc, piano.
       With: *Élégie: for Horn and Piano. Sonata for Flute and Piano. Trio for
         Oboe, Bassoon, and Piano.*
       See: B114.

D31   Angel 36370 mono. stereo S 36370. Also issues as HMV ALP2296.
       See: B157; B340; B382; B547. Also See: ARG 33/4:346; NYT 10-30-
         66,D:20.

D32   BASF G 22765 stereo.
       Re-issued as HNH 4045 and Musicmasters 20017.
       See: B125. Also See: ARG 40/7:52; NYT 8-28-77,II:22.

D33   CRD CD 3437. Compact disc. 1986.
       Thomas Allen, baritone; The Nash Ensemble; Lionel Friend, cond.

With: *Le Bestiaire. Sextuor. Trio for Oboe, Bassoon, and Piano.*
See: B87; B480. Also See: Fa 10/2:192.

D34   Esoteric 518.
See: B40. Also See: NYT 12-20-53,X:7; SR 33/17:49.

D35   Esoteric 2000.
See: B83; B324; B352; B398; B469. Also See: SR 33/17:49.

D36   HNH 4045 stereo. See: B216. Also See: NR 46/6:14.

D37   Musicmasters MM 20017 stereo. See: Fa 6/2:271.

D38   Véga C 35 A 35 mono.
Re-issued with Poulenc's *Stabat Mater* on Westminster XWN 18422 and
9618. Re-issued on Adès 14052-2 compact disc.

D39   Westminster XWN 18422 mono.
Re-issued as Westminster W9618.
See: B172; B300; B303; B355. Also See: ARG 24/4:155; ARG
31/6:556; AtM 200/6:186; LJ 92:1117.

Banalités

D40   Adès 14.114-2. Compact disc. 1988. Re-issues of recordings copyright
in 1958 and 1960.
Pierre Bernac, baritone; Francis Poulenc, piano.
With: *Le Bestiaire. Calligrammes. Chansons gaillardes. Deux mélodies:
Le Pont. Deux poèmes* (Apollinaire). *Epitaphe. La Grenouillère.
Montparnasse. Priez pour paix.*
See: B114.

D41   Columbia ML 4333 mono. MM 958 78rpm. See: B186; B187; B353.
Also See: ARG 17/7:252.

D42   EMI 2C-165.16231-35. See: B121; B493; B533.

D43   Musical Heritage Society MHS 1776 stereo.

See: StR 34/1:64.

D44   Odyssey 32-26-0009 mono.
       See: B350; B445; B450. Also See: AtM 220/6:128; HF/SR 19/6:120.

D45   Véga C 30 A 293 mono.

D46   Westminster XWN 19105 mono. WST 17105 stereo.
       See: B286; B294; B381. Also See: ARG 33/4:347; HF/SR 17/1:70; NR
       34/4:11.

Banalités: Hôtel; Sanglots

D47   Caprice CAP 1107. See: StR 37/1:132.

Banalités: Hôtel; Voyage à Paris

D48   Columbia ML5918 mono. MS6518 stereo.
       See: B99; B149; B223; B491. Also See: HF/SR 12/2:82.

D49   Hyperion A 66147. 1984.
       Felicity Lott, soprano; Graham Johnson, piano.
       With: See D5.
       See: B7; B482; B574.

D50   RCA LM 1793.
       See: ARG 20/11:377; LJ 80:148; NYT 7-4-54,X:6.

Banalités: Voyage à Paris

D51   Columbia ML 4158.
       See: ARG 15/11:350; LJ 74:1340; SR 32/26:54; SR 32/27:39.

D52   Philips PHS 9500.356.
       See: B537. Also See: NR 46/4:11; StR 41/2:146.

Le Bestiaire

D53   Adès 14.114-2. Compact disc. 1988. Re-issues of recordings copyright
       in 1958 and 1960.
       Pierre Bernac, baritone; Francis Poulenc, piano.
       With: See D40.
       See: B114.

D54   Angel 36370 mono. S36370 stereo. Also issued as HMV ALP2296.
       See: B157; B340; B382; B547. Also See: ARG 33/4:346; NYT 10-30-
       66,D:20.

D55   Columbia CBS M 37819 stereo. 1981.
       Marilyn Horne, mezzo-soprano; Mindu Katz, piano.
       In: Marilyn Horne Live at La Scala.
       See: Fa 6/6:260; HF 33/8:88; ON 48/3:69; StR 48/9:95.

D56   CRD CD 3437. Compact disc. 1986.
       Thomas Allen, baritone; The Nash Ensemble; Lionel Friend, cond.
       With: See D33.
       See: B87; B480.

D57   EMI 2C-165.16231-35. See: B121; B493; B533.

D58   Gramophone DB 6299. See: B441.

D59   Hyperion A 66149. 1985.
       Richard Jackson, baritone; Graham Johnson, piano.
       In: Le Bestiaire.
       See: Gram 64:296.

D60   Musical Heritage Society MHS 1776. See: StR 34/1:64.

D61   Nimbus NI 5029. Compact disc. 1987.
       Shura Gehrman, bass; Adrian Farmer, piano.

D62   RCA Victor 12-0426.
       Re-issue of Gramophone DB6299.
       See: B82; B307. Also See: ARG 15/6:186; Nation 168/9:258.

D63   Véga C 35 A 33.

D64   Westminster XWN 19105 mono. WST17105 stereo.
      See: B286; B294; B381. Also See: D622. ARG 33/4:347; HF/SR
      17/1:70.

Les Biches

D65   Angel 35932. See: ARG 29/7:510.

D66   Angel DS37848 stereo. Also released as HMV ASD4067. Re-issued as
      EMI ASD4067.
      With: *Bucolique; L'Éventail de Jeanne: Pastourelle; La Guirlande de
      Campra: Matelot provençale.*
      See: B31; B77; B483. Also See: Fa 5/4:218.

D67   Arabesque 8035 stereo. 1980.
      City of Birmingham Symphony Orchestra; Louis Frémaux, cond.
      See: Fa 4/5:218.

D68   Decca LXT 2720. See: B442.

D69   Denon CO 1519. Compact disc. 1987.
      Czech Philharmonic Orchestra; Vladimir Válek, cond.

D70   HMV ASD 2989. 1973. See: B383.

D71   London LLP 624.
      See: B239. Also See: ARG 19/3:82; SR 35/43:65.

D72   MGM E 3098. See: NR 22/4:3.

D73   MGM E 3415. See: Disques n79/5:381.

D74   Parlophone PMC 1004. See: Gram 32:197.

D75   Varèse/Sarabande VC 81096. See: ARG 43/5:53.

D76   Vox Prima MWCD 7152. Compact disc. 1987.
       Luxembourg Radio Orchestra; Louis de Froment, cond.

Bleuet

D77   EMI 2C-165.16231-35. See: B121; B493; B533.

D78   Hyperion A 66147. 1984.
       Felicity Lott, soprano; Graham Johnson, piano.
       With: See D5.
       See: B7; B482; B574.

D79   Nimbus 2118. Re-issued on compact disc Nimbus NI 5027.
       See: B105; B573.

Bucolique: contribution to *Variations sur le nom de Marguerite Long*

D80   Angel DS37848 stereo. 1981. Also released as HMV ASD 4067.
       Re-issued as EMI ASD 4067.
       Philharmonic Orchestra; Georges Prêtre, cond.
       With: See D66.
       See: B31; B77; B483.

Calligrammes

D81   Adès 14.114-2. Compact disc. 1988. Re-issues of recordings copyright
       in 1958 and 1960.
       Pierre Bernac, baritone; Francis Poulenc, piano.
       With: See D40.
       See: B114.

D82   Columbia ML 4484.
       See: B191; B534. Also See: NYT 4-20-52,X:10.

D83   EMI 2C-165.16231-35. See: B121; B493; B533.

D84   Odyssey 32-26-0009.

See: B350; B445; B450. Also See: AtM 220/6:128; HF/SR 19/6:120; LJ 96:597.

D85   Philips PHM 500148 mono. PHS 900148 stereo.
        See: B247; B263; B379. Also See: MT 109:44.

D86   Rizzoli 2003 digital. 1986.
        Glenda Maurice, mezzo-soprano; Dalton Baldwin, piano.
        In: French Songs.
        See: B6.

D87   Véga C 30 A 293.

Calligrammes: Voyage

D88   Hyperion A 66147. 1984.
        Anthony Rolfe Johnson, tenor; Graham Johnson, piano.
        With: See D5.
        See: B7; B482; B574.

Capriccio: D'apré La Bal masqué

D89   Chandos ABRD 1229. 1987.
        Seta Tanyel and Jeremy Brown, pianos.
        With: *Élégie. L'Embarquement pour Cythère. Sonata* (four hands). *Sonata*
        (two pianos).
        Re-issued on compact disc Chandos CHAN 8519.
        See: Fa 13/2:197; Gram 64:321.

D90   EMI 2C-165.12519-22. See: B479.

D91   Pianissime MAG 2005. See: Fa 8/1:394.

D92   Pierre Verany PV 83011. See: B571.

Ce doux petit visage

D93   EMI 2C-165.16231-35. See: B121; B493; B533.

D94   EMI EL 270296-1 digital. Compact disc CDC 7 47550-2. 1987.
       Mady Mesplé, soprano; Gabriel Tacchino, piano.
       With: See D9.
       See: B484.

D95   RCA LM 2279.

Chanson à boire

D96   Lyrichord LLST 7208. See: B270.

D97   Moss Music Group MMG 1104 stereo. Also released as HMV CSD 3740.
          Previously issued in part on Angel S 37025.
       See: B21.

Une Chanson de porcelaine

D98   EMI 2C-165.16231-35. See: B121; B493; B533.

Chansons françaises

D99   Berkshire Boy Choir (no number).
       See: ARG 34/9:844; NYT 2-18-68,II:31.

D100   EMI 2C-165.16231-35. See: B121; B493; B533.

D101   Hyperion A 66059 stereo. 1983.
       Light Blues.
       In: Tour de France.
       See: Gram 61:178; StR 48/11:84.

Chansons françaises: La Belle si nous étions; Clic, clac, dansez sabots

D102   Moss Music Group MMG 1104 stereo. Also released as HMV CSD 3740.
          Previously issued in part on Angel S 37025.
       See: B21.

Chansons françaises: Clic, clac, dansez sabots

D103   Lyrichord LLST 7208. See: B270.

Chansons françaises: Margoton va t'a l'iau; La Belle se siet au pied de la tour

D104   Lyrichord LLST 7177. No reviews.

*Chansons françaises: Margoton va t'a l'iau; La Belle se siet au pied de la tour;
C'est la petite fille du prince*

D105   Musical Heritage Society MHS 1078 stereo.
        Grenoble University Choir; Jean Giroud, cond.
        In: Contemporary Choral Music.
        With: *Un Soir de neige.*
        No reviews.

Chansons gaillardes

D106   Adès 14.114-2. Compact disc. 1988. Re-issues of recordings copyright
        in 1958 and 1960.
        Pierre Bernac, baritone; Francis Poulenc, piano.
        With: See D40.
        See: B114.

D107   EMI 2C-165.16231-35. See: B121; B493; B533.

D108   RCA LSC 3018 stereo. LM 3018 mono.
        See: B124; B217. Also See: NR 36/7:11.

D109   Véga C 35 A 34.

Chansons gaillardes: La Belle jeunesse; Invocation aux parques

D110   Gramophone DA 4894.

Chansons gaillardes: La Belle jeunesse; Sérénade

D111   1750 Arch S 1754 stereo.
        See: B550. Also See: ON 40/22:48; StR 36/5:128.

Chansons gaillardes: Sérénade (arr.)

D112   Period 708. See: ARG 19/8:270; MA 75/6:17.

Chansons villageoises

D113   Angel 36370 mono. S 36370 stereo. Also issued as HMV ALP2296.
        See: B157; B340; B382; B547. Also See: ARG 33/4:346; NYT 10-30-
        66,D:20.

D114   Columbia ML 4333 mono. MM 958 78rpm.
        See: B187; B353. Also See: ARG 17/7:252.

D115   EMI 2C-165.16231-35. See: B121; B493; B533.

D116   Odyssey 32-26-0009.
        See: B350; B445; B450. Also See: AtM 220/6:128; HF/SR 19/6:120.

D117   Philips PHM 500148 mono. PHS 900148 stereo.
        See: B247; B263; B379. Also See: MT 109:44.

Les Chemins de l'amour

D118   Columbia M 33933. See: NR 44/2:10; ON 40/20:32.

D119   Columbia M 36682 stereo. 1981.
        Elly Ameling, soprano; Dalton Baldwin, piano.
        In: Elly Ameling: Think On Me.
        See: Gram 59:1176; StR 46/8:100.

D120   EMI EL 270296-1 digital. Compact disc CDC 7 47550-2. 1987.
        Mady Mesplé, soprano; Gabriel Tacchino, piano.
        With: See D3.
        See: B484.

D121   Fanfare FL 6005 stereo. 1984.
        Rosemarie Landry, soprano; Dalton Baldwin, piano.
        In: Chansons d'Acadie et de France.
        With: *A sa guitare.*

See: B282.

D122   Golden Crest CRS 4230 stereo. 1984.
        Arranged for piano solo.
        Grant Johannesen, piano.
        In: Invitation to Love.
        See: Fa 8/3:344.

D123   Hyperion A 66147. 1984.
        Richard Jackson, baritone; Graham Johnson, piano.
        With: See D5.
        See: B7; B482; B574.

D124   Philips PHS 9500.356.
        See: B537. Also See: NR 46/4:11; StR 41/2:146.

D125   RCA LM 1793.
        See: ARG 15/1:25; ARG 20/11:377; LJ 80:148; NR 22/6:11; NYT 7-4-
        54,X:6.

D126   Townhall S 38 stereo. 1985.
        Carlson, mezzo-soprano; Hunter, piano.
        In: Réflexions de France.
        With: *La Grenouillère. Quatre poèmes: Avant le cinéma; Carte postale.*
        See: Fa 8/6:294.

Cinq poèmes (Eluard)

D127   Adès 14.115-2. Compact disc. 1988. Re-issued from recordings
        copyright in 1958 and 1960.
        Pierre Bernac, baritone; Francis Poulenc, piano.
        With: *Le Disparu. Deux poèmes* (Aragon): *"C". La Fraîcheur et le feu.
        Métamorphoses: C'est ainsi que tu es. Parisiana. Paul et Virginie. Tel
        jour, telle nuit. Le Travail du peintre.*
        See: B114.

D128   EMI 2C-165.16231-35. See: B121; B493; B533.

D129   Turnabout TV 4489. See: B119.

D130   Véga C 35 A 33.

Cinq poèmes (Jacob)

D131   EMI 2C-165.16231-35. See: B121; B493; B533.

D132   Westminster WST 17146.
        See: B361; B549. Also See: ARG 35/10:996; NYT 5-4-69,D:26.

Cinq poèmes (Jacob): *La Petite servante*

D133   Cambridge CRS 2777.
        See: B113; B128. Also See: ARG 46/2:42; HF/MA 31/10:88; NR
        50/6:11; StR 46/8:100.

Cinq poèmes (Jacob): *Souric et Mouric*

D134   Spectrum SR147 stereo. 1982.
        Maria Logios, soprano; Elizabeth Buccheri, piano.
        In: Songs of "Les Six."
        With: See D7.
        See: B113; B346.

Cocardes

D135   EMI 2C-165.16231-35. See: B121; B493; B533.

Colloque

D136   EMI 2C-165.16231-35. See: B121; B493; B533.

D137   Hyperion A 66147. 1984.
        Richard Jackson, baritone; Anthony Rolfe Johnson, tenor; Graham
        Johnson, piano.
        With: See D5.
        See: B7; B482; B574.

Concert champêtre

D138   Angel 35993 mono. S 35993 stereo. Also released as HMV ALP 1967
        mono. ASD 517 stereo.
        See: B18; B70; B149; B230; B299; B481; B488. Also See: ARG
        29/10:803; HF/SR 11/2:64; MA 83/9:47; NR 31/5:6; RasM 31/2:164.

D139   Angel DS 38122 digital stereo. 1984.
        Jean-Patrice Brosse, harpsichord; Monte Carlo Philharmonic Orchestra;
        Georges Prêtre, cond.
        With: *Concerto in D minor for Two Pianos*.
        See: B236. Also See: Gram 62:611.

D140   Angel S 37441. Also released as HMV ASD 3489.
        See: B18; B524. Also See: HF 28/11:122; StR 41/6:154.

D141   ARGO ZRG 878. See: B476. Also See: ARG 43/6:38.

D142   Erato NUM 75210 stereo. 1986.
        Ton Koopman, harpsichord; Rotterdam Philharmonic Orchestra; James
        Conlon, cond.
        With: *Concerto in G Minor for Organ, Strings, and Tympani*.
        Re-issued on compact disc Erato ECD 88141. 1987.
        See: B136. Also See: Fa 9/5:206; Gram 63:626.

D143   Erato STU 70637. See: B230.

D144   International Piano Archives IPA106-107.
        See: B183; B485. Also See: NR 44/12:5; NYT 2-20-77,II:19.

D145   Musical Heritage Society MHS 1595.
        See: B70. Also See: HF 23/10:109.

Concerto for Piano and Orchestra

D146   Angel 36426 mono. S 36426 stereo. 1967. Also released as HMV ALP
        2306.
        Gabriel Tacchino, piano; Orchestre de Société des Concerts du
        Conservatoire de Paris; Georges Prêtre, cond.
        With: *Aubade*.

Re-issued on compact disc Angel CDC 47369.
See: B229; B271; B295. Also See: NR 35/6:5.

D147   Angel CDC 47224. Compact disc. Also released as HMV ASD 1077851
       digital. 1983.
       Cécile Ousset, piano; Bournemouth Symphony Orchestra; Rudolf Barshai,
       cond.
       See: B226.

D148   Angel S 37246. Also released as HMV SQ ASD 3299.
       See: B17. Also See: ARG 40/5:30.

D149   Erato ECD 88140. Compact disc. 1986. Erato NUM 75203 stereo disc.
       François-René Duchable, piano; Rotterdam Philharmonic Orchestra;
       James Conlon, cond.
       With: *Aubade. Concerto in D minor for Two Pianos*.
       See: B136; B478. Also See: Fa 9/5:206.

D150   Period 563. See: B505. Also See: ARG 19/7:228.

Concerto in D minor for Two Pianos

D151   Angel 35993 mono. S 35993 stereo. Also released as HMV ALP 1967
       mono. ASD 517 stereo.
       See: B149; B299; B395; B481; B488. Also See: ARG 29/10:803; HF/SR
       11/2:64; LJ 92:1117; MA 83/9:47; NR 31/5:6; RasM 31/2:164.

D152   Angel CDC 47369. Compact disc. 1987.
       Gabriel Tacchino and Bernard Ringeissen, 2 pianos; Orchestre de
       Société des Concerts du Conservatoire de Paris; Georges Prêtre,
       cond.
       With: *Aubade. Concerto for Piano and Orchestra*.

D153   Angel DS 38122 digital stereo. 1984.
       Gabriel Tacchino and Bernard Ringeissen, 2 pianos; Monte Carlo
       Philharmonic Orchestra; Georges Prêtre, cond.
       With: *Concert champêtre*.
       See: B134; B236. Also See: Gram 62:611; StR 50/5:105.

D154   Capital P 8537 mono. S 8537SD stereo.

D155   Columbia ML 5792 mono. MS 6392 stereo.
        See: ARG 29/7:510; HF/SR 10/6:70; MA 83/9:47.

D156   Decca SXL 6551. See: B395.

D157   Erato ECD 88140. Compact disc. Record NUM 75203. 1986.
        François-René Duchable and Jean-Phillipe Collard, 2 pianos; Rotterdam
            Philharmonic; James Conlon, cond.
        With: *Aubade. Concerto for Piano and Orchestra.*
        See: B136; B478. Also See: Fa 9/5:206.

D158   Inedits O.R.T.F. 995.035. See: B71.

D159   London CS 6754. See: B71. Also See: NR 41/9:4.

D160   Musical Heritage Society MHS 3576. See: B13.

D161   RCA Victor DM 1235.
        See: B37; B462. Also See: ARG 15/1:14.

D162   Seraphim S 60214. No reviews.

D163   Supraphon 110.2074.
        See: B563. Also See: NR 46/5:4.

Concerto in G Minor for Organ, Strings, and Timpani

D164   Angel 35953 mono. S 35953 stereo. Re-issued on compact disc Angel
            CDC47723.
        See: B18; B70; B129; B173; B197; B215; B230; B249; B470. Also See:
            NR 29/4:7; SR 44/22:40.

D165   Angel S 37441. Also released as HMV ASD 3489.
        See: B18; B476; B524. Also See: HF 28/11:122; StR 41/6:154.

D166   ARGO ZRG 878.
        See: B280; B476. Also See: ARG 43/6:38.

D167   Columbia ML 4329 mono. C-MM 951 78rpm.
       See: B39; B85; B197; B249; B486. Also See: ARG 17/5:168.

D168   Columbia ML 5798. See: ARG 29/7:510; MA 83/9:47.

D169   Erato NUM 75210 stereo. 1986.
       Marie-Claire Alain, organ; Rotterdam Philharmonic Orchestra; James
          Conlon, cond.
       With: *Concert champêtre.*
       Re-issued on compact disc Erato ECD 88141. 1987.
       See: B136. Also See: Fa 9/5:206; Gram 63:626.

D170   Erato STU 70637. See: B230.

D171   Musical Heritage Society MHS 1595.
       See: B70. Also See: HF 23/10:109.

D172   Orion ORS 79346.
       See: B280; B359. Also See: ARG 43/6:38.

D173   Proprius PROP 7785. See: StR 44/2:128.

D174   RCA AGL 2445. Re-issued on compact disc RCA 5750-2-RC. See:
       B238.

D175   RCA LSC 2567 stereo. LM 2567 mono.
       See: B238.

D176   Telarc DG 10077.
       Re-issued on compact disc Telarc CD 80104.
       See: Fa 6/3:228; NYT 5-1-83,II:23; StR 48/5:71.

La Courte paille

D177   EMI 2C-165.16231-35. See: B121; B493; B533.

D178   EMI EL 270296-1 digital. Compact disc CDC 7 47550-2. 1987.
       Mady Mesplé, soprano; Gabriel Tacchino, piano.

With: See D3.
See: B484.

La Courte paille: La Reine de coeur

D179   Caprice CAP 1107. See: StR 37/1:132.

La Dame de Monte-Carlo

D180   EMI EL 270296-1 digital. Compact disc CDC 7 47550-2. 1987.
Mady Mesplé, soprano; Monte-Carlo Philharmonic Orchestra; Georges
    Prêtre, cond.
With: See D3.
See: B484.

Dernier poème

D181   EMI 2C-165.16231-35. See: B121; B493; B533.

D182   RCA LSC 3018 stereo. LM 3018 mono. See: B124; B127.

Deux marches et un interméde

D183   Angel S 36519.
See: B75; B158; B227; B373. Also See: AtM 223/3:154; HF/MA 19/2:
    100; MT 110:1047; SR 51/48:76.

D184   Aurora AUR 5065. See: B104.

D185   HNH 4027. See: StR 5/78:110.

D186   Louisville Orchestra LS 68-4. See: ARG 35/6:467.

D187   Westminster WGS 8310. See: B75.

Deux mélodies

D188   EMI 2C-165.16231-35. See: B121; B493; B533.

D189   Orion ORS 82422.
       See: B112. Also See: ARG 46/2:88; Fa 6/5:254.

D190   Turnabout TV 4489. See: B119.

Deux mélodies: Le Pont

D191   Adès 14.114-2. Compact disc. 1988. Re-issued from recordings
       copyright in 1958 and 1960.
       Pierre Bernac, baritone; Francis Poulenc, piano.
       With: See D40.
       See: B114.

D192   Musical Heritage Society MHS 1776. See: StR 34/1:64.

D193   Véga C 35 A 33.

D194   Westminster XWN 19105 mono. WST 17105 stereo.
       See: B286; B294; B381. Also See: ARG 33/4:347; HF/SR 17/1:70; NR
       34/4:11.

Deux mélodies 1956

D195   RCA LSC 3018 stereo. LM 3018 mono.
       See: B124; B217. Also See: NR 36/7:11.

Deux mélodies 1956: Nuages

D196   Turnabout TV 4489. See: B119.

Deux novelettes

D197   Angel S 36602. See: B202; B306; B523.

D198   London 417 438-2. Compact disc. 1987.
       Pascal Rogé, piano.
       With: *L'Éventail de Jeanne: Pastourelle. Improvisations: Nos. 1, 2, 3,
       6, 7, 8, 12, 13, 15. Novelette sur un thème de Manuel de Falla. Les
       Soirées de Nazelles. Trois mouvements perpétuels. Trois pièces. Valse.*

See: Fa 13/2:197; Gram 64:204; HF 3/88:64.

Deux poèmes (Apollinaire)

D199   Adès 14.114-2. Compact disc. 1988. Re-issued from recordings
       copyright in 1958 and 1960.
       Pierre Bernac, baritone; Francis Poulenc, piano.
       With: See D40.
       See: B114.

D200   EMI 2C-165.16231-35. See: B121; B493; B533.

D201   Pathé FALP 50036. See: B445; B450.

D202   Véga C 35 A 33.

Deux Poèmes (Apollinaire): *Dans le jardin d'Anna*

D203   Gramophone DB 6383-4.

D204   Pathé FALP 50036. See: B445; B450.

Deux poèmes (Aragon)

D205   Caprice CAP 1107. See: StR 37/1:132.

D206   EMI 2C-165.16231-35. See: B121; B493; B533.

D207   Gramophone DB 6267. See: B440.

D208   Hyperion A 66147. 1984.
       Anthony Rolfe Johnson, tenor; Graham Johnson, piano.
       With: See D5.
       See: B7; B482; B574.

Deux poèmes (Aragon): "C"

D209   Adès 14.115-2.   Compact disc.   1988.   Re-issued from recordings copyright in 1958 and 1960.
Pierre Bernac, baritone; Francis Poulenc, piano.
With: See D40.
See: B114.

D210   Columbia ML 5918 mono. MS 6518 stereo.
See: B99; B149; B223; B491. Also See: HF/SR 12/2:82.

D211   EMI EL 270296-1 digital. Compact disc CDC 7 47550-2. 1987.
Mady Mesplé, soprano; Gabriel Tacchino, piano.
With: See D3.
See: B484.

D212   Musical Heritage Society MHS 1776 stereo.
See: StR 34/1:64.

D213   Nimbus 2118. Re-issued on compact disc Nimbus NI 5027.
See: B105; B573.

D214   RCA Victor LCT 1158.
See: B348. Also See: HF 6/1:128; LJ 80:2593; NR 23/7:7; NYT 9-25-55,X:16; SR 38/35:41.

D215   1750 Arch S 1754.
See: B550. Also See: ON 40/22:48; StR 36/5:128.

D216   Véga C 35 A 34.

Dialogues des Carmélites

D217   Angel 3585 C/L.   1958.   Re-issued on compact disc EMI 7493312. 1988?
See: B52; B240; B251; B260. Also See: MT 109:828; SR 42/13:56.

Dialogues des Carmélites: Mes filles, voila que s'achève

D218   RCA LSC 3163.
        See: B257; B275; B458. Also See: ARG 37/5:296; HF 20/12:117; ON
        35/6:34.

Le Disparu

D219   Adès 14.115-2.   Compact disc.   1988.   Re-issued from recordings
        copyright in 1958 and 1960.
        Pierre Bernac, baritone; Francis Poulenc, piano.
        With: See D127.
        See: B114.

D220   EMI 2C-165.16231-35. See: B121; B493; B533.

D221   Véga C 35 A 34.

Élégie: For horn and piano

D222   Adès 14052-2. Compact disc. 1987.
        Lucien Thévet, horn; Francis Poulenc, piano.
        With: See D30.
        See: B114.

D223   Boston BST 1009. 1959?
        James Stagliano, horn; Paul Ulanowsky, piano.
        See: B301.

D224   Crystal S 374 stereo. 1982.
        Lowell Greer, horn; Arvi Sinka, piano.
        See: Fa 6/6:282; NR 51/5:7.

D225   Crystal S375. See: Fa 6/6:282. NR 50/9:7.

D226   EMI 2C-165.12519-22. See: B479.

D227   Musicmasters 60040W/41M. 2 compact discs. 1985. Also released as
        Musical Heritage Society MHS 827387.

The Chamber Music Society of Lincoln Center: Robert Routch, horn; Charles Wadsworth, piano.
In: Francis Poulenc: Complete Music for Wind Instruments and Piano.
With: *Sextuor. Sonata for Clarinet and Bassoon. Sonata for Clarinet and Piano. Sonata for Flute and Piano. Sonata for Oboe and Piano. Sonata for Two Clarinets. Trio for Oboe, Bassoon, and Piano. Villanelle.*
See: B243.

D228   Thorofon Capella MTH 257 stereo. 1984.
Sören Hermansson, horn; Horst Göbel, piano.
In: Music for Horn.
See: Fa 8/1:389; Gram 62:242.

Élégie: For two pianos

D229   Chandos ABRD 1229. 1987.
Seta Tanyel and Jeremy Brown, 2 pianos.
With: See D89.
Re-issued on compact disc Chandos CHAN 8519.
See: Fa 13/2:197; Gram 64:321.

D230   EMI 2C-165.12519-22. See: B479.

D231   Pierre Verany PV 83011 stereo. See: B571.

D232   RBM Records RBM 3069. 1983.
Edith Henrici and Hans-Helmut Schwarz, 2 pianos.
With: *L'Embarquement pour Cythère; Sonata* (four hands); *Sonata* (two pianos).
See: B570.

L'Embarquement pour Cythère

D233   Chandos ABRD 1229. 1987.
Seta Tanyel and Jeremy Brown, 2 pianos.
With: See D89.
Re-issued on compact disc Chandos CHAN 8519.
See: Fa 13/2:197; Gram 64:321.

D234   Charade Records CH 1012.

D235   Decca DL 9791. See: Gram 34:89; HF 6/3:80; LJ 81:1264.

D236   Decca SXL 6486. See: Gram 48:1178.

D237   EMI 2C-165.12519-22. See: B479.

D238   London CS 6694.
        See: B204. Also See: NR 39/4:12; StR 27/3:104.

D239   Orion ORS 76238. See: NR 45/7:12.

D240   Pianissime MAG 2005 stereo. 1984.
        Danielle and Marielle Renault, 2 pianos.
        With: *Capriccio: D'après Le Bal masqué.*
        See: B283. Also See: Fa 8/1:394.

D241   Pierre Verany PV 83011. See: B571.

D242   RBM Records RBM 3069. 1983.
        Edith Henrici and Hans-Helmut Schwarz, 2 pianos.
        With: *Élégie; Sonata* (four hands); *Sonata* (two pianos).
        See: B570.

Epitaphe

D243   Adès 14.114-2. Compact disc. 1988. Re-issued from recordings
        copyright in 1958 and 1960.
        Pierre Bernac, baritone; Francis Poulenc, piano.
        With: See D40.
        See: B114.

D244   EMI 2C-165.16231-35. See: B121; B493; B533.

D245   Véga C 35 A 34.

L'Éventail de Jeanne: Pastourelle (arr. for guitar by Marshall)

D246   Angel S 36053. See: StR 5/77:103.

L'Éventail de Jeanne: Pastourelle (Orchestra)

D247   Angel DS 37848. Also released as HMV ASD 4067. Re-issued as EMI
ASD 4067.
Philharmonic Orchestra; Georges Prêtre, cond.
With: See D66.
See: B31; B77; B483.

D248   Chandos ABRD 1119 stereo. Also issued as compact disc CHAN 8356.
1984.
Philadelphia Orchestra; Geoffrey Simon, cond.
In: French Ballet Music of the 1920's.
With: *Les Mariés de la Tour Eiffel.*
See: B151; B177; B472.

L'Éventail de Jeanne: Pastourelle (Piano)

D249   Angel S 36602. See: B202; B306; B523.

D250   Angel S 37303. See: NR 45/12:14.

D251   London 417 438-2. Compact disc. 1987.
Pascal Rogé, piano.
With: See D198.
See: Fa 13/2:197; Gram 64:204; HF 3/88:64.

D252   MGM E 3129.
See: ARG 21/5:169; NYT 12-26-54,X:8; SR 37/48:66.

D253   Orion ORS 83459 stereo. 1983.
Flavio Varani, piano.
With: *Intermezzo in A Flat. Nocturnes. Suite française. Trois pieces.
Valse-improvisation sur le nom de Bach.*
See: B138; B195.

Exultate Deo

D254   ARGO ZRG 883. See: B106. Also See: StR 42/1:110.

Fancy

D255   EMI 2C-165.16231-35. See: B121; B493; B533.

D256   Hyperion A 66136 stereo. 1984.
        Sarah Walker, mezzo-soprano; Graham Johnson, piano.
        In: Shakespeare's Kingdom.
        See: Fa 8/3:325; Gram 62:1006.

Feuillets d'album See D29.

Fiançailles pour rire

D257   EMI 2C-165.16231-35. See: B121; B493; B533.

D258   EMI EL 270296-1 digital. Compact disc CDC 7 47550-2. 1987.
        Mady Mesplé, soprano; Gabriel Tacchino, piano.
        With: See D3.
        See: B484.

D259   Etcetera ETC 1029 digital. 1984.
        Yvonne Kenny, soprano; Lawrence Skrobacks, piano.
        In: Recital at Wigmore Hall.
        See: B385. Also See: Gram 62:1268.

D260   Haydn Society 154. See: B558

D261   Westminster WST 17146.
        See: B361; B549. Also See: ARG 35/10:996; NYT 5-4-69,D:25.

Fiançailles pour rire: Il vole

D262   Spectrum SR 147 stereo. 1982.
        Maria Logios, soprano; Elizabeth Buccheri, piano.
        In: Songs of "Les Six."

    With: See D7.
    See: B113; B346.

Fiançailles pour rire: Violon

D263   Decca DL 10013.
       See: B378. Also See: NR 27/8:13; NYT 7-19-59,X:9; SR 42/24:44.

Figure humaine

D264   Erato STU 70924.

D265   Pierre Verany PV 2811. See: Fa 7/2:282.

D266   Proprius PROP 7839. See: B552.

La Fraîcheur et le feu

D267   Adès 14.115-2. Compact disc. 1988. Re-issued from recordings
       copyright in 1958 and 1960.
       Pierre Bernac, baritone; Francis Poulenc, piano.
       With: See D127.
       See: B114.

D268   Angel LPAM 34757. 1985. Remastered disc recorded 1969. Also
       released as HMV SXLP 30556.
       Jessye Norman, soprano; Irwin Gage, piano.
       With: *Miroirs brûlants: Tu vois le feu du soir.*
       See: B54; B86. Also See: NR 54/6:14.

D269   EMI 2C-165.16231-35. See: B121; B493; B533.

D270   Musical Heritage Society MHS 1776. See: StR 34/1:64.

D271   Orion ORS 82422.
       See: B112. Also See: ARG 46/2:88; Fa 6/5:254.

D272   Philips PHM 500148 mono. PHS 900148 stereo.

See: B247; B263; B379. Also See: MT 109:44.

D273   Véga C 35 A 33.

D274   Westminster XWN 19105 mono. WST 17105 stereo.
        See: B286; B294; B381. Also See: ARG 33/4:347; HF/SR 17/1:70; NR
        34/4:11.

Gloria

D275   Angel 35953 mono. S 35953 stereo. Re-issued on compact disc Angel
        CDC 47723.
        See: B17; B129; B173; B197; B215; B249; B313; B370; B470.
        Also See: Gram 1:58; NR 29/4:7; SR 44/22:40.

D276   Angel S 37246 stereo. Also released as HMV SQ ASD 3299.
        See: B17; B370. Also See: ARG 40/5:30.

D277   Argo ZRDL 1010 stereo. 1982.
        Sylvia Greenberg, soprano; Suisse Romande Radio Choir; Lausanne Pro
        Arte Choir; Orchestre Suisse Romande; Jésus López-Cobos, cond.
        See: B347; B371.

D278   Candide QCE 31104.
        See: ARG 42/8:15; Fa 2/5:34; NR 47/1:10; ON 43/10:33.

D279   Columbia M 34551.
        See: B73; B309; B313; B370. Also See: NR 45/12:9; NYT 2-19-78,II:17.

D280   RCA LSC 2822.

D281   Telarc DG 1077. Re-issued on compact disc Telarc CD 80104.
        See: B111. Also See: Fa 6/3:228; NYT 5-1-83,II:23; StR 48/5:71.

La Grenouillère

D282   Adès 14.114-2. Compact disc. 1988. Re-issued from recordings
        copyright in 1958 and 1960.

Pierre Bernac, baritone; Francis Poulenc, piano.
With: See D40.
See: B114.

D283   EMI 2C-165.16231-35. See: B121; B493; B533.

D284   Nimbus 2118. Re-issued on compact disc Nimbus NI 5027.
See: B105; B573.

D285   Philips PHM 500132 mono. PHS 900132 stereo.
See: B246; B254; B377.

D286   Philips PHS 9500.356.
See: B537. Also See: NR 46/4:11; StR 41/2:146.

D287   Townhall S 38 stereo. 1985.
Carlson, mezzo-soprano; Hunter, piano.
In: Réflexions de France.
With: See D126.
See: Fa 8/6:294.

D288   Turnabout TV 4489. See: B119.

D289   Véga C 35 A 34.

L'Histoire de Babar

D290   Angel 36357 mono. S 36357 stereo. Also released as HMV ALP 2286.
See: B228; B272; B308; B343; B396. Also See: NR 53/3:15.

D291   Les Discophiles Française (EMI Import Series) 425105.
See: B20.

D292   Golden Crest CRS 4133. See: StR 34/5:98.

D293   Pianissime MAG 2012 stereo. 1985.

Boris Ndedltchev and Michel Rabaud, piano four-hands; Jean de Brunhoff, narrator (in French).
See: B137. Also See: Fa 8/6:242.

D294   Spectrum SR 187 stereo. 1985.
Robert J. Lurtsema, narrator; Sanda Schuldman, piano; Harry Clark, cello.
See: B343.

Huit chansons polonaises

D295   EMI 2C-165.16231-35. See: B121; B493; B533.

D296   Turnabout TV 4489. See: B119.

Humoresque

D297   Golden Crest CR 4042. See: B101; B131; B174.

D298   Period 563. See: B505. Also See: ARG 19/7:228.

Hyde Park

D299   Hyperion A 66147. 1984.
Felicity Lott, soprano; Graham Johnson, piano.
With: See D5.
See: B7; B482; B574.

Hymne

D300   EMI 2C-165.16231-35. See: B121; B493; B533.

D301   RCA LSC 3018 stereo. LM 3018 mono.
See: B124; B217. Also See: NR 36/7:11.

Impromptus See D29.

Improvisations

D302   Lyrichord LL 61. See: NYT 1-19-58,X:17; SR 41/4:52.

D303   Period 563. See: B505. Also See: ARG 19/7:228.

Improvisations: Nos. 1, 2, 3, 6, 7, 8, 12, 13, 15

D304   London 417 438-2. Compact disc. 1987.
       Pascal Rogé, piano.
       With: See D198.
       See: Fa 13/2:197; Gram 64:204; HF 3/88:64.

Improvisations: Book II

D305   Golden Crest CR 4042. See: B101; B131; B174.

Improvisation No. 5 in A minor

D306   Angel 35261.
       See: B323. Also See: HF 5/8:106; NR 23/8:14; NYT 10-2-55,X:17.

Intermezzo in A Flat Major

D307   Orion ORS 83459 stereo. 1983.
       Flavio Varani, piano.
       With: See D253.
       See: B138; B195.

       Also See: D655.

Intermezzo in A Flat Major; Intermezzo in D Flat Major

D308   RCA LSC 2751 stereo. LM 2751 mono. Re-issued on compact disc
       RCA 5665-2RC.
       See: B155; B200; B393. Also see: Gram 56:1917; Harper's
       230/1377:134; NYT 11-29-64,X:26; SR 47/52:49.

       Also See: D655.

Laudes de Saint Antoine de Padoue

D309   Lyrichord LLST 7208. See: B270.

D310   Moss Music Group MMG 1104 stereo. Also released as HMV CSD 3740.
        See: B21.

D311   Music Guild S 870.
        See: B270. Also See: LJ 95:1460; NR 37/12:9.

Litanies à la vierge noire

D312   Abbey LPB 780. See: MT 118:828.

D313   ARGO ZRG 662. See: B68; B473. Also See: NR 39/7:8.

D314   Harmonia Mundi HMC 5149 stereo. 1985.
        Choeurs et Orchestre National de Lyon; Serge Baudo, cond.
        With: *Salve Regina. Stabat Mater.*
        Re-issued on compact disc Harmonia Mundi 905149.
        See: B477. Also See: Fa 8/6:242; StR 50/8:58.

D315   Pathé DTX 247.

D316   Pearl SHE 584. 1984.
        Choir of Trinity College, Cambridge; Richard Marlow, cond.
        See: Fa 9/2:299; NR 53/9:8.

Main dominée par le coeur

D317   Columbia ML 4484. See: B191; B534.

D318   EMI 2C-165.16231-35. See: B121; B493; B533.

D319   Musical Heritage Society MHS 1776. See: StR 34/1:64.

D320   Odyssey 32-26-0009.

See: B350; B445; B450. Also See: AtM 220/6:128; HF/SR 19/6:120.

D321   RCA LM 2279.

D322   RCA LSC 3018 stereo. LM 3018 mono.
       See: B124; B217. Also See: NR 36/7:11.

D323   Westminster XWN 19105 mono. WST 17105 stereo.
       See: B286; B294; B381. Also See: ARG 33/4:347; HF/SR 17/1:70; NR
       34/4:11.

Mais mourir

D324   EMI 2C-165.16231-35. See: B121; B493; B533.

Les Mamelles de Tirésias

D325   Angel 35090. See: B188; B241; B325.

D326   Seraphim M 60029. See: B120; B130; B211.

Les Mariés de la Tour Eiffel

D327   Angel S 36519.
       See: B158; B227; B375. Also See: AtM 223/3:154; HF/MA 19/2:100;
       MT 110:1047; SR 51/48:76.

D328   Chandos ABRD 1119 stereo. 1984.
       Philadelphia Orchestra; Geoffrey Simon, cond.
       In: French Ballet Music of the 1920's.
       With: *L'Éventail de Jeanne: Pastourelle.*
       See: B151; B177; B472.

Matelote provençale: contribution to *La Guirlande de Campra*

D329   Angel DS 37848 stereo. Also released as HMV ASD 4067. Re-issued
       as EMI ASD 4067.
       Philharmonic Orchestra; Georges Prêtre, cond.
       With: See D66.

See: B31; B77; B483.

Mazurka

D330   EMI 2C-165.16231-35. See: B121; B493; B533.

D331   Robert E. Blake Editions 2.
        See: B387. Also See: SR 33/17:49.

Mélancolie

D332   Columbia ML 5746 mono. MS 6346 stereo.

D333   MCA Classics MCAD 25969.
        Cristina Ortiz, piano.
        See: Fa 13/2:369; Gram 64:81.

Messe en sol majeur

D334   ARGO ZRG 883. See: StR 42/1:110.

D335   Columbia 69486/7. See: B339.

D336   Erato STU 70924.

D337   Lyrichord LL 127 mono. LLST 7127 stereo.
        See: B175. Also See: ARG 31/5:446; NR 32/10:12.

D338   RCA LM 1088 mono. WDM 1409 45rpm. DM 1409 78rpm.
        See: B84; B187; B386.

D339   Seraphim S 60085. See: B305. Also See: LJ 94:1473.

D340   Supraphon 112.1113.
        See: B16; B60. Also See: Gram 51:1406; HF 23/10:109.

Métamorphoses

D341   EMI 2C-165.16231-35. See: B121; B493; B533.

D342   EMI EL 270296-1 digital. Compact disc CDC 7 47550-2. 1987.
       Mady Mesplé, soprano; Gabriel Tacchino, piano.
       With: See D3.
       See: B484.

D343   Gramophone DB 6267. See: B440.

D344   Hyperion A 66147. 1984
       Anthony Rolfe Johnson, tenor; Graham Johnson, piano.
       With: See D5.
       See: B7; B482; B574.

D345   RCA Victor 12-0426.
       See: B82; B307. Also See: ARG 15/6:186; NR 16/12:10.

D346   Westminster WST 17146.
       See: B361; B549. Also See: ARG 35/10:996; NYT 5-4-69,D:26.

Métamorphoses: C'est ainsi que tu es

D347   Adès 14.115-2. Compact disc. 1988. Re-issued from recordings
       copyright in 1958 and 1960.
       Pierre Bernac, baritone; Francis Poulenc, piano.
       With: See D127.
       See: B114.

D348   Pro Arte PAD 231 stereo. 1985.
       Leontyne Price, soprano; David Garvey, piano.
       In: Leontyne Price at the Ordway. Recording of inaugural concert in
       Ordway Music Theater, Saint Paul, January 8, 1985.
       See: Fa 9/2:291; HF 36/1:62; NR 53/8:10.

D349   Véga C 35 A 34.

Métamorphoses: Reine des mouettes

D350   Philips PHM 500132 mono. PHS 900132 stereo.
        See: B254; B377; B246.

Métamorphoses: Reine des mouettes; C'est ainsi que tu es

D351   Musical Heritage Society MHS 1776. See: StR 34/1:64.

D352   Westminster XWN 19105 mono. WST 17105 stereo.
        See: B286; B294; B381. Also See: ARG 33/4:347; HF/SR 17/1:70; NR
        34/4:11.

Miroirs brûlants

D353   EMI 2C-165.16231-35. See: B121; B493; B533.

Miroirs brûlants: Je nommerai ton front; Tu vois le feu du soir

D354   RCA LM 2279.

Miroirs brûlants: Tu vois le feu du soir

D355   Adès 14.115-2. Compact disc. 1988. Re-issued from recordings
        copyright in 1958 and 1960.
        Pierre Bernac, baritone; Francis Poulenc, piano.
        With: See D127.
        See: B114.

D356   Angel LPAM 34757. 1985. Remastered disc recorded 1969.
        Also released as HMV SXLP 30556.
        Jessye Norman, soprano; Irwin Gage, piano.
        With: *La Fraîcheur et le feu.*
        See: B54; B86. Also See: NR 54/6:14.

D357   Columbia ML 4484. See: B191; B534.

D358   Hyperion A 66147. 1984.
        Anthony Rolfe Johnson, tenor; Graham Johnson, piano.
        With: See D5.

See: B7; B482; B574.

D359   Odyssey 32-26-0009.
        See: B350; B445; B450. Also See: AtM 220/6:128; HF/SR 19/6:120.

D360   Véga C 35 A 34.

Montparnasse

D361   Adès 14.114-2.   Compact disc.   1988.   Re-issued from recordings
        copyright in 1958 and 1960.
        Pierre Bernac, baritone; Francis Poulenc, piano.
        With: See D40.
        See: B114.

D362   Gramophone DB 6299. See: B441.

D363   Hyperion A 66147. 1984.
        Felicity Lott, soprano; Graham Johnson, piano.
        With: See D5.
        See: B7; B482; B574.

D364   Musical Heritage Society MHS 1776. See: StR 34/1:64.

D365   Pathé FALP 50036. See: B450; B445.

D366   Philips PHS 9500.356.
        See: B537. Also See: NR 46/4:11; StR 41/2:146.

D367   Véga C 35 A 33.

D368   Westminster XWN 19105 mono. WST 17105 stereo.
        See: B286; B294; B381. Also See: ARG 33/4:347; HF/SR 17/1:70; NR
        34/4:11.

Napoli: Suite for Piano

D369   Spectrum SR322. 1987.
        Martha Anne Verbit, piano.
        See: Fa 13/1:223.

        Also see: D29.

Nocturnes

D370   Angel S 36602. See: B202; B306; B523.

D371   Concert Hall CHS 1181.
        See: B169; B430. Also See: ARG 20/11:370; NYT 7-25-54,X:6.

D372   Orion ORS 83459 stereo. 1983.
        Flavio Varani, piano.
        With: See D253.
        See: B138; B195.

Nocturne in D Major

D373   Columbia ML 4399. See: B193; B212; B354.

D374   Odyssey Y 33792. See: B64; B122.

Novelette sur un thème de Manuel de Falla

D375   Angel S 36602. See: B202; B306; B523.

D376   London 417 438-2. Compact disc. 1987.
        Pascal Rogé, piano
        With: See D198.
        See: Fa 13/2:197; Gram 64:204; HF 3/88:64.

Parisiana

D377   Adès 14.115-2. Compact disc. 1988. Re-issued from recordings
        copyright in 1958 and 1960.

Pierre Bernac, baritone; Francis Poulenc, piano.
With: See D127.
See: B114.

D378   EMI 2C-165.16231-35. See: B121; B493; B533.

D379   Véga C 35 A 34.

Paul et Virginie

D380   Adès 14.115-2. Compact disc. 1988. Re-issued from recordings
       copyright in 1958 and 1960.
       Pierre Bernac, baritone; Francis Poulenc, piano.
       With: See D127.
       See: B114.

D381   EMI 2C-165.16231-35. See: B121; B493; B533.

D382   RCA LSC 3018 stereo. LM 3018 mono.
       See: B124; B217. Also See: NR 36/7:11.

D383   Véga C 35 A 34.

Petites voix

D384   RCA Victor 10-1409.
       See: B293; B367. Also See: ARG 14/10:322; NR 16/5:7.

Pièce brève sur le nom d'Albert Roussel. See: D665.

Poèmes de Ronsard

D385   EMI 2C-165.16231-35. See: B121; B493; B533.

Poèmes de Ronsard: Attributs; Le Tombeau

D386   Cambridge CRS 2777.

See: B113; B128.   Also See: ARG 46/2:42; HF/MA 31/10:88; NR 50/6:11; StR 46/8:100.

Le Portrait

D387   EMI 2C-165.16231-35.   See: B121; B493; B533.

D388   RCA LSC 3018 stereo.   LM 3018 mono.
         See: B124; B217.   Also See: NR 36/7:11.

Presto

D389   Angel S 36602.   See: B202; B306; B523.

D390   Columbia ML 4534.
         See: B268.   Also See: ARG 19/2:57; CRB 30/4:35; LJ 78:210; NYT 8-
         24-52,X:6.

D391   Columbia ML 5746 mono.   MS 6346 stereo.

D392   RCA LSC 3233.
         See: ARG 38/12:588; NR 39/9:12; NYT 10-10-71,II:26.

D393   RCA Victor 12-0428.
         See: ARG 15/2:56; Nation 167/17:474; SR 31/44:54.

Priez pour paix

D394   Adès 14.114-2.   Compact disc.   1988.   Re-issued from recordings
         copyright in 1958 and 1960.
         Pierre Bernac, baritone; Francis Poulenc, piano.
         With: See D40.
         See: B114.

D395   EMI 2C-165.16231-35.   See: B121; B493; B533.

D396   Hyperion A 66147.   1984.
         Anthony Rolf Johnson, tenor; Graham Johnson, piano.

With: See D5.
See: B7; B482; B574.

D397   Nimbus 2118 stereo. Re-issued as compact disc Nimbus NI 5027.
       See: B105; B573.

D398   Philips PHM 500132 mono. PHS 900132 stereo.
       See: B246; B254; B377.

D399   1750 Arch S 1754.
       See: B550. Also See: ON 40/22:48; StR 36/5:128.

D400   Véga C 35 A 34.

Promenades See D29.

Quatre chansons pour enfants

D401   EMI 2C-165.16231-35. See: B121; B493; B533.

Quatre chansons pour enfants: Nous voulons une petite soeur

D402   EMI EL 270296-1 digital. Compact disc CDC 7 47550-2. 1987.
       Mady Mesplé, soprano; Gabriel Tacchino, piano.
       With: See D3.
       See: B484.

D403   Hyperion A 66147. 1984.
       Richard Jackson, baritone; Graham Johnson, piano.
       With: See D5.
       See: B7; B482; B574.

Quatre motets pour le temps de Noël

D404   ARGO ZRG 5430. See: B434.

D405   Gallo 30.157. See: B569.

D406   Lyrichord LL 127 mono. LLST 7127 stereo.
        See: B175. Also See: ARG 31/5:446; NR 32/10:12.

D407   Pierre Verany PV 2811. See: Fa 7/2:282.

D408   Supraphon 112.1113.
        See: B16; B60. Also see: Gram 51:1406; HF 23/10:109.

Quatre motets pour le temps de Noël: Hodie Christus natus est; O magnum
   mysterium

D409   Crest NEC 104.
        See: HF 23/4:106; NR 41/4:10; StR 30/3:130.

Quatre motets pour le temps de Noël: Hodie Christus natus est; Quem vidistis
   pastores

D410   Seraphim S 60085.
        See: B70; B305. Also See: LJ 94:1473.

Quatre motets pour un temps de pénitence

D411   Angel 36121 mono. S 36121 stereo. Also released as HMV ALP 2034
            mono. ASD 583 stereo. Re-issued on compact disc Angel CDC 47723.
        See: B70; B99; B156; B287; B438; B475; B528. Also See: SR 47/4:54.

D412   ARGO ZRG 5430. See: B434.

D413   Lyrichord LL 127 mono. LLST 7127 stereo.
        See: B175. Also See: ARG 31/5:446; NR 32/10:12.

D414   Music Guild S 870 stereo. 1969.
        See: B270. Also See: LJ 95:1460; NR 37/12:9.

D415   Supraphon 112.1113.
        See: B16; B60; B70. Also See: Gram 51:1406; HF 23/10:109.

Quatre motets pour un temps de pénitence: Timor et tremor.

D416   RCA LSC 3081.
    See: B372. Also See: ARG 36/7:486; StR 25/5:112.

Quatre petites prières de Saint François d'Assise

D417   Caprice CAP 1230. See: Fa 5/1:224; NR 49/6:10.

D418   Erato STU 70924.

D419   Finlandia FA 908 stereo. 1984.
    Academic Male Choir of Helsinki; Westerlund, cond.
    In: Magnificat.
    See: Fa 8/3:318.

D420   Lyrichord LLST 7208. See: B270.

D421   Moss Music Group MMG 1104 stereo. Also released as HMV CSD 3740.
    See: B21.

D422   Pierre Verany PV 2811. See: Fa 7/2:282.

Quatre poèmes (Apollinaire)

D423   Columbia ML 4484.
    See: B191; B534. Also see: NYT 4-20-52,X:10.

D424   EMI 2C-165.16231-35. See: B121; B493; B533.

D425   Odyssey 32-26-0009.
    See: B350; B445; B450. Also See: AtM 220/6:128; HF/SR 19/6:120;
    LJ 96:597.

D426   Orion ORS 82422.
    See: B112. Also See: ARG 46/2:88; Fa 6/5:254.

Quatre poèmes: L'Angouille

D427   1750 Arch S 1754.
        See: B550. Also See: ON 40/22:48; StR 36/5:128.

Quatre poèmes: Avant le cinéma

D428   RCA LSC 3018 stereo. LM 3018 mono.
        See: B124; B217. Also See: NR 36/7:11.

D429   Turnabout TV 4489. See: B119.

Quatre poèmes: Avant le cinéma; Carte postale

D430   Townhall S 38 stereo. 1985.
        Carlson, mezzo-soprano; Hunter, piano.
        In: Réflexions de France.
        With: See D126.
        See: Fa 8/6:294.

Rapsodie nègre

D431   Angel 36370 mono. S 36370 stereo. Also issued as HMV ALP 2296.
        See: B157; B340; B382; B547. Also See: ARG 33/4:346; NYT 10-30-
        66,D:20.

Rosemonde

D432   EMI 2C-165.16231-35. See: B121; B493; B533.

D433   RCA LSC 3018 stereo. LM 3018 mono.
        See: B124; B217. Also See: NR 36/7:11.

Salve Regina

D434   ARGO ZRG 883.
        See: B106. Also See: StR 42/1:110.

D435   Harmonia Mundi HMC 5149 stereo. 1985.
        Choeurs et Orchestre National de Lyon; Serge Baudo, cond.

With: *Litanies à la vierge noire. Stabat Mater.*
Re-issued on compact disc Harmonia Mundi 905149.
See: B477. Also See: Fa 8/6:242; StR 50/8:58.

D436   Pierre Verany PV 2811. See: Fa 7/2:282.

Sarabande

D437   Angel S 36849. See: B529.

D438   Deutsche Grammophon 2531.382 stereo. 1982.
Narcisco Yepes, guitar.
In: Guitar Music of Five Centuries.
See: B132. Also See: Gram 60:945.

D439   Musical Heritage Society MHS 1916. No reviews.

Sécheresses

D440   Angel 3515B.
See: B42; B461; B463; B514. Also See: ARG 21/5:161.

Sept chansons

D441   Desto DC 6483. See: NYT 3-29-70,II:24; StR 25/2:90.

Sextuor

D442   Angel 35133.
See: B170. Also See: ARG 21/5:167; NYT 2-13-55,II:10; SR 37/52:50.

D443   Angel 36261 mono. S 36261 stereo.
See: B165. Also See: HF/SR 14/10:102; NR 33/6:9; SR 48/26:60.

D444   BIS LP 61. See: B213.

D445   Capital P 8258.

See: B41; B81; B116; B168; B400; B471; B511. Also See: ARG 20/11: 374; NR 23/1:9.

D446   Columbia ML 5613 mono. MS 6213 stereo.
        See: B252; B277; B302. Also See: HF/SR 6/6:68; LJ92:1117.

D447   Columbia ML 5918 mono. MS 6518 stereo.
        See: B99; B149; B223; B491. Also See: HF/SR 12/2:82; LJ 92:1117.

D448   Concert Disc CS 221 stereo.

D449   Concert Hall H 15. No reviews.

D450   CRD CD 3437. Compact disc. 1986.
        The Nash Ensemble; Lionel Friend, cond.
        With: See D33.
        See: B87; B480.

D451   EMI 2C-165.12519-22. See: B479.

D452   Everest 6081 mono. S 3081 stereo.
        See: B490. Also See: HF/SR 12/1:88; NR 31/8:7.

D453   Musicmasters 60040W/41M. 2 compact discs. 1985. Also released as
        Musical Heritage Society MHS 827387.
        Charles Wadsworth, piano; The Chamber Music Society of Lincoln
        Center.
        In: Francis Poulenc: Complete Music for Wind Instruments and Piano.
        With: See D227.
        See: B243.

D454   Nonesuch D 79045 stereo. 1983.
        Gilbert Kalish, piano; New York Woodwind Quintet.
        With: Sonata for Oboe and Piano. Trio for Oboe, Bassoon, and Piano.
        See: B93. Also See: NR 51/6:4; NYT 1-15-84,II:23; StR 48/11:85.

D455   Robert E. Blake Editions 7.
        See: B190. Also See: ARG 18/4:120; LJ 77:205.

D456   Turnabout TVS 34507. See: B69; B526.

D457   Westminster WGS 8259. See: StR 33/5:132.

D458   Westminster XWN 19097 mono. WST 17097 stereo.
        See: HF/MA 15/8:83; HF/SR 14/10:100; SR 48/22:56.

Sinfonietta

D459   Angel S 36519.
        See: B158; B227; B375. Also See: AtM 223:154; HF/MA 19/2:100; MT
        110:1047; SR 51/48:76.

Un Soir de neige

D460   Hungaroton SLPX 11779. See: B135.

D461   Musical Heritage Society MHS 1078 stereo.
        Grenoble University Choir; Jean Giroud, cond.
        In: Contemporary Choral Music.
        With: *Chansons françaises*.

Les Soirées de Nazelles

D462   International Piano Archives IPA 2002 mono. 1977.
        John Ranck, piano.
        Previously issued as Zodiac 1002. 195-.
        See: B63. Also See: Fa 2/1:92.

D463   London 417 438-2. Compact disc. 1987.
        Pascal Rogé, piano.
        With: See D198.
        See: Fa 13/2:197; Gram 64:204; HF 3/88:64.

D464   Zodiac 1002. See: B43; B509. Also See: D665.

Sonata for Cello and Piano

D465   EMI 2C-165.12519-22. See: B479.

D466   Golden Crest CR 40899. See: B256.

Sonata for Clarinet and Bassoon

D467   Angel S36586.
        See: B164; B373. Also See: MT 111:811; NYT 5-4-69,D:26.

D468   EMI 2C-165.12519-22. See: B479.

D469   Golden Crest CR 4076. See: NR 35/4:7.

D470   Golden Crest CRS 4115. See: StR 30/6:128.

D471   Grenadilla GS 1004. See: NR 44/5:6.

D472   Merlin MRF 80701. See: B564. Also See: StR 46/5:88.

D473   Musical Heritage Society MHS 3187. No reviews.

D474   Musicmasters 60040W/41M. 2 compact discs. 1985. Also released as
        Musical Heritage Society MHS 827387.
        The Chamber Music Society of Lincoln Center: Gervase de Peyer,
        clarinet; Loren Glickman, bassoon.
        In: Francis Poulenc: Complete Music for Wind Instruments and Piano.
        With: See D227.
        See: B243.

D475   Robert E. Blake Editions 7.
        See: B190. Also See: ARG 18/4:120.

Sonata for Clarinet and Piano

D476   Chandos ABRD 1100 stereo. 1984.
        Janet Hilton, clarinet; Keith Swallow, piano.
        See: B572. Also See: Gram 62:627.

D477   Chandos CHAN 8526. Compact disc.

Gervase de Peyer, clarinet; Gwenneth Pryor, piano.
See: ARG 3-4/88:45; Fa 13/2:285; Gram 64:436; HF 4/88:78.

D478   Crystal S 331. See: B65.

D479   Crystal S 645. See: Fa 6/2:302; NR 50/9:4.

D480   Desmar 1014G. See: B326.

D481   EMI 2C-165.12519-22. See: B479.

D482   Harlequin 3806. See: NR 42/4:7.

D483   Harmonia Mundi HMB 5121. See: B332; B568.

D484   Lyrichord 193 mono. 7193 stereo.
        See: B250; B304; B360. Also See: HF/SR 21/3:98.

D485   Mark MC 3344. See: B61.

D486   Merlin MRF 80701.
        See: B564. Also See: Fa 4/5:218; StR 46/5:88.

D487   Musicmasters 60040W/41M. 2 compact discs. 1985. Also released as
        Musical Heritage Society MHS 827387.
        The Chamber Music Society of Lincoln Center: Gervase de Peyer,
        clarinet; Charles Wadsworth, piano.
        In: Francis Poulenc: Complete Music for Wind Instruments and Piano.
        With: See D227.
        See: B243.

D488   Nonesuch H 1033 mono. H 71033 stereo.
        See: B15; B176; B296. Also See: ARG 31/9:868.

D489   Orion ORS 82426. See: Fa 6/1:254; NR 50/7:9.

D490   University of Michigan Records SM 0018 stereo. 1982.
David Shifrin, clarinet; William Doppman, piano.
In: 20th Century Classics for Clarinet and Piano.
See: B32.

Sonata for Flute and Piano

D491   Adès 14052-2. Compact disc. 1988.
Francis Poulenc, piano.
With: See D30.
See: B114.

D492   Angel 36261 mono. S 36261.
See: B165. Also See: HF/SR 14/10:102; NR 33/6:9; SR 48/26:60.

D493   BIS LP 140. See: NR 48/8:8.

D494   Denon CO 1476. Compact disc.
Alain Marion, flute; Pascal Rogé, piano.
In: La Flute à Paris.
See: NYT 7-19-87

D495   Desmar 1012G. See: StR 41/1:94.

D496   EMI 2C-165.12519-22. See: B479.

D497   Golden Crest RE 7010. See: B5.

D498   Jerusalem ATB 8401 stereo. 1984.
E. Talmi, flute; Y. Talmi, piano.
See: Fa 8/3:352; Gram 62:775.

D499   Musical Heritage Society MHS 9065.

D500   Musical Heritage Society MHS 4180 stereo. 1980.
Carol Wincenc, flute; András Schiff, piano.
In: The Naumburg Foundation Presents Carol Wincenc.
Re-issued on Musicmasters MM 20004.

See: B567.   Also See: HF/MA 30/10:96; NYT 4-12-81, II:28; StR
45/4:127.

D501   Musicmasters MM 20004. See: Fa 5/1:263.

D502   Musicmasters 60040W/41M. 2 compact discs. 1985. Also released as
Musical Heritage Society MHS 827387.
The Chamber Music Society of Lincoln Center: Paula Robison, flute;
Charles Wadsworth, piano.
In: Francis Poulenc: Complete Music for Wind Instruments and Piano.
With: See D227.
See: B243.

D503   Odyssey Y 33905. See: NR 44/2:6.

D504   Pandora PAN 106. See: B185.

D505   Stolat SZM 0119.
See: B90. Also See: Fa 5/5:271; StR 47/7:72.

D506   Supraphon 1111.2477.
See: B91. Also See: Gram 60:936.

Sonata for Flute and Piano: Cantabile

D507   Columbia CBS M 35176. See: NR 47/8:5.

D508   Desmar 1012G. See: B326. Also see: StR 41/1:94.

Sonata for Horn, Trumpet, and Trombone

D509   ARGO ZRG 731. See: NR 41/8:13.

D510   Crystal S 367. See: StR 24/3:120.

D511   Desto DC 6474-77. See: StR 24/3:120.

D512   EMI 2C-165.12519-22. See: B479.

D513   Grenadilla GS 1027. See: Fa 2/6:131; NR 47/8:4.

D514   Musical Heritage Society MHS 3753. No reviews.

D515   Night Music 103-04. See: Gramophone Shop Sept. 1947:8.

D516   Stradivari 605. See: B513. Also See: HF 2/1:58.

Sonata for Oboe and Piano

D517   Angel 36261.
       See: B165. Also See: HF/SR 14/10:102; NR 33/6:9; SR 48/26:60.

D518   Deutsche Grammophone 2555 013.

D519   EMI 2C-165.12519-22. See: B479.

D520   Jecklin 239 digital. 1985.
       George Paradise, oboe; Carl Rutti, piano.
       See: Fa 10/1:300.

D521   Lyrichord 193 mono. 7193 stereo.
       See: B250; B304; B360; B527.

D522   Lyrichord LLST7320 stereo.
       See: B93. Also See: Fa 6/2:299; Fa 7/1:235.

D523   Musicmasters 60040W/41M. 2 compact discs. 1985. Also released as
       Musical Heritage Society MHS 827387.
       The Chamber Music Society of Lincoln Center: Leonard Arner, oboe;
       Charles Wadsworth, piano.
       In: Francis Poulenc: Complete Music for Wind Instruments and Piano.
       With: See D227.
       See: B243.

D524   Nonesuch H 1033 mono. H71033 stereo.
        See: B15; B176; B296. Also See: ARG 31/9:868.

D525   Nonesuch D 79045 stereo. 1983.
        Gilbert Kalish, piano; New York Woodwind Quintet.
        With: *Sextuor. Trio for Oboe, Bassoon, and Piano.*
        See: B93. Also See: NR 51/6:4; NYT 1-15-84,II:23; StR 48/11:85.

D526   Pavane ADW 7007. See: Fa 6/6:280.

D527   Telarc S 5034. See: B93. Also See: Fa 7/1:235.

Sonata for Two Clarinets

D528   EMI 2C-165.12519-22. See: B479.

D529   Musicmasters 60040W/41M. 2 compact discs. 1985. Also released as
        Musical Heritage Society MHS 827387.
        The Chamber Music Society of Lincoln Center: Gervase de Peyer and
            Peter Simenauer, clarinets.
        In: Francis Poulenc: Complete Music for Wind Instruments and Piano.
        With: See D227.
        See: B243.

Sonata for Violin and Piano

D530   EMI 2C-165.12519-22. See: B479.

D531   Fantasy 85021.

D532   Ophelia OP 67103. Compact disc. 1986.
        Aurelio Perez, violin; Janis Vakerelis, piano.
        See: B78.

D533   Orion ORS 7292. See: B521.

D534   Sine Qua Non Superba SA 2016. See: StR 41/4:160.

Sonata (four hands)

D535   Chandos ABRD 1229. 1987.
        Seta Tanyel and Jeremy Brown, piano.
        With: See D89.
        Re-issued on compact disc Chandos CHAN 8519.
        See: Fa 13/2:197; Gram 64:321.

D536   Columbia ML 4854.
        See: B150; B512. Also See: ARG 20/9:284; NR 22/3:15.

D537   Decca LXT 6158 mono. SXL 6158 stereo. See: B394.

D538   Devon DV 7111 stereo. 1977.
        Jeffry and Ronald Marlowe, piano.
        In: Concert Favorites: Classic Beatles.
        See: NR 46/2:10.

D539   EMI 2C-165.12519-22. See: B479.

D540   Golden Crest CRS 4170. See: NR 31/10:14.

D541   Inter-American Musical Editions OAS 003.
        Nelly and Jaime Ingram, piano.
        In: Nelly and Jaime Ingram--Panamanian Piano Duo.

D542   London CM 9420 mono. CS 6420 stereo.
        See: HF/MA 15/12:112; NYT 10-17-65,X:30.

D543   Pierre Verany PV 83011. See: B571.

D544   RBM Records RBM 3069. 1983.
        Edith Henrici and Hans-Helmut Schwarz, piano.
        With: See D242.
        See: B570.

D545   RCA LM 1705 mono. WDM 1705 45rpm.
        See: ARG 19/1:26; NR 20/7:14; SR 35/35:50.

Sonata (two pianos)

D546   Chandos ABRD 1229. 1987.
        Seta Tanyel and Jeremy Brown, 2 pianos.
        With: See D89.
        Re-issued on compact disc Chandos CHAN 8519.
        See: Fa 13/2:197; Gram 64:321.

D547   Columbia ML 5068.
        See: B56; B297. Also See: ARG 22/5:81; NYT 12-18-55,X:17.

D548   Columbia ML 5918 mono. MS 6518 stereo.
        See: B99; B149; B223; B491. Also See: HF/SR 12/2:82; NYT 12-18-55,X:17.

D549   Command CC 11013. See: B100; B285.

D550   Decca LXT 6357. See: B329.

D551   EMI 2C-165.12519-22. See: B479.

D552   Golden Crest CR 4070 mono. S 4070 stereo.
        See: B100; B148. Also See: HF 14/2:83.

D553   Klavier KS 549. See: B66.

D554   London CS 6583. See: B218; B520.

D555   Mace M 9023 mono. SM 9023 stereo. 1966?.
        Liselotte Gierth and Gerd Lohmeyer, 2 pianos.
        See: HF/SR 16/5:92; NR 34/10:15.

D556   Musical Heritage Society MHS 854. No reviews.

D557   Musical Heritage Society MHS 3576 stereo. 1977.
        Joan Yarbrough and Robert Cowan, 2 pianos.
        With: *Concerto in D Minor for Two Pianos and Orchestra.*

See: B13.

D558   Orion ORS 76238. See: B62.

D559   Pierre Verany PV 83011. See: B571.

D560   RBM Records RBM 3069. 1983.
        Edith Henrici and Hans-Helmut Schwarz, 2 pianos.
        With: See D242.
        See: B570.

Stabat Mater

D561   Angel 36121 mono. S 36121 stereo. Also released as HMV ALP 2034
            mono. ASD 583 stereo.
        See: B99; B156; B278; B287; B438; B475; B477; B528.
        Also See: ARG 31/6:556; SR 47/4:54

D562   Harmonia Mundi HMC 5149 stereo. 1985.
        Choeurs et Orchestre National de Lyon; Serge Baudo, cond.; Michele
            Lagrange, soprano.
        With: *Litanies à la vierge noire. Salve Regina.*
        Re-issued on compact disc Harmonia Mundi 905149.
        See: B477. Also See: Fa 8/6:242; StR 50/8:58.

D563   Westminster XWN 18422. Re-issued as Westminster W9618. 1964.
        See: B172; B278; B300; B303; B355. Also See: ARG 24/4:155; AtM
            200/6:186.

Suite française (arr. for winds)

D564   Nonesuch D 78026 stereo. 1982.
        London Wind Orchestra; Denis Wick, cond.
        In: Music for Winds--Vol. 2.
        See: HF 35/5:71; NR 53/1:4.

D565   WEA Enigma Classics K 53574. See: B327.

Suite française (Orchestra)

D566   Angel S 36519.
       See: B158; B227; B375. Also See: AtM 223:154; HF/MA 19/2:100; MT
       110:1047; SR 51/48:76.

D567   Music Guild 39 mono. S 39 stereo.
       See: B50; B489. Also See: LJ 88:3657; NR 31/5:4.

Suite française (Piano)

D568   Angel S 36602. See: B202; B306; B523.

D569   Columbia ML 4399. See: B193; B212; B267; B354.

D570   Columbia ML 5746 mono. MS 6346 stereo.

D571   Golden Crest CR 4042. See: B101; B131; B174.

D572   Mercury MG 15007.
       See: B189. Also See: ARG 16/12:401; LJ 75:1848; Nation 171/6:134.

D573   Odyssey Y 33792. See: B64; B122.

D574   Orion ORS 83459 stereo. 1983.
       Flavio Varani, piano.
       With: See D253.
       See: B138; B195.

Suite française (transcribed for harp)

D575   Orion ORS 76231. See: B522.

Suite in C

D576   Griffon 1003. See: NR 19/7:12; SR 35/13:48.

D577   Hungaroton SLPX 12009-10. See: B432.

Tel jour, telle nuit

D578   Adès 14.115-2. Compact disc. 1988. Re-issued from recordings
        copyright in 1958 and 1960.
        Pierre Bernac, baritone; Francis Poulenc, piano.
        With: See D127.
        See: B114.

D579   BBC LP 25950 mono. 1 side. Recorded November 10, 1956.
        Pierre Bernac, baritone; Francis Poulenc, piano.

D580   EMI 2C-165.16231-35. See: B121; B493; B533.

D581   Golden Crest GCCL 202. No reviews.

D582   Gramophone DB 6383-4.

D583   Hyperion A 66147. 1984.
        Anthony Rolfe Johnson, tenor; Graham Johnson, piano.
        With: See D5.
        See: B7; B482; B574.

D584   Musical Heritage Society MHS 1776. See: StR 34/1:64.

D585   RCA LSC 3018 stereo. LM 3018 mono.
        See: B124; B217. Also See: NR 36/7:11.

D586   Véga C 30 A 293.

D587   Westminster XWN 19105 mono. WST 17105 stereo.
        See: B286; B294; B381. Also See: ARG 33/4:347; HF/SR 17/1:70; NR
        34/4:11.

Thème varié

D588   Golden Crest CR 40866. See: B203; B258.

D589   Golden Crest CRS 4201. See: Au 64/5:89.

       Also See: D655.

Toréador

D590   EMI 2C-165.16231-35. See: B121; B493; B533.

D591   Hyperion A 66147. 1984.
       Ann Murray, mezzo-soprano; Graham Johnson, piano.
       With: See D5.
       See: B7.

Le Travail du peintre

D592   Adès 14.115-2. Compact disc. 1988. Re-issued from recordings
          copyright in 1958 and 1960.
       Pierre Bernac, baritone; Francis Poulenc, piano.
       With: See D127.
       See: B114.

D593   BBC LP 26798 mono. 1 side. Recorded September 6, 1957.
       Pierre Bernac, baritone; Francis Poulenc, piano.

D594   EMI 2C-165.16231-35. See: B121; B493; B533.

D595   Philips PHM 500148 mono. PHS 900148 stereo.
       See: B247; B263; B379. Also See: MT 109:44.

D596   Turnabout TV 4489. See: B119.

D597   Véga C 30 A 293.

Trio for Oboe, Bassoon, and Piano

D598   Adès 14052-2. 2 compact discs. 1987.
       Francis Poulenc, piano.
       With: See D30.
       See: B114.

D599   Angel 36261 mono. S 36261 stereo.
       See: B165. Also See: HF/SR 14/10:102; NR 33/6:9; SR 48/26:60.

D600   Angel S 36586.
       See: B164; B373. Also See: MT 111:811; NYT 5-4-69,D:26.

D601   Columbia D 14213/4. See: B94.

D602   CRD CD 3437. Compact disc. 1986.
       The Nash Ensemble; Lionel Friend, cond.
       With: See D33.
       See: B87; B480.

D603   EMI 2C-165.12519-22. See: B479.

D604   Musical Heritage Society MHS 3187.

D605   Musicmasters 60040W/41M. 2 compact discs. 1985. Also released as
           Musical Heritage Society MHS 827387.
       The Chamber Music Society of Lincoln Center: Leonard Arner, oboe;
           Loren Glickman, bassoon; Charles Wadsworth, piano.
       In: Francis Poulenc: Complete Music for Wind Instruments and Piano.
       With: See D227.
       See: B243.

D606   Nonesuch D 79045 stereo. 1983.
       New York Woodwind Quintet; Gilbert Kalish, piano.
       With: *Sextuor. Sonata for Oboe and Piano*.
       See: B93. Also See: NR 51/6:4; NYT 1-15-84,II:23; StR 48/11:85.

D607   Robert E. Blake Editions 7.
       See: B190. Also See: ARG 18/4:120.

D608   Telefunken AW 6.42081. See: B214.

D609   Unicorn 1005.
        See: B171. Also See: ARG 22/2:28; NR 23/8:10.

Trois chansons de F. Garcia Lorca

D610   EMI 2C-165.16231-35. See: B121; B493; B533.

D611   Haydn Society 154. See: B558.

D612   Westminster WST 17146.
        See: B361; B549. Also See: ARG 35/10:996; NYT 5-4-69,D:26.

Trois mouvements perpétuels

D613   Angel S 36602. See: B202; B306; B523.

D614   Angel S 37303. See: B201. Also See: NR 45/12:14.

D615   Columbia ML 4399. See: B193; B200; B212; B267; B354.

D616   Concert Hall CHS 1181.
        See: B169; B430. Also See: ARG 20/11:370; NYT 7-25-54,X:6.

D617   London 417 438-2. Compact disc. 1987.
        Pascal Rogé, piano.
        With: See D198.
        See: Fa 13/2:197; Gram 64:204; HF 3/88:64.

D618   Meridian E 77018. See: Gram 57:885.

D619   Odyssey Y 33792. See: B64; B122; B201.

D620   RCA ARL 2 2359 stereo. 2 discs. 1979.
        Artur Rubinstein, piano.

In: The Artistry of Artur Rubinstein.
Previously issued as RCA Victor LSC2751. Re-issued on compact disc
  RCA 5665-2RC.
See: B351. Also See: ARG 31/7:648; ARG 42/8:43; Gram 56:1917.

D621   RCA LSC 2751 stereo. LM 2751 mono. Re-issued on compact disc
  RCA 5665-2RC.
See: B155; B200; B201. Also See: Harper's 230/1377: 134; NYT 11-
  29-64,X:26; SR 47/52:49.

D622   Supraphon 1111.3771-72 stereo. 2 discs. 1984.
  Joseph Pálenicëk, piano.
See: Fa 7/6:315.

  Also see: D663.

Trois mouvements perpétuels (Arr. for two pianos)

D623   Columbia ML 2197. arr. for 2 pianos.
See: ARG 18/3:88.

Trois mouvements perpétuels: No. 1 in B Flat Major (Transcribed for violin)

D624   RCA ARM 40944. See: HF 25/8:71.

Trois mouvements perpétuels: Nos. 1 and 3 (Transcribed for flute, harp, and
  strings)

D625   Angel S 37308.
  Transcribed by Ransom Wilson.
See: ARG 42/1:50; NR 46/5:5; StR 41/1:100.

Trois pièces

D626   Columbia ML 5746 mono. MS 6346 stereo.

D627   London 417 438-2. Compact disc. 1987.
  Pascal Rogé, piano.
  With: See D198.
See: Fa 13/2:197; Gram 64:204; HF 3/88:64.

D628   Orion ORS 83459 stereo.   1983.
       Flavio Varani, piano.
       With: See D253.
       See: B138; B195.

D629   Period 563 mono. See: B505.

D630   RCA FY 113 stereo.   1984.
       Marie-Catherine Girod, piano.
       In: French Piano Works.
       See: B225. Also See: Fa 7/6:311; Gram 62:509.

Trois pièces: Pastorale; Toccata

D631   Angel COLH 300.
       See: B205; B248.   Also See: ARG 32/2:129; Gram 42:449; HF/SR
       14/10:114.

Trois pièces: Toccata

D632   Angel S 36602. See: B202; B306; B523.

D633   Columbia M 32070. See: B76. Also See: NR 4/6:15.

D634   Meridian E 77018. See: Gram 57:885.

Trois poèmes (Louise de Vilmorin)

D635   EMI 2C-165.16231-35. See: B121; B493; B533.

D636   EMI EL 270296-1 digital. Compact disc CDC 7 47550-2.   1987.
       Mady Mesplé, soprano; Gabriel Tacchino, piano.
       With: See D3.
       See: B484.

D637   Westminster WST 17146.
       See: B361; B549. Also See: ARG 35/10:996; NYT 5-4-69,D:26.

Trois poèmes de Louise Lalanne

D638   EMI 2C-165.16231-35. See: B121; B493; B533.

D639   Hyperion A 66147. 1984.
        Anthony Rolfe Johnson, tenor; Graham Johnson, piano.
        With: See D5.
        See: B7; B482; B574.

D640   Westminster WST 17146.
        See: B361; B549. Also See: ARG 35/10:996; NYT 5-4-69,D:26.

Trois poèmes de Louise Lalanne: Chanson; Hier

D641   Cambridge CRS 2777.
        See: B113; B128. Also See: ARG 46/2:42; HF/MA 31/10:88; NR
        50/6:11; StR 46/8:100.

Valse

D642   Angel S 36602. See: B202; B306; B523.

D643   Golden Crest CR 4042. See: B101; B131; B174.

D644   London 417 438-2. Compact disc. 1987.
        Pascal Rogé, piano.
        With: See D198.
        See: Fa 13/2:197; Gram 64:204; HF 3/88:64.

D645   Period 563. See: B505. Also See: ARG 19/7:228.

Valse (Arr. for clarinet and orchestra)

D646   Columbia MM 865; 4 10" discs. LP C-ML 4260 mono.
        See: ARG 16/5:164; NR 17/12:12.

Valse-improvisation sur le nom de Bach

D647   Orion ORS 83459 stereo. 1983.

Flavio Varani, piano.
With: See D253.
See: B138; B195.

Also See: D655.

Villageoises

D648   Golden Crest CR 4042. See: B101; B131; B174.

Also See: D655.

Villanelle

D649   Musicmasters 60040W/41M. 2 compact discs. 1985. Also released as
        Musical Heritage Society HMS 827387.
        The Chamber Music Society of Lincoln Center: Paula Robison, piccolo;
        Charles Wadsworth, piano.
        In: Francis Poulenc: Complete Music for Wind Instruments and Piano.
        With: See D227.
        See: B243.

La Voix humaine

D650   Andante AD 72405 stereo. 1981.
        Carole Farley, soprano; Adelaide Symphony Orchestra; José Sérébrier,
        cond.
        Re-issued on compact disc Chandos CD 8331.
        See: B133; B474.

D651   Le Chant du Monde LDX 78733. See: Fa 6/6:203.

D652   RCA LSS2385 stereo. LS2385 mono. Re-issued as Voix de Son Maître
        CVA 918. Re-issued as EMI CDM 7 69696 2 compact disc. 1988.
        See: B8; B95; B103; B349; B374; B380; B510.

NON-COMMERCIAL SOUND RECORDINGS

Records:

D653   Collection Français de notre temps, no. 13. Paris: Dunod. 1 disc.
        197-?.
        Ma musique est mon portrait.
        Francis Poulenc.
        Motion Picture, Broadcasting and Recorded Sound Division. Library of
        Congress, Washington, D.C. Catalogue number: 13 FT62.

D654   *Concert champêtre.* No date [1948?].
        16" disc. 1 side. 33rpm. mono.
        Francis Poulenc, piano; New York Philharmonic Orchestra; Dmitri
        Mitropoulos, cond.
        Voice of America Broadcast.
        Motion Picture, Broadcasting and Recorded Sound Division. Library of
        Congress, Washington, D.C. Catalogue number: LWO 9670,
        r22A11-B1.

D655   *Intermezzo.* March 1933.
        Recorded at a live performance in Paris at the Comédie des
        Champs-Elysées.
        Bibliothèque de L'Arsenal LO 16201 (Bob. 2) nos. 327-29, 31-33.

D656   *Pierre Bernac: Mélodies and Lieder.*
        Friends of Pierre Bernac PB1/3 mono. 3 discs. ca1987. Available from
        Discurio, 9 Shepherd Street, London W1Y7LG.
        Pierre Bernac, baritone; with various artists.
        Contents: PB1--Gounod: *Ce que je suis sans toi. Au rossignol. Venise.
        Prière. Chanson de printemps. L'Absent. Viens, les gazons sont verts.
        Envoi de fleurs. Mignon* (with Francis Poulenc, piano. BBC broadcast
        October 9, 1957). Poulenc: *L'Histoire de Babar* (Graham Johnson,
        piano. BBC broadcast November 27, 1977).
        PB2--Liszt: *Freudvoll und leidvoll. Es muss ein Wunder-bares sein.
        Nimm einen Strahl der Sonne* (re-issued from HMV DA4914). Gounod:
        Au rossignol (HMV DB6250, 1946). *Ce que je suis sans toi* (HMV
        DA4915). Fauré: *Après un rêve* (HMV DA4931). *Le Secret. Aurore*
        (both issued for the first time). *Prison* (HMV DA4889). *Soir* (HMV
        DA1907, 1949). Debussy: *Trois chansons de France* (HMV DA4890).
        Trois ballades de Villon (HMV DB6385/6, 1948). *Colloque sentimental*
        (HMV DB6386, 1948). Satie: *La Statue de bronze. Le Chapelier* (HMV
        DA4893). All with Francis Poulenc, piano.

PB3--Poulenc: *Le Bestiaire* (HMV DB6299, 1946). *Chansons gaillardes: La Belle jeunesse; Invocation aux Parques* (HMV DA4894). *Tel jour, telle nuit* (HMV DB6383/4, 1948). *Deux poèmes* (Aragon). *Métamorphoses* (both from HMV DB6267, 1946). Ravel: *Don Quichotte à Dulcinée* (HMV DA1869, 1947). Vellones: *A mon vils* (HMV W1516). All with Francis Poulenc, piano. Beydts: *Le lyre et les amours*. Orchestra conducted by Louis Beydts.
See: B114; B482. Also See: MT 122:539.

Tapes: All in Motion Picture, Broadcasting and Recorded Sound Division. Library of Congress, Washington, D.C.

D657   *Concert champêtre*. Recorded November 14, 1948.
Francis Poulenc, piano; New York Philharmonic Orchestra; Dmitri Mitropoulos, cond.
Catalogue number: LWO 6359, r44B4-45B2.

D658   *Concert champêtre*. Recorded November 20, 1949.
Wanda Landowska, harpsichord; New York Philharmonic Orchestra; Leopold Stokowski, cond.
Catalogue number: LWO 6359, r70A4-71A2.

D659   *Concerto in D minor for Two Pianos*. Recorded January 21, 1961, in Symphony Hall, Boston, by WGBH.
Francis Poulenc and Evelyne Crochet, pianos; Boston Symphony Orchestra; Charles Münch, cond.
Catalogue number: LWO 12095, r37 cut 1.

D660   *Litanies à la vierge noire*. Recorded March 3 [no year], in Sanders Theater.
Radcliffe Choral Society; Nadia Boulanger, cond.
Catalogue number: LWO 9485, r14A2.

D661   Recital With Pierre Bernac. Recorded November 23, 1948.
Pierre Bernac, baritone; Francis Poulenc, piano.
With: Poulenc: *Deux poèmes: Fêtes galantes. Métamorphoses.* Gounod: *Au rossignol. Quand tu chantes.* Duparc: *Élégie. L'Invitation au voyage.* Ravel: *Chanson à boire. Chanson épique. Chanson romanesque.*
Catalogue number: T6110, reel 21.

ADDENDA

D662   Columbia 15041. See: B196.

D663   Columbia 13053. See: B196.

D664   NW Records 229 stereo. 1978.
Recording of Samuel Barber's *Mélodies passagères, Op. 27.*
Pierre Bernac, baritone; Francis Poulenc, piano.
Recorded 15 Feb 1952, in New York City for Columbia XLP9280; never
released.

D665   EMI C069-73101. 1982.
Gabriel Tacchino, piano.
*Suite française. Pièce breve sur le nom d'Albert Roussel. Les Soirées
de Nazelles. Thème varié. Trois Intermezzi. Valse-Improvisation sur
le nom de Bach. Villageoises.*
See: B178.

Bibliography

This is an annotated Bibliography of selected references. Because of the vast amount of material available about Poulenc, not all of which is of equal value to scholars, it was not possible to include everything in this Bibliography. Material included here was chosen because it revealed important information about the life and music of the composer. Additional references about individual works and performances of those works are listed in the "Works and Performances" and "Discography" sections. "See" references refer to individual works and particular performances of those works as described in the "Works and Performances" section (e.g., See: W10) and in the "Discography" section (e.g., See: D8). There are also cross references to additional information in the entries in the "Bibliography" section (e.g., See: B40).

B1   A.C.F. "London Concerts," *Musical Times* 90 (March 1949):90.

   Review of the first concert performance of *L'Histoire de Babar* on February 8, 1949. "As a private gift to his niece--which is how the work originated--it passes; but a paying public could justifiably expect more of Uncle Francis." See: W109.

B2   "Academy of Arts and Letters Honors Four Foreigners," *New York Times* January 7, 1959, p. 66.

   Announcement of Poulenc's selection to membership. "Honorary membership in the academy and institute is limited to fifty foreigners who have distinguished themselves in art, letters and music. . . . Poulenc, now in his sixtieth year, won attention for his compositions before he was 20." A photograph of Poulenc is included.

B3   Adema, Pierre-Marcel. "Les Mamelles de Tirésias: Essai bibliographi-
      que," *La Revue des lettres modernes*, Quatrième série, nos. 123-26
      (1965):55-63.

      Bibliography of performances of the play, including the premiere of
      Poulenc's musical setting, with sources for reviews of performances, lists
      of cast members, and production information. See: W2.

B4   Advertisement. *Chesterian* 2 (October 1919):58-59.

      A two-page advertisement for pieces recently published by Chester,
      including *Trois mouvements perpétuels, Le Bestiaire*, and *Cocardes*.
      "The music of Francis Poulenc may be likened in some ways to the art
      of Picasso; there is no perspective, as it were, and no elaborate detail.
      But it must not be surmised from this that he is a 'cubist' or 'furist'
      composer; he is too refined an artist and too great an individuality to be
      dismissed with one of these vaguely comprehensive labels." See: W61;
      W71; W144.

B5   Affelder, Paul. "Records In Review," *High Fidelity* 12 (April 1962):82-83.

      Review of a recording of *Sonata for Flute and Piano* on Golden Crest
      RE7010.   The music "makes for good listening . . . Especially is this
      true of the charming little Poulenc Sonata." Pellerite "is a master of his
      instrument. His tone is full and appealing in all registers, his technique
      secure." See: D497.

B6   Alfano, Vincent. "Glenda Maurice," *Fanfare* 10 (July 1987):215.

      Review of Rizzoli 2003, a recording of songs performed by Maurice, who
      "may not have the lightness of tone or the complete insight into the texts
      to make this recital a complete success, but the voice is full and steady,
      and she seems to know what she's singing about a good deal of the
      time. What she lacks . . . is the French touch to make these songs
      really come into their own." See: D86.

B7   ___. "The Songmakers' Almanac," *Fanfare* 10 (November 1986):261-62.

      Review of a recording of songs on Hyperion A66149. Richard Jackson
      "has a pleasing but not terribly interesting voice; light, clear, tonally
      dependable, but with limited colors, and the colors that are displayed are
      not among the most vibrant. . . . High praise for Graham Johnson--an
      accompanist to rank with the best technically, and the most impressive

interpretively."   See: D5; D49; D78; D88; D123; D208; D299; D344; D358; D363; D396; D403; D583; D639.

B8   "Allo, cheri?," *Saturday Review* 43 (May 28, 1960):62.

Review of a recording of *La Voix humaine* on RCA Victor Soria Series LS2385. "Like a skilled chef who undertakes to prepare a dish from a limited number of ingredients, it ends up more fluff than substance, an anecdote enlarged to a novelette without a sufficiency of matter to support the etc.-etc.'s that enter into the monologue. Any section of the music would endorse the high opinion commonly held of Poulenc, especially as a composer for texts." See: D652.

B9   Almond, Frank. *Melody and Texture in the Choral Works of Francis Poulenc*. Ph.D. dissertation, Florida State University, 1970.

Analysis of melody and texture in the choral works of Poulenc to determine characteristics which distinguish this genre of composition from others.   "In conclusion, the influences of tradition are everywhere apparent in the choral works. With regard to melody and texture, then, Poulenc's style is based not upon avant-gardism, but rather is more readily understood as an extension of traditionalism."

B10   Amis, John.   "In Search of Poulenc,"   *Music and Musicians* 22 (November 1973):44-49.

An account of the author's first meeting with Poulenc immediately after World War II, when the composer was in London for a recital. Amis writes about the recital, "Poulenc's piano-playing was fluent, avoided rubato and was thickly pedalled." He also relates his experiences while working on a documentary about Poulenc for the BBC-2 with the help of Poulenc's many friends. Several photographs of the composer and his house at Noizay are included.

B11   Anderson, Jack. "Cocteau Divertissement Opens Florence Gould Hall," *New York Times* April 8, 1988, III:5.

Review of a performance of *Les Mariés de la Tour Eiffel* at the opening of the Florence Gould Hall in New York City on April 6, 1988. The original creation of the work is retold, and the first performance compared to the present production: "Appropriately, therefore, in this staging, Marc Boisseau's costumes were grotesque and, as at the Paris premiere, the lines were recited by actors encased in constructions resembling old-fashioned phonographs. Michel Moinot and Christian

Aubert read them amusingly in a combination of French and English that made Cocteau's wit universally comprehensible. . . . One could imagine a production that made more of the fact than this one did that the camera's apparitions, the baby's tantrums and the family's stuffiness may symbolize the way art and youthful rebellion subvert middle-class values." See: W9.

B12   Anderson, Robert. "The Carmelites," *Musical Times* 124 (June 1983):374.

Review of the April 18, 1983, Covent Garden performance of this opera. "These Carmelites, portrayed with affection and economy, may at a bar's notice be whisked from their devotions to take part in an operetta or 'musical.' Poulenc's sincerity is patent, but his gifts are at odds with it." See: W1.

B13   Anderson, Steven. "Poulenc," *Fanfare* 1 (September 1977):42-43.

Review of the Musical Heritage Society MHS3576 recording of the *Concerto in D Minor for Two Pianos* and *Sonata* (two pianos). The performances by Yarbrough and Cowan are described as "infectious and neat. . . . The lullaby-like Larghetto [from the Concerto] is played especially sensitively." See: D160; D557.

B14   Anderson, W. R. "Round about Radio," *Musical Times* 90 (May 1949): 161-62.

Review of a radio broadcast of the violin sonata, characterized as "a mixture of the serious and the trivial; the trouble is, this composer does not seem to recognize the latter element for what it is." See: W120.

L'Approdo musicale. See: B210.

B15   Aprahamian, Felix. "Poulenc," *Gramophone* 43 (August 1965):107.

Review of the Nonesuch H1033 recording of *Aubade, Sonata for Clarinet and Piano*, and *Sonata for Oboe and Piano*. "Who better than Jacques Février, Poulenc's old two-piano partner, for the piano parts? Here is the authentic touch, crisp, brittle, rhythmic, just like the composer's own playing, except, perhaps, that Francis would have been less sparing of the pedals and one or two wrong notes would have been hit with the greatest authority." See: D26; D488; D524.

B16   Aprahamian, Felix. "Poulenc," *Gramophone* 50 (April 1973):1912.

Review of performances of choral works performed by Kühn's Mixed Choir. "The splendid performances on this record are beyond reproach. . . . Their enunciation is clear, and they bring the same impact to Poulenc's choral writing . . . good, firm vocal tone in all sections of the choir, no lapses in intonation, and close observance of Poulenc's markings of tempo and dynamic throughout." See: D340; D408; D415.

B17   ___. "Poulenc," *Gramophone* 54(December 1976):1041.

The majority of this review is devoted to a comparison of performances of *Gloria* on HMV ASD3299 and the earlier recording on Angel conducted by Prêtre. "Both the old and the new versions of Poulenc's adorable *Gloria* come from the same stable and compete very fairly. Poulenc himself was present at the Paris recording sessions of the French version, but his spirit was surely hovering over those at Birmingham too, for Louis Frémaux cedes nothing to Georges Prêtre in his idiomatic projection of this music." The reading of the Piano Concerto on the reverse side was characterized as "a sparkling performance." See: D148; D275; D276.

B18   ___. "Poulenc," *Gramophone* 56 (June 1978):55.

The reviewer compared the most recent recording of the organ concerto and *Concert champêtre* on HMV ASD3489 with the earlier versions by Duruflé and van de Wiele. "The authenticity of the initial recording (Duruflé's) can never be set aside. On the other hand, the new Preston/ Previn version, slightly more deliberate, is the clearest of all, and . . . the most revealing in detail. And, of course, unlike the French recording, it's impeccably in tune." In the *Concert champêtre* "we find Preston's playing, once again, clear and precise . . . Aimée van de Wiele proves the most conscientious interpreter of the solo part." See: D138; D140; D164; D165.

B19   Ardoin, John A. "Gérard Souzay, Gold and Fizdale," Musical America 84 (February 1964):37.

Review of a concert presented by Souzay, Gold, and Fizdale on January 25, 1964, in New York City. Souzay performed three cycles and seven additional songs with the pianist, Dalton Baldwin. "Each song was a miniature drama, acted out with both voice and body. His understanding of not only the poetry but of its musical setting was all-encompassing and knowing." Gold and Fizdale performed both of the piano passing and knowing." Gold and Fizdale performed both of the piano sonatas and the New York premieres of *Elégie* and the *Capriccio d'aprés Le Bal masqué*. See: W55B; W151.

B20   Ardoin, John A. "Poulenc's 'Babar'," *Musical America* 84 (February 1964):47.

Ardoin liked the performance by the composer on Les Discophiles Française 425105 but stressed that the piece was not intended for concert use. Rather, it was intended for radio broadcast, "where it was premiered by Poulenc and Pierre Bernac," or for recorded sound. See: D291.

B21   Arnold, Denis. "French Songs," *Gramophone* 51 (July 1973):222.

Review of the HMV CSD3740 recording of *Chanson à boire, Chansons françaises, Laudes de Saint Antoine de Padoue*, and *Quatre petites priéres de Saint François d'Assise*. The reviewer praised the "sure intonation" of the choir in their performances of these choral works characterized by difficult, chromatic harmonies. See: D97; D102; D310; D421.

B22   Auric, Georges. "Apollinaire et la musique," *La Revue musicale* 26 (January 1952):147-49.

Discussion of the poetry of Apollinaire and the importance of the poet to the songs of Poulenc. Auric concludes that Poulenc "was [Apollinaire's] musician, the composer of songs of inspiration so spontaneous and strong" that they could dissipate for Auric the melancholy he felt when recalling his last meetings with Apollinaire.

B23   ____. "Paris--The Survival of French Music," *Modern Music* 22 (March-April 1945):157-60.

An essay on the public performances of music in Paris during and immediately following World War II. "Two artists in particular developed an unusually zealous following. The composer, Francis Poulenc, had the happy idea of joining forces with the singer, Pierre Bernac. Their recitals of contemporary song have rapidly achieved a rare and unquestioned success. The quality of the works they selected, the perfect preparation, and their intelligent interpretations are now recognized by everyone. No one will forget, either, the fine courage they have always displayed in rejecting the least compromise, the least concession, the least hint of propaganda."

B24   Auric, Georges.   "A Personal Memoir of 'Les Six'," *New York Times* February 7, 1954, II:7.

A personal memoir concentrating on the early years and first successes of the group. Auric remembers the premiere of *Les Mariés de la Tour Eiffel*: "What an uproar from the stalls to the upper gallery. Everyone was mad at us! Critics dissatisfied or reserved; confreres reserved or dissatisfied . . . Finally, here was a public of two minds, caught between the enjoyment of a good laugh and the fear of being hoaxed. . . . A short time afterward a writer in the highly respectable review, *Le Mercure de France*, coolly pointed out that the explanation of such an evening was much simpler than one imagined. We, with Louis Durey, were in reality . . . six 'little amateurs' possessing just a few very vague ideas of their craft. . . . As for the 'Six'--well, after all, they have had their day, which is already a matter for satisfaction." See: W9.

B25   B. V.   "Sonate for Two Clarinets (B Flat and A),"*Musical Times* 66 (1925):522.

Analytical essay with musical examples. "Some time ago a wicked story was being whispered about a new orchestral work of Schönberg's which the trumpeters of the orchestra played--owing to a mistake of the copyist--in the wrong key, the error passing unperceived by the players, the conductor, and the composer. Now the same story . . . is told about the Sonate . . . [Poulenc] does not believe in the past, and the Sonate for horn, trumpet, and trombone makes fun of the old sonatinas. He does not believe in the present, and whenever he gets hold of a little trick which appears to him good, he repeats it over and over again." See: W119.

B26   Bagar, Robert. "Concerto champêtre for Piano and Orchestra," *New York Philharmonic Program Notes* November 14, 1948.

Program notes for a performance on November 14, 1948, with Poulenc as pianist. "[The work] is not, as the composer assures us, a virtuoso piece, but rather a sort of study in sonorities. The melodic element in the music is of a popular character and related, if only spiritually, to random folk and rural airs." See: W28.

B27   Bancroft, David. "Two Pleas for a French, French Music," *Music and Letters* 48 (April 1967):109-19; (July 1967):251-58.

In part I of this brilliant essay on the philosophical state of French music at the beginning of the 1920s, the author discussed Cocteau's work, *Le Coq et l'Arlequin*, "popularly accepted for many years as a statement of the code of aesthetics of that group of musicians referred to as 'Les Six'." He evaluated Cocteau's opinions on musical aesthetics and questioned his emphasis on Satie as the leader of a new aesthetic while rejecting the importance of Stravinsky as a source of influence. In part II he explores the ideas of Jean-Aubry that the sources for a French, French music were found in nationalistic composers such as Grieg, Sibelius, and Bartok; and the recognition of the French quality in works by the composers Debussy, Ravel, d'Indy, Roussel, Schmitt, and Ducasse.

B28　Barraud, Henry. "Contrasting Modern Operas Hold Parisian Stages," *Musical America* 71 (October 1951):6.

In his review of two operas produced in Paris, one of which was Poulenc's *Les Mamelles de Tirésias*, Barraud compares the opera with the *Stabat Mater*, "the most beautiful work yet written by this composer. The grandeur of the Stabat Mater is the more touching because it is achieved so naturally, with the most economical means. It is accomplished in art, and luminous and serene in thought." See: W2; W54.

B29　___. "French Religious Music: Precursors and Innovators," *Musical America* 72 (February 1952):26.

The premiere of *Stabat Mater* at the Strasbourg Festival on June 13, 1951, was the impetus for this article treating some aspects of the development of religious music in France. The author's assessment of Poulenc's religious music is that "Poulenc does not practice the mortifications of the cloister . . . [but composes] pure and moving music that always seems to come from the heart. My only regret is that he does not prolong musical ideas sufficiently, but passes too rapidly from one to another without allowing them time to develop fully." See: W54.

B30　Bathori, Jane. "Les Musiciens que j'ai connus." Translated by Felix Aprahamian. *Recorded Sound*, no. 15 (July 1964):238-45.

Reminiscences about Satie and his influence on Les Six, especially Milhaud, Honegger, and Poulenc. Bathori relates that she was first introduced to Poulenc by Ricardo Viñes at the Vieux-Colombier. "His open face--simple, naíve, almost child-like--had something distracted in its expression." The author recounts Poulenc's study with Charles Koechlin. This article is also useful as a source for information about contemporaries of Poulenc and Bathori.

B31   Bauman, Carl. "Poulenc: Les Biches," *American Record Guide* 45 (June 1982):54-56.

Review of the EMI ASD4067 recording of *Les Biches; Hommage à Marguerite Long: Bucolique; L'Éventail de Jeanne: Pastourelle*; and *La Guirlande de Campra: Matelote provençale*. The reviewer praised the performance of *Les Biches*, especially for the fact that the conductor recorded the full score. "The short works . . . are interesting. Each is Poulenc's contributions to a work honoring another person, and composed collectively with each of several composers contributing one movement." See: D66; D80; D247; D329.

B32   Bauman, John. "Twentieth Century Classics for Clarinet and Piano," *Fanfare* 5 (May 1982):277-78.

Review of a recording of the *Sonata for Clarinet and Piano* on the label of the University of Michigan School of Music SM0018. "Shifrin plays with a finer tone than does André Boutard, whose Nonesuch disc has long been a favorite, but Boutard and Jacques Février bring a certain Gallic flair that is missing in the present issue." See: D490.

B33   Beard, Harry R. "Reports from Abroad: Milan," *Musical Times* 100 (1959):216.

Review of the one-act opera produced in Milan. "Poulenc's setting of Cocteau's *La Voix humaine* I found disappointing. Cocteau's text is nothing more than a piece of raw material for a great star to turn into an effective act. One can imagine a dozen actresses each giving a different interpretation. Poulenc's music imposes a fixed and insufficiently varied pattern on the artist." See: W4.

B34   Bellas, Jacqueline. "Francis Poulenc ou le 'son de voix de Guillaume'," *La Revue des lettres modernes*, Troisième série, nos. 104-07 (1964): 130-48.

In this essay the author attempts to define Poulenc's "true melodic style," that Poulenc believed he had found when he began to set the poems of Apollinaire, and traces the development of his melodic style. Bellas finds in the songs of Poulenc the "son de voix de Guillaume" ("the vocal sound of Guillaume" Apollinaire).

B35   ___. "Les Mamelles de Tirésias en habit d'Arlequin," *La Revue des lettres modernes*, Quatrième série, nos. 123-26 (1965):30-54.

Discussion of the text and history of the drama before Poulenc set it as an opera. Includes analysis of Poulenc's approach to the dramatic treatment of the text. Musical examples are included. See: W2.

B36   Béraud, Henri. "Théâtre," *Mercure de France* 149 (July-August 1921): 449-54.

Review of the premiere performance of *Les Mariés de la Tour Eiffel* on June 18, 1921. "Their comedy, vaudeville, absurd, anecdote, parade ballet is nothing less than a hoax of the avant-garde." See: W9.

B37   Berger, Arthur. "Reviews Of the Month," *Saturday Review* 31 (September 25, 1948):48.

Review of the Whittemore and Lowe performance of the *Concerto in D Minor for Two Pianos* on RCA Victor 1235. "One marvels at so much craftsmanship applied to so small a purpose, but it does entertain-- modestly and with snickers rather than guffaws." A photograph of Poulenc is included. See: D161.

B38   ___. "Scores and Records," *Modern Music* 22 (March-April 1945): 199-201.

In this essay Berger reports that recording and publishing companies are slowly returning to activity after the war. Among other new works by European and American composers, he cites the violin sonata by Poulenc, recently published by Eschig in Paris. "As a song composer, Poulenc is perhaps unsurpassed in our time. In a less concise form, however, the seductive lyricism animating his songs is also encountered in his instrumental works. The *Violin Sonata* is a delightful example. By frankly accepting what others are, quite understandably, laboriously engaged in rejecting, Poulenc is able to achieve a warm, impetuous flow which is very much needed these days." See: W120.

B39   ___. "Spotlight On the Moderns," *Saturday Review* 34 (January 27, 1951):57.

Review of a recording of the organ concerto on Columbia ML 4329. "The sweet, sympathetic personality of the author of his Organ Concerto makes itself felt. As in all of his large instrumental efforts the form is somewhat weak and the quality of material uneven. But there are exciting and moving episodes. . . . The performance is an intense and animated one under Richard Burgin's direction." See: D167.

B40   Berger, Arthur. "Spotlight On the Moderns," *Saturday Review* 36 (November 28, 1953):87.

Review of a recording of *Le Bal masqué* on Esoteric 518. "One of the gem's of contemporary music on LP . . . the Poulenc sounds more than ever like champagne." See: D34.

B41   ___. "Spotlight On the Moderns," *Saturday Review* 37 (June 26, 1954):57.

Review of the Capital P8258 recording of *Sextuor*. "In this superb reading . . . the sextet serves the ear as fine wallpaper serves the eye." See: D445.

B42   ___. "Spotlight on the Moderns: 'Les Six' Up To Date," *Saturday Review* 37 (December 25, 1954):50.

Review of a recording on Angel 3515B entitled *Le Groupe des Six*. Included is a performance of *Sécheresses*. "The album's finest work is Poulenc's *Sécheresses* . . . We know . . . how eloquently Poulenc can handle tender words. Given more imposing forces, he has achieved a work of depth and power that is very moving." See: D440.

B43   ___. "Spotlight On the Moderns," *Saturday Review* 38 (March 26, 1955):59.

Review of a recording of *Les Soirées de Nazelles* performed by John Ranck, piano, on Zodiac 1002. "At last someone has had the good sense to delve into Poulenc's piano music of the thirties. . . . [Ranck] has a flair for this music." The performer cut three-and-a-half pages "where the composer suggests an optional cut of one-and-a-half. If he did so with Poulenc's approval, it should have been stated in the notes." See: D464.

B44   Berkeley, Lennox. "Obituary," *Musical Times* 104 (March 1963):205.

"It was as a song-writer that he was at his best. In them his melodic invention, his power of expressing subtle and intimate feeling, together with a natural ability for the musical treatment of words and prosody are everywhere in evidence." Included are a brief biography and a photograph of Poulenc with Berkeley.

B45   Bernac, Pierre. "A Certain Grace," *Opera News* 41 (February 5, 1977):28-32.

Poulenc remembered by a life-long friend and colleague. The composer's development as a pianist and composer is stressed in a brief biography, followed by description of Poulenc--appearance, personality, house at Noizay and apartment in Paris, and the composer's daily routine. Much of the article is devoted to analysis of the vocal music, especially the songs, but Bernac discusses also opera and choral works. Illustrations include a caricature of Poulenc in his early twenties by La Fresnaye, and photographs of Bernac and Régine Crespin.

Bernac, Pierre. *En guise d'introduction*. See: B577.

B46   ___. *Francis Poulenc: The Man and His Songs*. Translated by Winifred Radford, with a foreword by Lennox Berkeley. New York: Norton, 1977.

This work, by the leading interpreter of Poulenc's songs and close friend of the composer for many years, is an invaluable guide to the song literature. Included are chapters on performance and interpretation and a description of Poulenc's method of composing songs. The majority of the text is devoted to information about each song, including date of composition, performance suggestions, translations of texts into English, and notes on interpretation. The indexes are excellent, including a list of songs with date of composition, poet, publisher, vocal range, and titles of songs in each cycle; an index of titles; and an index of first lines. A short biography of the composer and numerous photographs are included.

B47   ___. "Poulenc," *Recorded Sound*, no. 41 (January 1971):698-704.

Text of a lecture about Poulenc given on January 20, 1971, as an informal and familiar portrait of the composer. "He had such a devotion to Debussy that once, when he was in a shop with his mother, he suddenly recognized Debussy who had put his hat on a chair. Little Francis, without being noticed, went up to the hat and kissed it." Eight photographs illustrate the article.

B48   ___. "Poulenc's Songs," *Recorded Sound*, no. 18 (April 1965):315-21.

Text of a lecture in which Bernac discusses Poulenc's early songs, his first meeting with the composer, and their subsequent recitals together.

B49   Bernac, Pierre. "The Songs of Francis Poulenc," *NATS Bulletin* 21 (February 1965):2-6.

The article includes a brief biography and discussion about the composer's interest in and approach to the composition of songs. Comments about individual works, based on Poulenc's *Journal de mes mélodies*, concern the composition of each song and how Poulenc felt about the song. There is some analysis of the music. Bernac concludes with a catalogue of songs, listing for each the date of composition, source of text, whether for male or female voice, and publisher.

B50   Bernheimer, Martin. "Poulenc: Suite française pour orchestre," *Saturday Review* 16 (July 27, 1963):44.

Review of Music Guild S-39, the first available recording of the *Suite française* in the instrumental version. The piece "does not represent its composer at his most inspired. . . . The performances are knowledge-able, though understated." See: D567.

B51   Bloomfield, Arthur. "Our Critics Abroad: San Francisco," *Opera* 31 (February 1980):173-76.

Review of San Francisco Opera's triple-bill production of *Il prigioniero, La Voix humaine*, and *Gianni Schicchi* on October 3, 1979. "Magda Olivero can do very little wrong in my book, and her account of the befurred protagonist of Poulenc's lyric monologue was remarkable for its magnetism, its dramatic edge, its knee-scratching realism, also a steadiness and dynamic control amazing in a singer who, by the most conservative estimates, is approaching 70." See: W4.

B52   Blyth, Alan. "Poulenc," *Gramophone* 66 (July 1988):198.

Review of the EMI reissue on compact disc of the original Angel recording of Dialogues. "This is a very welcome reissue of a classic and irreplaceable recording made in 1958 at the time of the first French performances of the work. . . . In the history of French opera it is a worthy successor to Pelleas and indeed its touching heroine Blanche shares much of the troubling, troubled, out-of- this-world, fey personality of her predecessor. It is evident from these records that the singers were inspired by the piece to give of their considerable best. With the benefit of hindsight we can judge that this was a final flowering of the authentic school of French singing. . . . As compared with the vocal score, there are a few cuts and changes in the voice parts, both sanctioned by Poulenc." See: D217.

B53   Bobbitt, Richard B. *The Harmonic Idiom in the Works of "Les Six."*
       Ph.D. dissertation, Boston University, 1963.

       This study treats the principal harmonic devices used by members of Les
       Six, with emphasis on the techniques peculiar to each composer. The
       author concludes that "Les Six were not innovators in the usual sense
       of the word, but were, rather, by-products of the general transition in the
       arts from cohesion towards abstraction . . . Les Six were important as
       representatives of the Satie-Cocteau aesthetic, and as a significant force
       in the establishment of the avant-garde . . . Les Six were the musical
       manifestation of the French rejection of Austro-German, post-romantic
       Expressionism."

B54   ___. "Song Recital," *Gramophone* 60 (January 1983):857.

       Review of the HMV Concert Classics SXLP30556 recording of songs. "I
       believe this to have been Jessye Norman's first record, made in 1970 by
       EMI Electrola but never issued here before. . . . Jessye Norman has
       delved deeper into Poulenc's world since making this disc. The
       emotions are rather too generally emitted here, the French language not
       so firmly encompassed as it has become, but the tone is as rich and
       resonant as it is in the Lieder." See: D268; D356.

B55   Bonavia, F. "4 Concertos in Search of Composer: New Works of
       Poulenc, Vaughan Williams, Arthur Benjamin and Szymanowski, Heard
       in London," *New York Times* February 26, 1933, IX:6.

       Review of performances of four new concerti in London, including
       Poulenc's *Concerto in D Minor for Two Pianos*. "Quite apart from the
       crudity of his technical equipment, Francis Poulenc lags a long way
       behind Szymanowski. Nothing of his that has been heard here has
       given him a claim to be taken seriously. . . . If we deduct from the
       concerto all that is cheap and undistinguished, nothing remains. . . .
       Modern music needs not irony but plain honesty and courage . . .
       A second-rate musician hiding under the cloak of intellectuality is a
       ludicrous figure." See: W29.

B56   "Bowles: A Picnic Cantata. Poulenc: Sonata for Two Pianos 1953," *New
       Records* 23/11 (January 1956):13.

       Review of the Columbia ML5068 recording. The Sonata is a "lovely work
       which will appeal to many persons . . . Gold and Fizdale display an
       obvious feeling for the work as well as sure and impeccable dexterity on
       the keyboards." See: D547.

B57   Brandes, Jeffrey Harold. *The Organ as an Ensemble Instrument: Concerto Techniques in the Sinfonia of Cantata BWV 169 by Johann Sebastian Bach, Concerto for Organ and Chamber Music, Op. 46, No. 2, by Paul Hindemith, and Organ Concerto in G Minor by Francis Poulenc.* DMA dissertation, Ohio State University, 1977.

Brandes examines these three works for their use of concerto techniques and for the function of the organ as an ensemble instrument. A historical survey of the evolution of the term, concerto, is followed by analysis and comparison of the three organ concerti. See: W30.

B58   Breitrose, Henry. "Conversation with Milhaud," *Music Educators Journal* 56 (March 1970):55-56.

Interview in which Milhaud stated Les Six were united by friendship: "It was a group for whom the differences never interfered, although we were writing music extremely different from each other." Milhaud met Poulenc only after the war. "He was still in the army. I met him at the house of a poet, René Chalupt, and he played me his music, which immediately I liked very much."

B59   "Britten Honored by Music Critics: Acclaimed in 2 Categories--Poulenc Choral Hailed," *New York Times* May 20, 1964, p. 37.

Britten's *War Requiem* shared honors in the choral category with Poulenc's *Sept répons des Ténèbres* in the annual citations of the New York Music Critics Circle. See: W52.

B60   Bronston, Levering. "Choral," *New Records* 41/5 (July 1973):5-6.

Review of a recording of choral works on Supraphon 112 1113. "Of the group of French composers belonging to the generation just after Debussy . . . Francis Poulenc remains, for me, the most consistently inspired. His Mass in G is a gentle, lyrical, deeply-felt work, well sung by this choir from Prague. The lovely 'Penitence Motets' are often heard, but the 'Christmas Motets' are new to me. All of them are shot through with Poulenc's special brand of lyricism." See: D340; D408; D415.

B61   ___. "Miscellaneous," *New Records* 40/12 (February 1973):14.

Review of a recording of the *Sonata for Clarinet and Piano* on Mark MC3344. "Some of the playfulness in Poulenc's Sonata are [sic] missing in Paul Drushler's careful and generally clean performances. His phrasing in the second movement of the Poulenc is lovely." See: D485.

B62   Bronston, Levering. "Piano," *New Records* 45/7 (September 1977):12.

Review of the Orion ORS76238 recording of *Sonata* (two pianos). "The best comes last: a lovely and vital performance of the attractive Poulenc sonata, a work shot through with the composer's unique blend of wit and wistfulness. The pianists' phrasing here is especially lucid, with a fresh crispness where necessary and an appealing tenderness in the central section." See: D558.

B63   ___. "Piano," New Records 46/1 (March 1978):12.

Review of International Piano Archives 2002 recording of *Les Soirées de Nazelles*. "This is witty, whimsical, gay, reflective music, very appealing-- another way of saying music characteristic of Francis Poulenc." See: D462.

B64   ___. "Poulenc Plays Poulenc and Satie," *New Records* 44/5 (July 1976):11.

Review of the recording of *Trois mouvements perpétuels, Nocturne in D Major*, and *Suite française* on Odyssey Y33792. "Poulenc's playing was straightforward, uncluttered and charming. He plays all the music beautifully, but I'm losing interest in Satie; Poulenc was a much more enjoyable composer." See: D374; D573; D619.

B65   ___. "Poulenc: Sonata for Clarinet and Piano," *New Records* 43/10 (December 1975):8.

Review of the Crystal S331 recording of the *Sonata for Clarinet and Piano*. "James Campbell is a gifted player. The perky sonata by Poulenc is done with a proper mixture of lyricism and humor. In fact, Campbell's disc is one of the most spectacular clarinet displays to come my way in some time." See: D478.

B66   ___. "Rachmaninoff: Suite No. 1, Op. 5; Poulenc: Sonata for (2) Pianos (1953)," *New Records* 43/12 (February 1976):14.

Review of a recording of the *Sonata* (two pianos) on Klavier KS549. "The Gordons are an excellent team and play both pieces with great brilliance and virtuosity. The Poulenc is a charming work." See: D553.

B67   Brooks, Laura Jeanice. *Poulenc and Surrealism: The Choral Cantatas on Texts of Eluard*. MA thesis, The Catholic University of America, 1985.

From the thirty-two poems by Paul Eluard which Poulenc chose as texts for songs and three choral works, the author selected the two cantatas, *Figure humaine* and *Un Soir de neige*, for analysis. A first-rate chapter on Eluard and surrealism in France traces the development of the surrealist movement, explaining Eluard's style in relation to it. Following chapters include analysis of the poetry and Poulenc's musical settings for the two cantatas. Extensive musical examples are included, along with complete texts and scores for both works. See: W40; W53.

B68   Brown, Royal S. "Classical Reviews," *High Fidelity* 21 (November 1971):118.

Review of a recording of *Litanies à la vierge noire* on Argo ZRG662. The music is of a "markedly sophisticated and highly dramatic character . . . The aesthetic level does not quite converge with the spiritual plane, but musically the Litanies stands among Poulenc's best compositions." The recording was "sensitively produced and beautifully performed. . . . The choir has excellent depth, and the fine, assured performances elicited here from their director . . . manifest a strong identification with the music." See: D313.

B69   ___. "Classical Reviews," *High Fidelity* 23 (September 1973):120-21.

Review of a recording of *Sextuor* performed on Turnabout TV34507. "The verve and wit of [Poulenc's] approach to the sextet's toccata-like opening theme and to the third movement's jazzy beginning are matched by the winds in superbly balanced performances of incredible élan. . . . The sextet strikes me as basically a virtuoso succession of rhythmic, melodic, instrumental, and stylistic ideas--all of them ingratiating." See: D456.

B70   ___. "Classical Reviews," *High Fidelity* 23 (October 1973):109-10.

Comparisons of performances of the organ concerto by Marie-Claire Alain on Musical Heritage Society MHS1595, by E. Power Biggs on Columbia MS6398, and by Maurice Duruflé on Angel S35953; of the *Concert champêtre* by Robert Veyron-Lacroix on Musical Heritage Society MHS1595 and Aimée van de Wiele on Angel S35993; and the *Motets pour un temps de pénitence* by Kühn's Mixed Choir on Supraphon 112 1113, by the Festival Singers of Toronto on Seraphim S60085, and by the Duclos Chorus on Angel S36121. Veyron-Lacroix's execution of the harpsichord part in the *Concert champêtre* "scintillates in its incredible virtuosity of the fingerwork and in the perfectly apropos, infectious spirit he imparts to the work." In the organ concerto, "Alain seems more equal to standards previously set by Biggs and Duruflé. But Alain's trump card is the lush, up-close organ sound obtained by Erato's engineers and preserved in the Musical Heritage transfer. . . . Sound from both the ensemble and engineers, is likewise the strong point of the Kühn's Mixed Choir . . . The ensemble has depth and training . . . to sound like a single instrument . . . unlike the Duclos Chorus whose Penitential Motets is singularly unmusical. In comparison, the Festival Singers of Toronto sound thin and pinched." See: D138; D145; D164; D171; D410; D411; D415.

B71   Brown, Royal S. "Classical Reviews," *High Fidelity* 24 (February 1974):99.

Review and comparison of two recordings of the *Concerto for Two Pianos and Orchestra in D Minor* on Inédits ORTF 995035 and London CS6754. "Poulenc's two-piano concerto is an absolute delight of shifting moods and styles, ranging from 'perpetuum mobile' to Chopin and back again." See: D158; D159.

B72   ___. "Classical Reviews," *High Fidelity* 24 (August 1974):100.

Review of the recording of *Aubade* on Orion ORS74139. "The over-all emotional and musical atmosphere grows out of the sharp contrasts between the unbridled wit and brilliance of some sections and the Gallic melancholia of others. . . . You will not find a livelier or more clearly played rendition." See: D27.

B73   ___. "Classical Reviews," *High Fidelity* 28 (May 1978):107-08.

Review of the Columbia M34551 recording of *Gloria*. The reviewer contrasts the Poulenc with a composition by Stravinsky on the reverse side. "There is more Stravinsky than one might expect in Poulenc, whose career as a composer began in a Paris still dazzled by the music of the Russian émigré. (There is also, from time to time, a bit of Poulenc in Stravinsky, such as in the latter's Sonata for Two Pianos)." See: D279.

B74   ___. "French Music Since Debussy and Ravel," *High Fidelity/Musical America* 23 (September 1973):50-65.

The author concludes that "a good deal of what has transpired in French music in this century has therefore been, at least to some degree, the product of revolt against an entire way of life and not simply against musical tradition." He finds that *Les Mamelles de Tirésias* "represents not only the greatest product of the group's [Les Six's] original aesthetic but also one of the most delightful comic operas ever written." See: W2.

B75   Brown, Royal S. "French Orchestral Miniatures," *High Fidelity/Musical America* 25 (September 1975):98-101.

Review of a recording of *Deux marches et un intermède* on Westminster Gold WGS8310. "The works here receive fine, well-polished performances. The conductor is perhaps at his best in the sumptuous, very stringy, and rather melancholic (especially in the second march) Poulenc. . . . He is far more successful than Prêtre (Angel S36519) in striking a balance between the harmonic and instrumental opulence, on the one hand, and the ingenuousness of the musical conception, on the other." See: D183; D187.

B76   ___. "Philippe Entrémont: A la Française," *High Fidelity/Musical America* 23 (August 1973):110.

Review of the recording of "Toccata" from *Trois pièces* on Columbia M32070. "Entrémont performs the Toccata splendidly, skillfully highlighting its almost hidden lyricism while maintaining the essential momentum inherent to the genre." See: D633.

B77   ___. "Poulenc," *Fanfare* 5 (January 1982):154.

Review of the EMI ASD4067 reissue of an earlier recording. "As a devout admirer of Francis Poulenc's music, I would not want to be without this disc. . . . Georges Prêtre, the Philharmonia Orchestra, and the Ambrosian Singers offer such a warm, expansive, and full-bodied interpretation of 'Les Biches,' and all involved are seconded by such sumptuous sound reproduction, that this EMI version is quite hard to resist. Making the release even more appealing is the inclusion of three vignettes." See: D66; D80; D247; D329.

B78   ___. "Poulenc," *Fanfare* 10 (July 1987):161.

Review of a recording on Ophelia OP67103. "If the violin sonata does not, perhaps, speak its piece with as much warmth and originality as other Poulenc compositions, it nonetheless offers a most refreshing medium within which to revel in the composer's familiar style. Violinist Aurelio Perez and pianist Janis Vakerelis make a particularly good case for the sonata in a well- balanced performance that captures quite nicely the kaleidoscopic mood changes so characteristic of the composer." See: D532.

B79   Bruyr, José. *L'Écran des musicians*. Preface by André Coeuroy. Paris: Des Cahiers de France, 1930.

This volume is comprised of essays, each devoted to one of the young French musicians who came into prominence in the 1920s. The short essay on Poulenc, pages 40-47, includes analysis of his musical style in the early works and a list of published compositions with the publisher of each work.

B80   C. S. S. "Alice Esty," *Musical America* 84 (February 1964):34.

Review of a concert sponsored by Alice Esty devoted to the music and memory of Poulenc. The program included his *Dernier poème, La Courte paille, Dans l'herbe*, and *La Fraîcheur et le feu*. The reviewer describes   Poulenc's music as the "work of a   master--somber, whimsical, tranquil and stormy. The writing was inventive and direct." See: W72; W73; W81; W82.

B81   Canby, Edward Tatnall. "The New Recordings," *Harper's* 209 (September 1954):110.

Review of a recording of *Sextuor* on Capitol P8258. "An amusing but somewhat erratic example of that composer's nose-thumbing anti-- Romanticism with moments of plain banality as well as many of real expression under the snazzy surface. . . . sharply etched playing, a bit on the rigid side but admirably precise." See: D445.

B82   ___. "The New Recordings," *Saturday Review* 32 (April 2, 1949):38.

Review of the Bernac-Poulenc recording of *Métamorphoses* and *Le Bestiaire* on RCA Victor 12-0426. The former are described as "well-built, non-dissonant French songs, well and nasally sung." The latter songs are an "Ogden Nash-like musical zoo. An exceptionally good piano-accompaniment recording: solid, legato, well balanced." See: D62; D345.

B83   Canby, Edward Tatnall. "The New Recordings," *Saturday Review* 33 (June 17, 1950):47.

Review of the Esoteric ES2000 recording of *Le Bal masqué*. "Poulenc up to his usual tongue-in-cheek . . . this work has more stuffing than most. Excellent singing of surrealist like verses; deliciously decadent." See: D35.

B84   ___. "The New Recordings," *Saturday Review* 34 (February 10, 1951):35.

Review of the Robert Shaw Chorale performance of the Mass in G on RCA Victor LM1088. "Poulenc has evidently undergone a massive struggle to break from the snazzy satirical style (so limited) that occupied the French for so long after War I. His success here is moving. The Mass, a capella, is of the difficult modern sort with . . . some intensely beautiful moments; the singing is orchestral in its perfection." See: D338.

B85   ___. "The New Recordings," *Saturday Review* 34 (February 10, 1951):35.

Review of the recording of the organ concerto performed by E. Power Biggs on Columbia C-MM951. The work "combines astonishing boldness of 'borrowing'--the Bach G minor Fantasia, an almost pure-Stravinsky allegro, the Tchaikowsky 'Pathétique' finale--with a far deeper expression." See: D167.

B86   Carno, Daniel. "Lieder Recital," *New Records* 54/6 (August 1986):14.

Review of the Angel LPAM34757 recording. "Poulenc songs are delivered with elegant dignity, in relatively straight-forward interpretations. Norman's voice-placement does not lend itself to perfect French diction, but given the wonderful sounds that she makes, I'm not complaining." See: D268; D356.

B87   ___. "Poulenc: Le Bal masqué; Le Bestiaire," *New Records* 55/1 (January 1987):23-24.

Review of the CRD 3437 compact disc recording. "I promise that you will find no part of this recording tedious. Credit is due to the programing itself, which balances nicely between vocal and instrumental selections and to the performances which are always interesting and entertaining." Thomas Allen's "diction is exemplary, his rich baritone miraculously scaled down and focused, his delivery conversational and free of exaggerations. Interpretations are appropriately low-keyed, artfully nuanced, indicating an intelligence, sensitivity, and courage foreign to many 'international' singers today." See: D33; D56; D450; D602.

B88   Carter, Elliott.   "Vacation Novelties, New York," *Modern Music* 15 (January-February 1938):96-103.

Essay on new music heard in New York, including Poulenc's *Concerto in D minor for Two Pianos*: "A pastiche of music ranging from Scarlatti, Mozart, Schumann, Chabrier to Stravinsky and popular songs, the concerto is convincing only because of its great verve which, with Poulenc's remarkable sensitivity to harmonic and orchestral sonorities, ends by captivating the most stubborn listener." *Sept chansons* was performed by the Lehman Engel Singers: "As so often in modern choral music, the demands made on the singers in the matter of intonation was very great and director Engel saw fit to double the chorus with a piano. This robbed the chorus of its flexibility and made it difficult to come to a decision about the music. The style of writing for the most part is like the French madrigals, harmonic, with occasional difficult modulations and dissonant chords." See: W29; W51.

B89   "Carter, Foss and Poulenc Works Get Music Critics Circle Awards," *New York Times*, April 19, 1961, p. 34.

Poulenc's *Gloria* was given the Music Critics Circle Award for the best choral work during the period for all of 1960 and the first four-and-a-half months of 1961. "The decisions were much more clear-cut than they have been in recent years. All won on the first ballot. . . . The only other work to receive votes in the choral category was Frank Martin's *Le Vin herbe*. In the opera category, votes were cast for . . . Poulenc's *La Voix humaine*. The Circle voted to give no award in the opera category." See: W4; W41.

B90   Chase, William W. "Chamber Music," *New Records* 50/4 (June 1982):5.

Review of the Stolat SZM0119 recording of the *Sonata for Flute and Piano*. "Boyd is an accomplished artist, fluent in technique and secure in her approach to the music. . . . Ms. Schmidt's accompaniment is sufficient, if somewhat heavy-handed." See: D505.

B91   ___. "Prokofiev: Sonata for Flute and Piano, Op. 94; Poulenc: Sonata for Flute and Piano," *New Records* 51/2 (April 1983):6.

Review of the Supraphone 1111.2477 recording. "Their approach to Poulenc's sonata is to make of it a more robust and dramatic work than others are wont to do; to some the performance may seem a bit hard-edged, but it avoids the watering-down to which that work is prey." See: D506.

B92   Chevaillier, Lucien. "Un Entretien avec Francis Poulenc," *Le Guide du concert et des théâtres lyriques*, no. 30 (April 26, 1929):855-57.

In this conversation with Chevaillier, Poulenc reminisces about his piano study with Ricardo Viñes, his study of counterpoint with Charles Koechlin, and his work with Landowska on the *Concert champêtre*, "measure by measure, note by note," not to change a single note of the melodic line, but to clarify the writing and to simplify the voicing. Included are photographs of Poulenc and one of Poulenc and Landowska at Saint-Leula-Forêt in the summer of 1928. Also on page 854, preceding this article, is an advertisement for the score of *Concert champêtre* and an announcement that Landowska and L'Orchestre Symphonique de Paris will premiere the work on May 3, 1929. See: W28.

B93   Chien, George. "Poulenc," *Fanfare* 7 (September 1983): 235.

Review of the Nonesuch 79045 recording of the *Sonata for Oboe and Piano, Sextuor*, and *Trio for Oboe, Bassoon, and Piano*. "The performances on this Nonesuch digital release are uniformly excellent, and Roseman's reading of the sonata [for oboe] is comparable in every way to those of Bourgue (Harmonia Mundi France), Lucarelli (Lyrichord), and Mack (Telarc non-digital)." See: D454; D522; D525; D527; D606.

B94   Chislett, W. A. "Neglected Composers: Francis Poulenc," *Gramophone* 6 (November 1928):236.

A brief biography of Poulenc and a list of his compositions is followed by a review of the Columbia D14213/4 recording of the *Trio for Oboe, Bassoon, and Piano*, "so far as I can ascertain . . . the only work by which Poulenc is represented on the gramophone. It is a firmly knit, mature work, quite Haydnesque in its simplicity and naivety and XVIIIth Century in character, all three movements of which are delightfully melodious. . . . Both playing and recording are magnificent." See: D601.

B95   Clark, John W. "Poulenc in Soria Series," *Musical America* 80 (May 1960):23.

Review of the RCA Victor Soria Series LS/LSS2385 recording of *La Voix humaine* with Duval and Prêtre. "The newest significant composition by

France's most illustrious living musician . . . *La Voix humaine* presses forward as an irresistible *pièce de théâtre*, blood-thick with immediacy. Couched in a setting of luxurious melody, clinically apt orchestration, and a colloquial prosody to be envied by all aspiring lyricists, the work is a fascinating success." See: D652.

B96   Cocteau, Jean. "Les Biches, Les Fâcheux," *La Nouvelle revue française* 22 (1924):275-78.

Cocteau briefly discusses these two new ballets performed in Monte Carlo on January 6 and 9, 1924, comparing the works with *Le Sacre du printemps* by Stravinsky and describing the beauty and success of the productions. See: W7.

B97   ___. *Le Coq*, nos. 1-4 (May-November 1920).

A news sheet edited by Cocteau that appeared in four numbers--May, June, July-August-September, and November of 1920. Number 3 was entitled *Le Coq Parisien*. The issues contained articles and reviews by Cocteau, Raymond Radiguet, Paul Morand, Louis Durey, Poulenc, Lucien Daudet, and others; drawings by La Fresnaye; and compositions by Satie and the members of Les Six. *Le Coq* promoted Cocteau's theories about a new art and the compositions of Les Six. It was in part a reply to "391," a publication that championed "antidadaism."

___. Drawing, "Cocteau and Les Six." See: B210.

___. *Les Mariés de la Tour Eiffel*. See: B210.

B98   Coeuroy, André. "Jeune musique française: Salade, Les Biches, Les Fâcheux," *La Revue universelle* 18 (July 1, 1924):380-84.

Review of the premiere of *Les Biches* on January 6, 1924. "The whole is formed from a suite of pieces cut out from classicism. . . . Schloezer writes the truth when he writes, 'The great difficulty and danger for Poulenc is that his music is essentially aristocratic; it is art of the court on the whole which, because of circumstances, finds itself obliged to turn toward the masses.' The proof of this is in the Adagietto, in which the elegiac grace and melodic flexibility are truly masterful. . . . It is certain that Poulenc in his maturity will write works with more personal material, but he will not reveal more clearly the exquisite finesse of his sensibility which bonds to the dreamy and the elegiac, the joyous." See: W7.

B99   Cohn, Arthur. "The Art of Francis Poulenc," *American Record Guide* 30
       (March 1964):622-23.

       Reviews of two recordings of compositions by Poulenc. Concerning the
       Columbia ML5918 (MS6518) recording of *Hôtel, Voyage à Paris, "C,"
       Sonata for Two Pianos,* and *Sextuor:* "Very satisfying as a miniature
       anthology. . . . Though this youthful art has been mellowed by the years,
       it has not been enfeebled by age. Music of such exuberance, vitality,
       and élan survives." The reviewer of the Angel 36121 recording of *Stabat
       Mater* and *Quatre motets pour un temps de pénitence* found the pieces
       "poetic rather than intellectually probing. . . . [*Stabat Mater*] has the
       strength of simplicity; its traditional dignity remains unimpaired even
       when contemporary dissonance is added to the harmonic vocabulary."
       See: D48; D210; D411; D447; D548; D561.

B100   ___. "Concert for Two Pianos," *American Record Guide* 30/9 (May
       1964):815.

       Review of the recording of the sonata for two pianos on Golden Crest
       CR4070. "The Lang sisters miss all the subtlety and confuse Poulenc's
       spirit of abandon with an invitation to play loudly." The reviewer prefers
       the performance of this work on Command 11013. See: D549; D552.

B101   ___. "Poulenc," *American Record Guide* 28 (April 1962):649.

       Review of the Golden Crest CR4042 recording of *Humoresque,
       Improvisations* (Book II), *Suite française, Valse in C, Les Animaux
       modèles* (arranged by Johannesen from the piano score of the original
       work), and *Villageoises. Villageoises* "consists of tunes to whistle with
       slightly salty harmonies, set in directly defined forms; waltz, march, etc.
       In the ballet suite there is charm and some inserted folk tunes, but little
       personality, and the music goes on for a long time. . . . Poulenc remains
       the life of the contemporary music party." See: D19; D297; D305; D571;
       D643; D648.

       Collaer, Paul. *"Le Coq et l'arlequin* di Jean Cocteau." See: B210.

B102   Collaer, Paul. *A History of Modern Music.* Translated by Sally Abeles.
       Cleveland: World Publishing Co., 1961.

       This survey of developments in the history of music from about 1910 to
       1960 includes chapters on "Erik Satie and the Six" and "Milhaud,
       Honegger, Auric, Poulenc: After the Six." Pages 265-71 are devoted to

an examination of the compositions of Poulenc with some stylistic analysis.

Collaer, Paul. "'Sei': Studio dell'evoluzione della musica francese dal 1917 al 1924." See: B210.

B103   Conly, John M.   "They Shall Have Music," *Atlantic Monthly* 205 (June 1960):160-62.

Interview with Poulenc conducted while he was in New York to supervise both a touring production of *La Voix humaine* and the RCA Victor recording of the opera.   The article includes descriptions of the composer's appearance and personality and quotes by Poulenc about his compositions and their musical style. See: W4; D652.

B104   Cooper, Martin.   "French Orchestral Works," *Gramophone* 56 (July 1978):206.

The reviewer describes *Deux marches et un intermède* recorded on Aurora AUR5065 as "a witty tribute to Chabrier followed by a very Parisian expedition to the countryside and back to Paris again for the second march." See: D184.

B105   ___. "French Songs," *Gramophone* 56 (April 1979):1762.

Review of the Nimbus 2118 recording of songs. "Of five Poulenc songs *Priez pour paix* shows the composer at his neo-medieval best and is admirably characterized here. . . . [Cuénod's] programme is skillfully chosen to exhibit what have always been some of his strongest points--his impeccably clear, yet unaffected verbal enunciation, his admirable sense of timing and a wit that can only be called infectious." See: D6; D79; D213; D284; D397.

B106   ___. "Peeters; Poulenc," *Gramophone* 56 (June 1978):96.

Review of the Argo ZRG883 recording of choral works. "Poulenc's deep affection for the music of the French past is shown at its best in his haunting setting of the *Salve Regina*, beautifully phrased and dynamically shaded in this performance. *Exultate Deo* is conceived as an explosion of energy and its robust rhythms are well reproduced in this recording." See: D254; D434.

B107   Copland, Aaron. "Scores and Records," *Modern Music* 14 (November-December 1936):39-42.

In a review of recently released recordings Copland includes the Columbia issue of *Aubade*. "It's a long work for Poulenc--six ten-inch sides. But if you are not too exacting (and certainly Poulenc isn't) you will probably discover moments of charm and 'allegresse;' also pages of warmed-over neo-classicism." See: D21.

B108   ___. "Scores and Records," *Modern Music* 15 (May-June 1938):244-48.

Review of new music, recently recorded or published. "Who could have foreseen that Poulenc, of all people, would turn up with a Mass for unaccompanied voices . . . He has changed his medium, but not his style. Eclectic as ever, charming as ever, musical as ever, this *Mass* is not at all severe and forbidding. *Au contraire*. It was meant to be sung in all simplicity in a sunny church in southern France. Even in an ordinary concert hall it may be counted on to win its auditors." See: W44.

Le Coq. See: B97.

B109   "Critics Give Prize to Smit Symphony: 'Carmelites' by Poulenc and Stravinsky's 'Agon' Are Other Top Scores of '57," *New York Times*, January 15, 1958, p. 23.

The Music Critics Circle selected *Dialogues des Carmélites* as the best new opera of the year. Poulenc's *Les Mamelles de Tirésias*, which had recently premiered in New York, was also nominated. But Carmélites won over both Tirésias and Benjamin Britten's Albert Herring. "This is the second critics' award that the French composer has won. His *Stabat Mater* received the circle's award as the best choral work 1952." See: W1; W54.

B110   Croce, Arlene. "Dancing," *New Yorker* 59 (March 21, 1983):109.

A revival of *Les Biches* by the Dance Theater of Harlem was the occasion for the author to compare the revival with earlier versions and interpretations of this work. Emphasis in the article is on the dance, but some information about Poulenc's views of the work is included. See: W7.

B111   Crumb, Rupert W. "Choral," *New Records* 50/12 (February 1983):8-9.

Review of the Telarc DG1077 recording of *Gloria*. "Shaw's present recording is similar to his earlier one--typically Shaw: vigorous and commanding, rather than subtle. The orchestra is bright and energetic, and Sylvia [sic] McNair is a light but attractive soloist." [McNair's given name is Patricia.] See: D281.

B112   ___. "Mélodies," *New Records* 50/8 (October 1982):14.

Review of the Orion ORS82422 recording of songs. "Carol Kimbell, more alto than mezzo-soprano, sings French mélodies as to the manner born. By her diction one might mistake her for a native Frenchwoman; she has just the right lilt, rhythmic vitality, light satiric touch, and pressing warmth. . . . Thomas Grubb assists her with deft and insightful pianism." See: D189; D271; D426.

B113   ___. "Vocal," *New Records* 50/6 (August 1982):11-12.

Review and comparison of two recordings of songs, Spectrum SR147 and Cambridge CRS2777. "In respect to Poulenc, the earlier set [Cambridge] was more satisfying, for I miss some of the soaring, lyrical melodies that were featured on the Cambridge record. . . . The songs of Les six have found a perfect interpreter . . . in Maria Lagios [on Spectrum]. She combines a beautiful voice, and equally beautiful diction, with an elegantly quick-silver style. She is superbly partnered at the piano by Elizabeth Buccheri." See: D7; D11; D15; D133; D134; D262; D386; D641.

B114   Crutchfield, Will. "A Wellspring from Poulenc's Song Legacy," *New York Times*, January 17, 1988, II:22.

Reviews of several collections of recorded songs and other works (Friends of Pierre Bernac PB1-3; Adès 14114-2, 14115-2, 14052-2; Clio 001) recently released from "unissued broadcasts, miscellaneous and hard to find 78 r.p.m. disks, live performances and LP's only briefly in circulation. The pianist is Francis Poulenc himself, the singers his chosen collaborators, Pierre Bernac and Denise Duval. The performances are breezy, precise, filled with feeling: wonderful. . . . Poulenc, like Britten, was one of the great accompanists; such high energy and virtuosity have been combined with such refinement of touch and sensibility only in three or four other pianists known to the recorded song literature." The Clio 001 recording with Poulenc and Duval is a recording of a live performance given in Bordeaux in 1958. Duval "is a delightful, full-hearted and un-self-conscious interpreter . . . the composer makes a hilarious vocal appearance, contributing the lines of the beleaguered husband in 'Les Mamelles de Tirésias'." Photographs of the composer, Bernac, and Duval are included. See: D30; D40; D53; D81; D106; D127; D191; D199; D209; D219; D222; D243; D267; D282; D347; D361; D377; D380; D394; D491; D578; D592; D598; D656.

B115   Cutler, Helen Miller. "Freshened Repertoire Marks 66th Ann Arbor May Festival," *Musical America* 79 (June 1959):3-5.

Review of the United States premiere of *Sécheresses* in Ann Arbor, Michigan, with Thor Johnson, conductor, and the University Choral Union, directed by Lester McCoy. The reviewer praised the music and the performance. See: W50.

B116   D. S. "Hindemith; Poulenc," *Gramophone* 32 (January 1955):354-55.

Review of the Capitol recording of *Sextuor*. "Enthusiasts in the restricted but attractive realm of modern wind music will welcome this excellent disc. . . . The two works offer an interesting contrast in style: Hindemith representing the cerebral craftsman, and Poulenc the witty virtuoso. The pianist in the latter work makes an effective contribution to the ensemble." See: D445.

B117   Davies, Margaret E. "The Voice of Paris," *Opera News* 23 (May 4, 1959):28.

Review of the world premiere of *La Voix humaine* at the Opéra-Comique in Paris on February 6, 1959. "While the addition of music slows down the urgency of the play's action and allows singer and audience less freedom, it also increases the emotional depth of the performance." See: W4.

B118   Davis, Peter G. "Ann Haenen's Skillful 'Voix'," *New York Times*, December 8, 1976, C:22.

Review of a New York performance of *La Voix humaine*. "To make its full effect, the role requires a soprano with magnetic stage presence and the vocal abilities of an accomplished diseuse--one false move and the piece can degenerate into a bathetic embarrassment. Miss Haenen sustained the 35-minute work with considerable dramatic skill and managed to be wholly convincing as a woman at the end of her emotional tether." See: W4.

B119   Davis, Peter G.   "Classical Reviews," *High Fidelity* 22 (September 1972):98.

Review of the Turnabout TV4489 recording of songs by Rose Dercourt, soprano, and Francis Poulenc, piano. "This disc is pretty excruciating when heard in the chill light of day." Davis found the singer's technique insecure and her intonation chancy. "Poulenc's poised, rhythmically supple accompaniments provide the chief historical interest here and the repertoire is unusual." See: D14; D129; D190; D196; D288; D296; D429; D596.

B120   ___. "The New Releases," *High Fidelity* 17 (February 1967):42.

Review of the release of a recording of *Les Mamelles de Tirésias* on Seraphim 60029 with Denise Duval and Jean Giraudeau. "Poulenc never wrote anything better; there's a superb sense of timing, subtle musical humor, and unerring compositional technique. . . . The performance brilliantly catches the flavor of the piece." See: D326.

B121   ___. "Recordings: Examining in Detail the Alluring 'Mélodie' of France," *New York Times*, January 25, 1981, IIA:26.

Review of the EMI 2C-165.16231-35 recordings of songs sung by Elly Ameling, Gérard Souzay, Nicolai Gedda, Michel Sénéchal, and William Parker with Dalton Baldwin, pianist. "Poulenc was perhaps the last great French composer of songs. For their combination of wit, sophistication, melodiousness, gaiety, profundity and sheer inventiveness, these fastidiously fashioned gems seem to sum up everything that makes the 'mélodie' unique." The album includes English translations of the texts. See: D2; D8; D42; D57; D77; D83; D93; D98; D107; D115; D128; D131; D135; D136; D177; D181; D188; D200; D206; D220; D244; D255; D257; D269; D283; D295; D300; D318; D324; D330; D341; D353; D378; D381; D385; D387; D395; D401; D424; D432; D580; D590; D594; D610; D635; D638.

B122   ___. "Recordings View: When Composers Perform Their Own Music," *New York Times*, May 16, 1976, II:19.

Review of Poulenc's performances on Odyssey Y33792 of his *Mouvements perpétuels, Nocturne in D Major*, and *Suite française* with piano works of Satie, including *Descriptions automatiques, Gymnopedie No. 1, Sarabande No. 2, Gnossienne No. 3, Avant-dernières pensées*, and *Croquis et agaceries d'un gros bon homme en bois*. "As a pianist, Poulenc was a perfect mirror of his music--urbane, witty and full of unexpected little expressive quirks. . . . On this disk Poulenc gives sparkling renditions of his [pieces]. They are slight pieces, perhaps, but deliciously piquant and delightfully ingenuous." See: D374; D573; D619.

B123   Davis, Peter G. "Régine Crespin Lends Fire to 'Carmelites'," *New York Times*, February 4, 1977, C:1.

Review of the Metropolitan Opera's production of this opera with Crespin in the role of the First Prioress, although her "customary role in the opera . . . was that of the more lyrical Second Prioress; Poulenc had even tailored the music specifically for her voice when he wrote the opera in 1956." Crespin relates the story of Poulenc's asking her to sing in the first Paris production and tells in her own words how she interprets the role. See: W1.

B124   ___. "Souzay--And More Poulenc," *High Fidelity* 17 (June 1967):20.

Souzay's recording of songs on RCA Victor LSC3018 inspired the reviewer to describe the recording session in New York's Town Hall and to discuss Souzay's friendship with the composer. "Poulenc has always been very close to Souzay--who was only thirteen when he first met the composer, through Pierre Bernac, a close friend of the Souzay family . . . 'I heard most of the songs in their first performances--by the composer himself,' Mr. Souzay recalled. 'He loved to sing but he had a monstrous voice'." See: D13; D108; D182; D195; D301; D322; D382; D388; D428; D433; D585.

B125   ___. "Surprising Disks From Familiar Musicians," *New York Times*, August 28, 1977, D:22.

Review of the Fischer-Dieskau performance of *Le Bal masqué* on BASF G22765. "Fischer-Dieskau has recorded very few French songs, which makes his new recital . . . of more than passing interest. . . . Fischer-Dieskau is too intelligent and musically aware to fail entirely in this program, but he lacks the requisite light touch and ease with the language to project the finer points of . . . Poulenc's sassy inspiration." See: D32.

B126   Dean, Winton. "Poulenc," *Musical Times* 111 (July 1970):733.

Review of the double-bill performance of Poulenc's two one-act operas by the Park Lane Group at Camden Town Hall. Dean wrote about *La Voix humaine*, "A great composer might just have brought it off, but Poulenc's bitter-sweet orchestral commentary, short on memorable phrases, is too narrow in range for a 40-minute work in which the single character has little tangible to react against. Both as drama and music it outruns its ideas. . . . *Les Mamelles de Tirésias* . . . is also thinly spread, but it has genuine high spirits and a savvy wit." See: W2; W4.

B127   Demuth, Norman. "The French Position Today," *Chesterian* 26 (October 1951):5-9.

"Milhaud in his latest Symphonies and Quartets has proved himself a giant and has left far behind him Francis Poulenc (1899), whose later works are mainly in the same idiom as those in the 1920's. . . . Posterity will remember Milhaud and Honegger alone of the band known as 'Les Six'."

B128   Dettmer, Roger. "Vocal," *Fanfare* 4 (July 1981):205.

Review of the Cambridge 2777 recording of songs. "Hardly another American artist is so adept at the sounding of French vowels as Carole Bogarde; buttressed by a lovely musical intelligence and an obedient voice. . . . From Poulenc we catch a whiff of 'vin ordinaire' after a night in the cafés, not unpleasantly aromatic although none here are his finest songs." See: D11; D133; D386; D641.

B129   Discus. "Music in the Round," *Harper's* 223 (August 1961):94.

Review of the Angel 35953 recording of *Gloria* and the organ concerto performed by Duruflé, organ. In this favorable review of both of these performances, the reviewer points out that Poulenc has been active in recording his own works, usually as a pianist, but has done little conducting. He has worked closely with the conductors and musicians who have recorded his compositions. This recording of *Gloria* was made under Poulenc's supervision. See: D164; D275.

B130   ___. "Music in the Round," *Harper's* 234 (June 1967): 113.

Review of the recording of *Les Mamelles de Tirésias* reissued on Seraphim M60029 performed by Denise Duval and Jean Giraudeau. "Les Mamelles is an opera bouffe to a poem by Apollinaire, and it is very high camp indeed. The opera aroused some consternation its first swing around the United States. It was considered naughty. And so it is; but how innocent its naughtiness appears today! The score is Poulenc at his wittiest, which means the best light-weight music of the century." See: D326.

B131   "Disks: Frijsh and Others," *New York Times*, February 11, 1962, XII:11.

Review of a recording of piano music performed by Grant Johannesen on Golden Crest CR4042.   "The music is a constant delight to the senses, and Mr. Johannesen plays it beautifully."   See: D19; D297; D305; D571; D643; D648.

B132   Ditsky, John. "Guitar Music of Five Centuries," *Fanfare* 6 (May 1983): 274-75.

Review of the Deutsche Grammophon 2531.382 recording of *Sarabande*. "We expect excellence from a Yepes recital, and we get it here. But what helps set this disc even further off from competing recital discs is its intelligently chosen program." The Poulenc *Sarabande* is described as "technically impressive." See: D438.

B133   ___. "Poulenc," *Fanfare* 7 (May 1984):256-57.

Review of the Andante AD72405 recording of *La Voix humaine*. "Farley acquits herself well here; her French, if not by definition in the running with Duval's, is serviceable; her voice as sturdy, if lacking in the histrionic intensity . . . of Duval's. Yes, Duval 'is' the better actress, but Farley is no less a singer. Poulenc's understated scoring gets careful treatment from Sérébrier and his Aussies." See: D650.

B134   ___. "Poulenc: Concerto in D minor for Two Pianos and Orchestra," *Fanfare* 8 (January 1983):219-20.

Review of the Angel DS38122 recording. "Georgie Priest! does this version race along! Luckily, the brilliance of the instrumentalists' virtuosity keeps pace with the conductor's breakneck abandon." See: D153.

B135   ___. "20th Century Choral Music," *Fanfare* 3 (November 1979):153.

Review of the Hungaroton SLPX11779 recording of *Un Soir de neige*. "Francis Poulenc's suite tries to match the snowy subject of Paul Eluard's texts, and succeeds with a notable absence of flashiness, of conspicuous exoticisms--just explorations within his unmistakable personal style." See: D460.

B136   Donner, Jay M. "Concerto," *New Records* 54/3 (May 1986):6.

Reviews of two recordings, Erato 75203 (*Concerto in D Minor for Two Pianos, Aubade*, and *Piano Concerto*) and 75210 (organ concerto and *Concert champêtre*). "The two Erato albums contain Poulenc's complete concerted works, nicely matched. The music is indispensable to the true collector and even those whose library already contains the three piano compositions, which astoundingly have never previously been available together, should grab this version forthwith. Jean-Philippe Collard might have been one of my choices for soloist, but he merely plays second banana to François-René Duchable in the Two Piano Concerto. It is the unfamiliar Duchable . . . who steals the show, aptly capturing the Gallic flavor and humor, yet adroitly managing to balance the romanticism and neo-classicism dabbed with a modern brush. . . . The inimitable Marie-Claire Alain is not as flamboyant as the Organ Concerto demands, but she is less straitlaced than I might have expected and actually does a rather commendable job. . . . Throughout James Conlon is master of the proceedings." See: D22; D142; D149; D157; D169.

B137   Donner, Jay M. "Poulenc: Histoire de Babar," *New Records* 53/3 (May 1985):15-16.

Review of Magne 2012, a performance of Babar on piano four hands, with narration in French. The reviewer recommends the recording by Peter Ustinov instead of this one, because Ustinov narrates the tale in English. See: D293.

B138   ___. "Poulenc: Nocturnes," *New Records* 52/2 (April 1984):14.

Review of the Orion ORS83459 recording of piano pieces. The pianist, Flavio Varani, "is fluent and glisteningly Gallic in his treatment of Poulenc. Especially noteworthy are the Nocturnes . . . I have rarely heard a more sensitive approach to night pieces from any composer, including Chopin." See: D253; D372; D307; D574; D628; D647.

B139   Downes, Olin. "Chat With Poulenc: French Composer Discusses Musicians of Own Time and Other Periods," *New York Times*, November 7, 1948, II:7.

In this discourse on composers whose works or influence Poulenc believed important, he named Milhaud as the greatest living composer of France. He liked Franck; Tchaikovsky; Richard Strauss ("*Don Juan* I find amazing. This is overwhelming genius"); Stravinsky (Stravinsky and French composers had both profited by mutual interchange of ideas); Hindemith ("He wrote too much and too fast"); and Schoenberg (He paid homage to Schoenberg for his sincerity, his immense influence upon contemporary music, and the beauty of certain works, but he admired the music of Alban Berg more than that of his master). "There was only one law for the composer, he [Poulenc] said, namely, to be only himself, to ape no one, to find out by experience in writing what he really thought and felt." Downes points out that Poulenc spoke English "at moments" during the conversation.

B140 Downes, Olin. "Furor in Paris: Poulenc's New Work at Opéra-Comique Raises a Critical Storm," *New York Times*, August 24, 1947, II:5.

"Poulenc, in Paris, has occasioned a fine row--something to which he never objected--with his opera bouffe,'Les Mamelles de Tirésias.' When this piece was produced at the Opéra-Comique the 'steady patrons' objected to a work which, in the estimate of the conservatives, was fit only for the burlesque stage--if for that--and not for this famous theatre." A synopsis of the plot is given. See: W2.

B141 Dragadze, Peter. "New Poulenc Opera Proves Exciting in Milan," *Musical America* 77 (March 1957):3.

Review of the world premiere on January 26, 1957, of *Dialogues des Carmélites* at La Scala, including   pictures of the production and the composer, a synopsis of the plot, and a favorable review of the "first-class singing and impressive staging." See: W1.

B142 ___. "One Act Operas Succeed at Piccola Scala," *Musical America* 79 (April 1959):26.

Review of productions of three one-act operas by Goffredo Petrassi, *Il Cordovano*; de Falla, *El Retablo de Maese*; and *La Voix humaine*. The reviewer was disappointed in Poulenc's opera: "The music is trivial, monotonous, and does not do credit to this important composer." See: W4.

B143 Drew, David. "Modern French Music." In *European Music in the Twentieth Century*, edited by Howard Hartog. New York: Frederick A. Praeger, 1957.

Poulenc's compositions are discussed on pages 260-67. Brief remarks about the style of each work are included. "More versatile than Duparc, less accomplished than Fauré, Poulenc has no single ancestor amongst French composers. He is very much a child of our time, and the boundaries of his talent--that of a largely self-taught composer-pianist whose creative successes tend to rely on the inspiration of a text or scenario--suggest parallels with the talent of only one other contemporary artist, George Gershwin. But whereas Gershwin's strength and originality are singularly uninvolved, there is something equivocal about every aspect of Poulenc's music--not least, its originality."

B144   Dumesnil, René. *La Musique en france entre les deux guerres, 1919-1939.* Genève: Éditions du Milieu du Monde, 1946.

This work presents an overview of musical life in France during a twenty-year period. The author covers not only important facts (composers and performers who were active; performances in theatres, concert halls, and radio; statistics about concerts) but also reveals the atmosphere which prevailed in the arts during this era. Poulenc is included, especially as his compositions relate to the factual information on public performances. Poulenc's early works are briefly discussed.

B145   Durey, Louis. "Francis Poulenc," *Chesterian* 25 (September 1922):1-4.

An essay on style in Poulenc's compositions proceeding from the idea that one of the most difficult questions a young composer faces is that of style. Durey finds in Poulenc's early works two quite distinct categories of music, "the first deliberately bare and neatly, frankly, precisely, even a little dryly written; the second full of a freedom and an exuberance that burst through the frames imposed by discipline. . . . In all these works, from the fist to the last and from the best to the weakest, may be discerned an extremely marked personality composed of grace and flexibility, and of so engaging a charm and fascination that it would be impossible to confuse these qualities with those of anyone else." All the early works are listed and briefly discussed.

B146   Durgin, Cyrus. "Poulenc Premiere," *Musical America* 81 (March 1961):24.

Review of the premiere of *Gloria* on January 20, 1961, by the Boston Symphony Orchestra, Charles Münch, conductor. The reviewer found the work "bright and joyous and a heartfelt utterance of glory to God. The musical style is varied to the point of eclecticism, but characterized by two Poulenc principles: real diatonic melody and tonal harmony." Poulenc was present not only to hear the premiere but also to perform his *Concerto in D Minor for Two Pianos*, "a waggish piece designed for sheer enjoyment." See: W29; W41.

B147   Ebensberger, Gary Lee. *The Motets of Francis Poulenc.* DMA dissertation, University of Texas, 1970.

Stylistic analysis, including textual treatment, of the eleven a cappella motets. See: W36; W39; W46; W47; W54.

B148   Ericson, Raymond. "Recent Disks in Review," *New York Times* October 27, 1963, X:19.

Review of the Golden Crest 4070 recording of the *Sonata for Two Pianos* performed by Judith and Doris Lang. "They play with a great deal of dash and enthusiasm, but not much rhythmic subtlety." See: D552.

B149   ___. "Recordings: A Batch of Moderns," *New York Times* November 10, 1963, X:14.

Review of performances of *Sextuor, Sonata for Two Pianos*, and the songs, "*C,*" *Hôtel*, and *Voyage à Paris*, on Columbia ML5918; also of the *Concerto for Two Pianos* and the *Concert champêtre* on Angel 35993. "The Sextuor . . . is wittily conceived for this kind of ensemble, full of bright ideas and a great deal of fun to listen to."   The *Concert champêtre*, "strikes the listener afresh with its airy loveliness and inventive use of the harpsichord and small orchestra." See: D48; D138; D151; D210; D447; D548.

B150   ___. "Records in Review," *High Fidelity* 4 (July 1954): 54.

Review of the recording of *Sonata* (four hands) performed by Arthur Gold and Robert Fizdale on Columbia ML4854. In comparison with recordings by other duo-piano teams (Bartlett and Robertson; Vronsky and Babin; Luboshutz and Nemenoff), Gold and Fizdale "offer the subtlest, most delicate interplay of truly musical temperaments. . . . Poulenc's early Sonata parades the affection for the music-hall style of melody and rhythm that he has incorporated so engagingly and expertly in so much of his music." See: D536.

B151   ___. "2 French Ballets by 15 Composers," *New York Times* July 21, 1985, II:9.

Review of the recording of *Les Mariés de la Tour Eiffel* and *L'Éventail de Jeanne* on Chandos ABRD1119, both recorded in their entirety for the first time. Ericson relates the story of the commission of the ballet by the Swedish Ballet. Cocteau wrote the libretto for *Les Mariés* and asked the members of Les Six to provide the music. After the original perfor-mances of the work in 1921, the score was lost until its discovery in 1956 in the Stockholm Dance Museum. See: D248; D328.

B152   "Etudes musicales analytiques: *Concert champêtre*--Francis Poulenc," *Le Guide du concert et des théâtre lyriques*, no. 30 (April 26, 1929): 870-74.

Analysis of the form and discussion of the use of the instruments in this composition. The main themes of the work are given in the musical examples. See: W28.

B153   Eyer, Ronald. "American Premiere of Poulenc Opera Presented by San Francisco Opera in Opening Week," *Musical America* 77 (October 1957):3.

Review of the American premiere of *Dialogues des Carmélites* on September 20, 1957, conducted by Erich Leinsdorf. Included are pictures of the production, a complete list of the cast, and analysis of the text setting and musical style. "It is a work of immense elegance, of true artistic economy and absolutely no bombast. It is, I think, an honest piece which makes the most of a difficult subject and does it in a way to grip the imagination and the emotions of the spectator." See: W1.

Ferrand, Mon. Louis. "En guise de conclusion." See: B577.

B154   Fingleton, David.   "Glyndebourne: La Voix humaine," *Music and Musicians* 25 (August 1977):50-51.

Review of the Glyndebourne performance of the opera with Graziella Sciutti as Elle. "The music is certainly full of atmosphere and wit, and, as is customary with the composer, is meticulously constructed. What troubles me, however, is the extent to which Poulenc really did anything for the play." Sciutti "sang the role with clarity, accuracy of intonation and skilful deployment of her vocal resources. . . . Much of the production's success sprang from Martin Battersly's exquisitely careful period setting. It hit precisely the right note of stylish, but slightly vulgar, art-deco." Includes a photograph of Sciutti in the role of Elle. See: W4.

B155   Flanagan, William. "Artur Rubinstein: A French Program," *HiFi/Stereo Review* 14 (March 1965):106-07.

Review of the RCA Victor LSC2751 recording of *Trois mouvements perpétuels, Intermezzo in A Flat Major*, and *Intermezzo in D Flat Major*. In the Poulenc pieces Rubinstein "finds all the right jokes . . . and at the same time he can indulge the composer's music-hall lushness and sentimentality without patronizing this side of him." See: D308; D621.

B156   Flanagan, William. "Poulenc," *HiFi/Stereo Review* 12 (March 1964):76.

Review of the Angel 36121 recording of *Stabat Mater* and *Quatre motets pour un temps de pénitence*. "Change the language from Latin to French, the texts from sacred writings to the poetry of Apollinaire, and any one of several moments in the *Stabat Mater* becomes, as musical style, no different from some of Poulenc's most lavishly hedonistic art songs." Nevertheless, the reviewer found the *Stabat Mater* "a magnificent work and a moving one. It may very well be a masterpiece." The four motets are "welcome encores." See: D411; D561.

B157   ___. "Poulenc," *HiFi/Stereo Review* 17 (December 1966):98-100.

Review of the Angel S36370 recording of *Chansons villageoises, Rapsodie nègre, Le Bal masqué*, and *Le Bestiaire*. The instrumental song accompaniments were orchestrated by the composer himself, "so there is no one else to blame but Poulenc" for what the reviewer hears as "a lessening of the material's quality." *Le Bal masqué*, conceived for instrumental accompaniment, "holds its own." See: D31; D54; D113; D431.

B158   ___. "Poulenc," *Stereo Review* 22 (March 1969):100-02.

Review of the Angel S36519 recording of *Sinfonietta, Suite française, Deux marches et un intermède*, and *Les Mariés de la Tour Eiffel*. "Poulenc viewed the Sinfonietta as a belated, symbolic farewell to youth." The reviewer found "the ravishing pastoral third movement . . . Poulenc at his best." See: D183; D327; D459; D566.

B159   ___. "Poulenc's *Les Mamelles de Tirésias* Introduced at Brandeis Festival," *Musical America* 73 (July 1953):5.

Review of the American premiere of Poulenc's first opera on June 13, 1953, at the Festival of Creative Arts at Brandeis University under the general direction of Leonard Bernstein. "The Poulenc score was a smooth progression of uninterrupted pleasure . . . a combination of sardonic romanticism and lovely fragments of pure popular song." See: W2.

B160   Flanner, Janet [Genêt]. "Letter From Paris," *New Yorker* 29 (November 21, 1953):187-92.

Review of a concert of music of Les Six organized by Jean Cocteau at the Théâtre des Champs-Elysées. Each of the original members of the group attended except for Honegger, "too ill to be there . . . None of the young Paris intellectuals attended. The enormous audience was composed of people who were young thirty-five years ago, when Les Six were le dernier cri." Poulenc's cantata, *Sécheresses*, performed on the program, was characterized as "magnificently melodic, and had, sure enough, an undulating musical line like a horizon." See: W50.

B161   Flanner, Janet [Genêt]. "Letter From Paris," *New Yorker* 33 (July 20, 1957):62-68.

Review of the French premiere of *Dialogues des Carmélites* at the Paris Opéra on June 21, 1957. "Since Poulenc, who was present, felt that the Italian treatment was too worldly and operatic for his pious intentions, the recent Paris presentation became, instead, practically a miracle of impressionistic, controlled musical nuances . . . His opera score is marked by his characteristic ecstasy of expression and subtlety of harmony; by lofty reaches of mounting melodic grace; by the rich polyphony of his chorals . . . and by an all too brief last-act overture of really passionate loveliness." See: W1.

B162   ___. "Letter From Paris," *New Yorker* 35 (March 21, 1959):154-60.

Review of an Opéra-Comique production of *La Voix humaine* in Paris, including a brief discussion of the work in its version as a stage play. "What Poulenc has written is poignant music for a victim--music that has the quick, insistent rhythm of a heartbeat." See: W4.

B163   ___. *Paris Journal: 1944-1965*. Edited by William Shawn. New York: Atheneum, 1965.

Flanner lived much of her life in Europe where she observed and commented on the musical scene, especially in a regular column for the New Yorker. In this memoir Flanner discussed premieres of Poulenc's works that she heard and evaluated the contributions of Poulenc and other French composers to the development of music in the twentieth century.

B164   Fleming, Shirley. "The New Releases," *High Fidelity* 19 (September 1969):100.

Review of recordings of the *Trio for Oboe, Bassoon, and Piano*; and the *Sonata for Clarinet and Bassoon* on Angel S36586. "The members of the Melos Ensemble do a superb job with these works . . . both the Trio and the Sonata, abounding in Poulenc's inevitable sassiness, simply dare you not to like them. The utter cocksureness of the first movement of the Clarinet and Bassoon Sonata sets some kind of record even by Poulenc's standards, and also provides one of the happiest examples I know of counterpoint a la the 1920s." See: D467; D600.

B165   Fleming, Shirley. "Records in Review," *High Fidelity* 15 (August 1965): 77-78.

Review of the recording of *Sextuor; Trio for Oboe, Bassoon, and Piano*; and *Sonata for Flute and Piano* on Angel 36261. "A wonderful reflection here of the two faces of Poulenc--conveying the bumptious and irreverent sauciness of the 1920s and '30s by way of the Trio and Sextet . . . and the free songfulness of the Flute Sonata." See: D443; D492; D599.

B166   "Francis Poulenc Is Dead at 64," *New York Times* January 31, 1963, p. 7.

This obituary noted that Poulenc, "had been one of the brightest lights of the French musical world for almost half a century. . . . All his adult life he was a prominent member of the French capital's intellectual and artistic life. He was friendly and outgoing and was able to combine a large musical output with a busy social program." A photograph of the composer taken in 1948 is included.

B167   Frankenstein, Alfred V. "Chicago Premieres," *Modern Music* 11 (January-February 1934):103-06.

Review of the first Chicago performance of *Aubade* presented by the Woman's Symphony Orchestra of Chicago: "Poulenc had the misfortune to make his reputation as a wild man fifteen years ago, with the result that so disarmingly simple and melodious a composition as the *Aubade* is likely to be laughed at. . . . As a matter of fact, the Poulenc of the *Aubade* and the *Trio for Oboe, Bassoon and Piano*, is a natural melodist." See: W6.

B168   ___. "Records in Review," *High Fidelity* 4 (August 1954):44.

Review of a recording of *Sextuor* on Capital P8258. The work is "typical in its exploitation of suave, flattering tunes, music hall echoes, and the elegantly banal." The recording was described as excellent. See: D445.

B169   ___. "Records in Review," *High Fidelity* 4 (October 1954):66.

Review of the Concert Hall CHS1181 recording of the eight *Nocturnes* and *Trois mouvements perpétuels* performed by Grant Johannesen. "Everything about this recording conveys an air of maturity, ripeness, generosity, balance, and good sense. This applies with equal force to the recording, the choice of material, and the performance." See: D371; D616.

B170   Frankenstein, Alfred V. "Records in Review," *High Fidelity* 4 (January 1955):57.

Review of the Angel 35l33 recording of *Sextuor*. "Poulenc is a past master of the tuneful, witty, and elegant, and this sextet is in his finest, subtlest vein. The recording is something extra special." See: D442.

B171   ___. "Records in Review," *High Fidelity* 5 (September 1955):66.

Review of the Berkshire Wind Ensemble performance of the *Trio for Oboe, Bassoon, and Piano* on Unicorn UNLP1005. "In all of these pieces, French lucidity and charm are displayed in highly entertaining forms. All . . . are music about other music, handling old themes or ideas with wit and point and flattering the hearer by means of reminiscence . . . the Poulenc [is] about Mozart." See: D609.

B172   ___. "Records in Review," *High Fidelity* 7 (December 1957):80.

Review of the Bernac-Poulenc recording of *Le Bal masqué* and *Stabat Mater* conducted by Louis Frémaux on Westminster XWN18422. The former work "is one of the masterpieces of Poulenc's early style. . . . The music reflects ragtime, popular songs, and 'Parisian folk lore' in the approved tradition established by The Six many years earlier." *Stabat Mater* "is still the work of a melodist, but light effects give way to massive ones, 'Parisian folk lore' gives way to medieval polyphony and Bach, and complex rhythms are superseded by a marching relentlessness. . . . The performance of Le Bal masqué is magnificent, that of the Stabat Mater very good." See: D39; D563.

B173   ___. "Records in Review," *High Fidelity* 11 (August 1961):5.

Review of the Angel 35953 recording of the *Gloria*, Rosanna Carteri, soprano, and the organ concerto performed by Maurice Duruflé. "The Gloria sounds like a mixture of Saint-Saëns and Carl Orff, although its lovely quiet ending recalls the fact that Poulenc was once capable of writing beautiful music. The Concerto is pure Saint-Saëns of the most

pompous and windy kind.   The performances are both magnificent."
See: D164; D275.

B174   Frankenstein, Alfred V. "Records in Review," *High Fidelity* 12 (May 1962):
        80.

Review of the Golden Crest CR4042 recording of piano music performed
by Grant Johannesen. "The exceptional work in this collection is the
Suite française . . . These [dances] are enchanting in their songful,
modal quality, their simplicity, and their direct emotional appeal." The six
Improvisations "run a considerable gamut of color and expressivity, but
remain always within the characteristic Poulenc framework of tunefulness, clarity, and point. The other pieces [*Humoresque, Valse in C,
Villageoises, Les Animaux modéles*] are all in Poulenc's wide-eyed,
false-naive style." See: D19; D297; D305; D571; D643; D648.

B175   ___. "Records in Review," *High Fidelity* 15 (January 1965):82.

Review of a recording of the Mass and eight Motets by the Whikehart
Chorale on Lyrichord LLST7127. "The Mass in G may well be Poulenc's
finest choral work. . . . a completely angelic work demonstrating that
brevity is not only the soul of wit but the soul of worship too. It is
modern music nurtured in Gregorian chant and Renaissance polyphony.
As bright and colorful as the famous illuminations in the Duc de Berry's
Book of Hours, it is a rare and perfect thing--and this interpretation does
full justice to it." The eight Motets, "are also very beautiful, although
listening to all eight of them in succession may be a bit too much
because of their consistent blandness." See: D337; D406; D413.

B176   ___. "Records in Review," *High Fidelity* 15 (February 1965):88-89.

Review of the Nonesuch H1033 recording of *Sonata for Clarinet and
Piano, Sonata for Oboe and Piano*, and *Aubade*. "The Clarinet Sonata,
in memory of Prokofiev, is full of Prokofievian effects. Its first movement
employs a theme derived from the first movement of the Russian's Flute
Sonata, its slow movement is a very 'Russian' adagio, and its finale is a
diabolical scherzo like the one in Prokofiev's First Violin Concerto. The
Oboe Sonata is dedicated to the memory of Honegger but contains
. . . no Honeggeresque touches; it is full of the warm tuneful lyricism
characteristic of Poulenc at his best . . . All three pieces are beautifully
performed." See: D26; D488; D524.

B177   Freed, Richard. "Collections," *Stereo Review* 50 (October 1985):86.

Review of the Chandos ABRD1119 recording of *L'Éventail de Jeanne* and *Les Mariés de la Tour Eiffel*. The music is "stylishly entertaining" and "filled with that peculiarly Gallic wit and warmth of heart." See: D248; D328.

B178   Freed, Richard. "A Glowing New Poulenc Collection from Pianist Gabriel Tacchino," *Stereo Review* 48 (June 1983):72.

Review of a recording on EMI C069-73101. "Everything here glistens with freshness and glows with heart--as Poulenc wrote it, as Tacchino plays it." See: D665.

B179   ___. "Tacchino's Inspired Poulenc," *Stereo Review* 51 (June 1986):123.

Review of the EMI 173196-1 recording of piano pieces. "EMI/France has now released the fourth and final volume in Tacchino's survey of Poulenc's solo-piano works, and you may be sure that he takes nothing for granted in the music. There is no relaxation of the total commitment that has so vivified all of the previous volumes in the series, which began in 1966. The tiniest pieces here--such as the five Impromptus--yield unexpected substance, and the three movements of the Napoli suite fairly blaze with the flush of inspiration that must have produced them." See: D29.

B180   Freeman, John W. "Song of the Scaffold," *Opera News* 30 (March 5, 1966):14-15.

Discussion of the plot of *Dialogues des Carmélites*, including musical examples. "The real subject is the growth of the characters in sureness of themselves, of each other, of their purpose and destiny. For a composer's operatic testament and guarantee of immortality, it could not be more appropriate." See: W1.

B181   Fritschel, James Erwin. *The Study and Performance of Three Extended Choral Works*. Ph.D. dissertation, State University of Iowa, 1960.

Stylistic analysis and study in the preparation and performance of three choral works. The Mass in G of Poulenc was chosen for inclusion, because it "represents the peak of Poulenc's sacred a cappella works." See: W44.

B182   Fuller, Donald. "Airborne Over New York: Spring 1946," *Modern Music* 23 (Spring 1946):116-23.

Reviews of New York performances of new music during the spring. "Poulenc's moving song cycle, *Tel Jour, Telle Nuit*, was sung by Maggie Teyte, and choral works were presented by the Lehman Engel Singers. *Salve Regina* shows Poulenc in his mystical religious mood. It is music of deep conviction, often quite powerful in its gaunt but resonant sonorities. The *Sept Chansons* reveal the heartwarming Poulenc, poet of daily emotions. The exquisitely tender alternates with the exquisitely gay; the evocations of love are often violent and impassioned. Surely Poulenc's mastery of choral technique and effect is unsurpassed today." See: W49; W51; W101.

B183   Garvelmann, Donald M.   "Rare Treasures from the Recent Past," *American Record Guide* 40 (February 1977):17.

Review of Wanda Landowska's performance of *Concert champêtre* reissued by International Piano Archives. "The work is like a wonderful, exciting excursion to a colorful rustic carnival, flashily brilliant and pompously funny, with a gorgeous second movement Sicilenne spelled out here by excellent strings. . . . This album, enhanced by several photographs and the annotations of Landowska's longtime friend, Denise Restout, is an extremely important document of performance style." See: D144.

B184   Gavoty, Bernard."*La Voix humaine*:   Un chef-d'oeuvre de Francis Poulenc," *Journal musical français* (March 17, 1959):20.

Review of the first production of the opera. "A masterpiece--perhaps even *his* masterpiece . . . Now that I have seen Denise Duval in the role . . . I can scarcely imagine any other interpretation than hers." See: W4.

B185   Gaynor, Richard. "The Platinum Flute," *Fanfare* 1 (November 1977):63.

Review of the Pandora 106 recording of *Sonata for Flute and Piano*. "Mr. Tipton and Ms. Norris seem very much at ease with this music. The recording, while lacking a bit in naturalness, still presents a clear view of the music and the first class playing of the soloists." See: D504.

B186   Gelatt, Roland. "Building Your Record Library," *High Fidelity* 5 (September 1955):65.

In suggesting a basic record collection of French music, Gelatt states about Poulenc, "At least one of this group [Les Six] is destined, in my view, to be esteemed by posterity. He is Francis Poulenc, a highly uneven musician, but at his best (that is, in his vocal music) a composer of great poetic power." The recording of *Banalités* by Bernac and Poulenc on Columbia ML4333 is recommended for inclusion in a basic collection. See: D41.

B187   Gelatt, Roland. "Champagne for New Years," *Saturday Review* 33 (December 30, 1950):43.

Reviews of the Columbia ML4333 recording by Bernac and Poulenc of songs by Poulenc and Ravel and of the RCA Victor LM1088 recording of the Mass. Concerning the Columbia recording: "If any reader is still unaware that Poulenc is the contemporary heir to the lyric mantle of Schubert, Wolf, and Ravel, these cycles--Banalités and Chansons villageoises--should set him right forthwith. The recording is a fine technical achievement. As for the interpretation, it calls for that much misused adjective 'perfect'." The Mass was performed by the Robert Shaw Chorale "with precision and understanding. I find this composition less original than the songs, embodying more craft then real invention. Certainly the Mass belongs among the few first-rate religious works of the past quarter century." See: D41; D114; D338.

B188   ___. "Fare From France," *Saturday Review* 37 (May 29, 1954):50.

Review of the Angel 35090 recording of *Les Mamelles de Tirésias* with Denise Duval, soprano, and Jean Giraudeau, tenor. "Apollinaire's fancy stimulated Poulenc to his kaleidoscopic best. . . . [Performed] with the zip Les Mamelles requires." See: D325.

B189   ___. "Le Gout Houstonien," *Saturday Review* 33 (July 29, 1950):41.

Review of Jean Germain's recording of *Suite française* on Mercury MG15007. "Charming and buoyant as this music may be it falls short of Poulenc's vocal attainments." See: D572.

B190   ___. "Major Debussy, Minor Poulenc," *Saturday Review* 34 (December 29, 1951):46.

Review of the REB Editions 7 recording of *Sextuor; Trio for Oboe, Bassoon, and Piano*; and *Sonata for Clarinet and Bassoon*. The works by Poulenc are, "of questionable value. Every now and then one of Poulenc's melting, bitter-sweet tunes fights its way clear of the bright instrumental chatter, but all too seldom." See: D455; D475; D607.

B191   Gelatt, Roland. "Music Without Notes," *Saturday Review* 35 (April 26, 1952):64.

Review of the Bernac-Poulenc recording of songs on Columbia ML4484. In this recording the artists, "are at the top of their form." Bernac remains "without a peer among practicing recitalists in his ability to project the quintessence of French song." See: D82; D357.

B192   ___. "A Vote for Francis Poulenc," *Saturday Review* 33 (January 28, 1950):57-58.

An interview with the composer on the occasion of his arrival in the United States for a three-month visit. The author assessed Poulenc's importance as a composer: "I must still express my growing conviction that the name of Francis Poulenc will appear on concert programs a century hence." Poulenc evaluated his piano music: "It came too easily. Being a pianist, I found myself engrossed only in exploiting the possibilities of the instrument, and the result was music of brilliance but little significance."

B193   ___. "With a French Accent," *Saturday Review* 34 (August 25, 1951):50.

Review of Poulenc's performances of his piano music and that of Satie on Columbia ML4399. The *Suite française* is described as Poulenc's best writing to date for solo piano: "His playing of the *Pavane* section provides an object lesson in endowing chords with flowing movement, and his zestful rhythm in the *Petite marche militaire* is a potent musical translation of the word *elan*." See: D373; D569; D615.

B194   George, André. "Francis Poulenc," *Chesterian* 6 (March-April 1925): 141-46.

Essay on the youthful compositions of Poulenc with analysis of musical style and comments on the influences on the works. "Poulenc is not without an elegiac side. The entrancing Adagietto in *Les Biches* is so for its most perfect expression. . . . In his heart of hearts, there is a little of Schubert in him, possibly more than people would suspect." See: W7.

B195   Gerber, Leslie. "Poulenc," *Fanfare* 7 (March 1984):227.

Review of the Orion ORS83459 recording of piano pieces. "The major work . . . is the set of *Nocturnes*, pieces which don't necessarily fit one's ideas of what music with that title will sound like. They are not all slow and quiet. I find the cycle of unusual interest among Poulenc's piano works, for its variety and the unassuming but constant interest of its materials. Varani . . . gives a fine impression . . . He plays cleanly and expressively, totally without pretense and exaggeration." See: D253; D372; D307; D574; D628; D647.

B196   Gilbert, Robert. "Honegger, Poulenc & Milhaud," *Disques* 1 (June 1930): 119-20.

Reviews of the Columbia D15041 recording of *Le Bestiaire* sung by Croiza, with Poulenc as accompanist, and the Columbia D13053 recording of *Trois mouvements perpétuels*, played by Poulenc. "Exquisite singing," described Croiza's performance. "Poulenc is a capable pianist and plays his charming pieces deftly." See: D662; D663.

B197   Glass, Herbert. "A Poulenc Masterpiece," *American Record Guide* 27 (August 1961):652-53.

Review of the Angel S35953 recording including *Gloria* and the organ concerto. "Without further introduction, let me say that I feel Poulenc's *Gloria* to be that composer's masterpiece (to date) and one of the supreme choral-liturgical works of this century. . . . [with] some of the most sublime melodic inspirations of our age, ethereal and supremely moving in their simple beauty." Glass found the organ concerto impressive--more so in this version than that of Biggs on Columbia ML4329. See: D164; D167; D275.

B198   Goddard, Scott. "London Letter," *Chesterian* 32 (Spring 1958):117-20.

Review of the premiere of *Dialogues des Carmélites* at Covent Garden. "The music sounded very French in its refusal ever to become pompous or imposing for its own ends; mainly it was memorable for its clarity and for the fluent manner in which it moved from episode to episode." See: W1.

B199   Goldbeck, Frederick. "Poulenc's 'Dialogues des Carmélites': Paris Première," *Musical Times* 98 (1957):448-49.

In this review Goldbeck looks back at the "bad boy" reputation of Les Six. In evaluating the opera the reviewer found that, "Harmonically--well, there are more common chords, dominant sevenths and diminished sevenths than in any other contemporary score I have ever seen or heard of. In consequence, musical archaism is the most characteristic element . . . both the main constituent of its style and the mainspring of its success." See: W1.

B200   Goldsmith, Harris. "Artur Rubinstein: A French Program," *High Fidelity* 15 (February 1965):96.

Review of Artur Rubinstein's performances of Intermezzos nos. 1 and 2 and *Trois mouvements perpétuels* on RCA Victor LSC2751.   "The simplicity and directness of the two Poulenc Intermezzos . . . should be the envy of every pianist, while the *Mouvements perpétuels* contrasts instructively with Poulenc's own recorded version on Columbia. Rubinstein rightly strives for clarity, while the composer, in my opinion, took his *gris* markings far too seriously and thereby muddied these humorous tidbits by using too much pedal. Inasmuch as Poulenc gave overwhelming approval to Rubinstein's performances of his music, one can only assume that he was less doctrinaire than most composers in determining how others were to play his work." See: D308; D621; D615.

B201   ___. "Classical Reviews," *High Fidelity* 28 (November 1978):132-33.

Review of the Angel S37303 recording in which Goldsmith characterized the playing of *Trois mouvements perpétuels* as "clear-cut and sympathetically idiomatic even if it lacks the patrician tapered line of Rubinstein's version [RCA LSC2751] or the moist ambiance of the composer's own [Odyssey Y33792]." See: D614; D619; D621.

B202   ___. "The New Releases," *High Fidelity* 19 (November 1969):102.

Review of Gabriel Tacchino's performances of piano music on Angel S36602.   "Tacchino enters into the very specialized world of this composer with striking affinity. Indeed, he almost goes too far in his ultrabrisk treatment of that second *Mouvement perpétuel.* . . . He puts a lot of incisive vigor into his technically brilliant, well-reproduced performances." See: D197; D249; D370; D375; D389; D568; D613; D632; D642.

B203   ___. "The New Releases," *High Fidelity* 20 (January 1970):114.

Review of the Golden Crest CR40866 recording of *Thème varié* performed by Johannesen. "The performances are pretty much what one would expect from one of this country's most distinguished middle-generation pianists . . . clear-cut, unaffected style and a tonal and technical approach similar to his mentor Robert Casadesus." See: D588.

B204   Goldsmith, Harris. "Recitals and Miscellany,"   21 (September 1971):
        112-14.

        Review of the London CS6694 recording of *L'Embarquement pour
        Cythère*. "The present, overlanguorous, underenergized treatment misses
        the fun and swinging rhythm this charmer must have." But the reviewer
        admired the ensemble precision of the team of Eden and Tamir: "Their
        togetherness verges on the uncanny, with the subtly gauged rubatos and
        intricate tonal balance and blend approaching supernatural perfection."
        See: D238.

B205   ___. "Vladimir Horowitz: Piano Recital," *High Fidelity* 15 (September
        1965):114.

        Review of a recording of *Pastourelle* and *Toccata* performed by Vladimir
        Horowitz on Angel COLH300, a reissue from HMV originals recorded
        between 1932 and 1936. "Now that Horowitz has embarked on yet
        another phase in his exciting concert career, the souvenirs from his
        youthful years prove more fascinating than ever. . . . The Poulenc is
        rendered with almost a supernatural limpidity and ease." See: D631.

B206   Goléa, Antoine. "French Music Since 1945." Translated by Lucile H.
        Brockway. *Musical Quarterly* 51 (January 1965):22-37.

        Survey of developments in the French musical world following WWII.
        "Certainly the situation of composers who have never set themselves the
        problems that Martinet and Nigg [two serial composers] have set
        appears more simple, clear-cut, and comfortable.   There are the
        composers of the older generation, who have continued to write
        according to the esthetics and technique of their youth, sometimes
        evolving in a very interesting way: among them Milhaud, Poulenc, Auric,
        Sauguet. Works like . . . the opera Voix humaine . . . are the fruit of
        sincere and authentic talents and carry the indelible mark of the
        personality of their composers." See: W4.

B207   Goodwin, Noël. "The Edinburgh Festival," *Musical Times* 101 (October
        1960):644.

        Review of the British premiere of *La Voix humaine* on August 30, 1960,
        with Denise Duval, soprano. "I found the work as a whole excessively
        tiresome . . . Poulenc's watery whole-tone musical convolutions add no
        new dimension to a stage work already existing on its own right as a
        dramatic monologue." See: W4.

B208   Goodwin, Noël. "Poulenc: The Ballet and the Church," *About the House* 5 (Spring 1980):46-47.

The premiere of the ballet, *Gloria*, choreographed to Poulenc's score of the same title by Kenneth MacMillan, took place at the Royal Opera House, London, on March 13, 1980.   This article traced Poulenc's development as a ballet composer. A list is included of all compositions of Poulenc used for ballet music and all the original ballet scores, including choreographer and year of the premiere. See: W41.

Gouverné, Yvonne. "Hommage à Francis Poulenc." See: B577.

B209   Gruen, John. "Poulenc," *Musical America* 80 (April 1960):6-7.

Interview with Poulenc. In the brief introductory essay to the interview, Gruen described the composer's music: "At the age of 61, a composer whose music is still full of youth, vigor, individuality, and, above all, full of the lyricism and elegance that is so uniquely his own." The composer gave up writing songs. "I am too old," he said. "Today, poets do not write in a manner that inspires me to song . . . to write more [songs] would be to force myself in a direction in which I really have nothing further to say."

B210   *Il gruppo dei sei*.   Special issue of *L'Approdo musicale*, nos. 19-20 (1965).

The entire issue of this Italian periodical is devoted to the "French Six." The contents are:

Cocteau, Jean. "Le Coq." Facsimile of the four numbers of the news sheet, *Le Coq*, published by Cocteau in 1920. The folded sheets are inserted in an envelope in the back of the periodical. See: B97.

Cocteau, Jean. "Les Mariés de la Tour Eiffel." Pages 145-48. Reprint of Cocteau's program notes for the first performance of the work. See: W9.

Cocteau, Jean. Drawing: "Cocteau and the Six," page 10.

Collaer, Paul. "I 'Sei:' Studio dell'evoluzione della musica francese dal 1917 al 1924." Pages 11-78. An essay filled with facts, anecdotes, and pictures. Especially important are the reproduction of an oil painting "I Sei" by Jacques-Emile Blanche now in the Rouen Museum of Art, and photographs of the Group with Cocteau from 1925 and 1953.   This article also includes biographical information, extracts from letters, and discussion of compositions.

Collaer, Paul. "Le Coq et l'arlequin di Jean Cocteau." Pages 79-91. A discussion of the ideas expressed in an essay written by Cocteau. The essay was published in Paris in 1918. One of the earliest attempts to articulate a new aesthetic philosophy following the war, the essay became the creed of the French Six.

Laurencin, Marie. Watercolor design for Poulenc's ballet, *Les Biches*, later reproduced on the cover of the first publication of the score, Paris 1924. Following page 140. See: W7.

Mantelli, Alberto. "Introduzione." Pages 5-8. The Introduction sets the scene for the formation and early years of development of the group of young musicians. Included is important information about individuals who were not composers of the group but who were associated with them in the early years, especially Jane Bathori, Henri Sauguet, and Jean Cocteau.

Photograph of Poulenc taken in 1922 following page 80.

Radiguet, Raymond. "Les Mariés de la Tour Eiffel." Pages 149-52. Reprint of a review of the work that appeared in *Les Feuilles libres*, no. 25, February 1922. See: W9.

Rognoni, Luigi. "Due colloqui con Arthur Honegger." Pages 131-40. Information about the early relationships among the members of the Group, their activities, and their early compositions.

B211   H. K. "Alla Breve: Satire, Camp," *New York Times* January 29, 1967, D:29.

Review of the Denise Duval and Jean Giraudeau recording of *Les Mamelles de Tirésias* reissued on Seraphim 60029. "This gem of lyric theater satire was a marvel when it was first recorded in 1954 and still takes the breath away with its bawdy spoofing of morals and manners. The performance is unimpeachable, the sound quite good." See: D326.

B212   Haggin, B. H. "Music," *The Nation* 173 (August 4, 1951): 98-99.

Review of the Columbia ML4399 recording of Poulenc performing his piano compositions (*Trois mouvements perpétuels*, *Suite française*, and *Nocturne in D Major*) and piano works by Satie. "Of the piano pieces of Satie played by Poulenc the *Tyrolienne Turque* is very amusing, but the rest aren't up to their funny titles. Poulenc's music . . . I don't care for." See: D373; D569; D615.

B213   Hall, Albert. "Beethoven: Quintet for Piano and Winds . . . Poulenc: Sextuor," *Fanfare* 2 (November 1978): 24.

Review of the BIS LP61 recording. "The Poulenc sextet is . . . routine, being negotiated by all concerned with a 'brio' that feels forced rather than genuinely engendered by the music." See: D444.

B214   ___. "Poulenc: Trio for Oboe, Bassoon, and Piano," *Fanfare* 3 (May 1980):194-95.

Review of the Telefunken 6.42081 recording. The performers "expand the possibilities of Poulenc's charming trio beyond the composer's wildest dreams of liveliness and technical perfection yet they remain firmly in style. . . . They turn a minor 'jeu d'esprit' into a small master-piece." See: D608.

B215   Hall, David. "Impressive Poulenc," *HiFi/Stereo Review* 7 (July 1961): 60-61.

Review of the Angel S35953 recording of *Gloria* and the organ concerto. "Certainly both the Organ Concerto and the *Gloria*, as representative of Poulenc's 'big' style, are deeply rooted in aspects of French musical style that go as far back as the grand baroque manner of Marc-Antoine Charpentier and Lalande. . . . Excellent as the Gloria is, the Organ Concerto is what would make me buy this disc." The reviewer judged the concerto to be "a full-blown neo-romantic utterance cast in a modern-baroque frame, filled with grandiose rhetoric, lyric sentiment, and feverish nervous tension." See: D164; D275.

B216   Hamilton, David. "Classical Reviews," *High Fidelity* 28 (April 1978):112.

Review of Fischer-Dieskau singing *Le Bal masqué* on the HNH 4045 recording. "The amiable grotesqueries of the Poulenc-Max Jacob cantata suffer not only from the singer's tone-heavy articulation, but also from the excessively sober rhythmic address of the instrumentalists." See: D36.

B217   ___. "The New Releases," *High Fidelity* 18 (October 1968):122.

Review of a recording of songs by Gérard Souzay, baritone, and Dalton Baldwin, piano, on RCA LSC3018. "Souzay's voice was apparently not in its best condition for this recording, and the close Victor miking emphasizes the rough sound and incipient tremolo as well as some imprecise pitching . . . Elegance is even more important in this literature than voice, and too many of the sounds we hear on this disc are inelegant." See: D13; D108; D182; D195; D301; D322; D382; D388; D428; D433; D585.

B218   Hamilton, David. "The New Releases," *High Fidelity* 19 (April 1969): 67.

Review of the Bracha Eden and Alexander Tamir recording of the Sonata for two pianos (1953) on London CS6583. The reviewer found the dynamic range limited and the tonal color monotonous. He pointed out several departures from the printed score, "including additional measures in the last movement, which presumably come from an authentic source (perhaps from Gold and Fizdale, to whom the piece is dedicated); possibly the reduced dynamics and increased tempo (half again as fast as indicated) of the opening pages have similar authority." See: D554.

B219   Hanson, John Robert. *Macroform in Selected Twentieth-Century Piano Concertos*. Ph.D. dissertation, Eastman School of Music, University of Rochester, 1969.

Formal analysis of selected concerti, including the Piano Concerto by Poulenc. "The analyses appear in chart form and concern the large, over-all or 'macro' form of the movements as determined by the statement and subsequent use of the main thematic elements." See: W31.

B220   Harding, James. *The Ox on the Roof: Scenes from Musical Life in Paris in the Twenties*. London: Macdonald, 1972.

Dedicated to the memory of Poulenc, this work treats the group of composers, Les Six, and their contributions to the history of French music in the 1920s. The author explores the entire musical scene in Paris during this era and those associated with the avant-garde in French music. Discussion about Poulenc and his music is related to Parisian musical life. This work is indispensable in placing Poulenc in the environment of his compositional youth, in revealing his relationships with his contemporaries, and in illustrating how the ideas of this era influenced his early works.

B221   Hargrove, Guy Arnold, Jr. *Francis Poulenc's Settings of Poems of Guillaume Apollinaire and Paul Eluard*. Ph.D. dissertation, University of Iowa, 1971.

An analysis of Poulenc's compositional techniques in setting texts by Apollinaire and Eluard to music. Included are biographies of the two poets. In addition, the author defines and explains the Surrealist movement and comments on interpreting the songs of Poulenc based on his study of this material with Bernac while on a Fulbright grant.

B222   Harrison, Jay S. "New York Music Scene," *Musical America* 84 (February 1964):24.

Review of the January 14, 1964, performance of *Dialogues des Carmélites* presented by the American Opera Society. "The work itself is a masterpiece, especially as it deals with a subject open to fakery and falsity of emotion. . . . The characters who live and die in his work are real and holy. That is why, I suspect, the opera is so touching and so painfully true in its sentiment." The opera shows the composer's "inordinate skill at curving a vocal line so that its meaning is complete in every detail. . . . The interpretation was lovely in the extreme. It brought to full and vigorous life every passage of the faultless work." See: W1.

B223   ___. "Paris Distilled," *Musical America* 84 (January 1964):61.

Review of the Columbia MS6518 recording of *Hôtel* and *Voyage à Paris* from *Banalités,* "*C,*" *Sextuor,* and Sonata for two pianos. "[Poulenc] was in his way, a genius, for he managed to distill in his music the essence of Paris, which was his city and his life. Poulenc was sad like Paris, gay like Paris, moody like Paris and ineffably lovely like Paris. On the occasion of his death, the city lost its leading voice." In this record review Harrison said of the Sextet, "The piece is dry, snappy and tongue-in-cheek--it revels in its own fun. 'C' stands in this rendition as one of the great mélodies of our time. Its limpidity, warmth and sheer beauty of phrase would strangle any degree of comparison." In the two piano sonata "stinging clash of dissonances and subsequent tonal fragrance of themes is astounding." See: D48; D210; D447; D548.

B224   Harrison, Lou. "New Music in Recitals and Symposiums," *Modern Music* 23 (Winter 1946):50-53.

Review of a song recital sung by Janet Fairbank, including Poulenc's *Tel jour, telle nuit*. "Poulenc's just pre-war songs are lovely, with their primer-like and delicate homophony. Coming after the genuine polyphony of the Bergsma, they showed how little the French understand counterpoint. Also how well they avoid its use. Several of the songs were reserved but powerful; the lyrical ones were quite veiled and evocative." See: W101.

B225   Harrison, Max. "French Piano Works," *Gramophone* 62 (October 1984): 509-10.

Review of the RCA FY113 recording including *Trois pièces*.   "A persuasive account is given of Poulenc's *Pastourelle*, [sic] although this is less engaging than the one he contributed to *L'entail [sic] de Jeanne*. The *Hymne* I have always found rather turgid, and the *Toccata* is much the best movement.   Here Girod lacks poise yet achieves notable brilliance." See: D630.

B226   ___. "Poulenc," *Gramophone* 61 (December 1983):780.

Review of the recording of the Piano Concerto by Cécile Ousset on HMV ASD1077851. "Poulenc's sole Piano Concerto is . . . a *divertissement* in the form of a procession of agreeable melodies, some on the piano and some in the orchestra, dressed in bright colours. Too bright for some tastes, perhaps, for while in Boston for the world première in 1950 Poulenc wrote, 'I lead an austere existence in this very Puritan town'." See: D147.

B227   Hart, Philip. "The New Releases," *High Fidelity* 19 (February 1969):100.

Review of a recording devoted to orchestral works, (*Sinfonietta, Les Mariés de la Tour Eiffel, Deux marches et un intermède, Suite française*) on Angel S36519. "This collection from the composer's relatively small output of works for orchestra reminds us of the lighter side of Poulenc, who, especially in his youth, was inclined to bright wit and acid mockery. The major work here, the Sinfonietta of 1947, is a throwback to the youthful style . . . Though eclectic in style and free in form, the piece displays extraordinary craftsmanship and its materials are both honest and interesting." See: D183; D327; D459; D566.

B228   Harvey, Trevor. "Harsanyi; Poulenc," *Gramophone* 44 (December 1966): 316.

Review of the HMV ALP2286 recording of *L'Histoire de Babar*. "Poulenc has failed by miles. He writes mood music instead of character music and most of it goes on far too long (and quite a lot of it is dull anyway). . . . Who is going to enjoy this record then? Certainly the Ustinov fans (including me)." See: D290.

B229   ___. "Poulenc," *Gramophone* 44 (April 1967):525-26.

Review of the HMV ALP2306 recording. "I enjoyed Side 1, the Piano Concerto, enormously and would recommend the record for that alone. The concerto choréographique (as Poulenc described his Aubade), like a good deal of ballet music, doesn't stand on very firm feet as concert music. . . . Surely no praise could be too high for the piano playing of Gabriel Tacchino throughout this record. It has just the right precision and clean finger-work, together with a ravishing melting quality . . . that is yet never romantic in the wrong way." See: D20; D146.

B230   Harvey, Trevor. "Poulenc," *Gramophone* 49 (July 1971):197.

Review of the Erato STU70637 recording of the organ concerto and *Concert champêtre* compared with performances by Duruflé and van de Wiele. "I prefer Amiée Van de Wiele's slower but delightfully rhythmic playing to some of Veyron-Lacroix's hectic speeds. Not that he isn't rhythmic but such speeds rob the music of much of its attractiveness. And anyway, Miss Van de Wiele's tempi are usually almost precisely those suggested by the composer. . . . I definitely prefer Marie-Claire Alain's account of the Organ Concerto, again helped by a very clean acoustic. True, Maurice Duruflé (the work's original soloist) is also good but it's not such a striking performance as this new one nor, in some soft passages, so moving." See: D138; D143; D164; D170.

B231   Hell, Henri. *Francis Poulenc*. Translated and Introduced by Edward Lockspeiser. New York: Grove Press, 1959.

This book is an abridged version of the original published in French. There is some biographical information, but the author concentrates on the musical life of the composer, beginning with the earliest compositions and ending with *Dialogues des Carmélites*. The special circumstances surrounding the composition and premieres of each work are explained. In his musical analysis Hell stresses the strengths of each piece, but he acknowledges the weaknesses where they exist. He often quotes Poulenc's remarks about individual pieces. Included are illustrations, a catalogue of works, and a discography. For a review of the book by David Cox see *Musical Times* 101:25.

B232   ___. "La Musique religieuse de Francis Poulenc," *La Revue musicale* 26 (1952):53-58.

Essay on the religious compositions, a genre in which Hell finds that Poulenc "has written his most accomplished, most ample, and most serious works." He cites the Mass, *Quatre motets pour un temps de pénitence, Figure humaine*, and *Stabat Mater* as examples. He contrasts style in the early compositions--"charming, gracious, and agile"--with the religious music where "all is interior, simple, and sincere."

B233   Henahan, Donal. "Music: 'La Voix Humaine'," *New York Times* February 20, 1988, I:14.

Review of a concert version of the work sung by Jessye Norman with the New York Philharmonic on February 18, 1988. "In its staged version, the single, unremittingly emotional scene can be an overwhelming tour de force, and in any version it is one of opera's great dramatic challenges in building and sustaining a character. . . . Miss Norman's range of expression was too restricted to draw the picture of a woman nearly out of control . . . Miss Norman, with her sumptuous soprano, sang the music more thrillingly than a Denise Duval ever could dream of doing." See: W4.

B234   ___. "Poulenc's 'Dialogues of the Carmelites' Sung at Madison Ave. Baptist Church," *New York Times* May 15, 1973, p. 28.

Review of a performance of the opera in English. "Poulenc's rather banal but melodious opera came to life remarkably well, thanks to a large, generally able cast that had been intensively rehearsed. . . . The chromatic wanderings of Poulenc's score and the comic-strip predictability of his characters might strain the resources of more renowned artists." See: W1.

B235   Henry, Leigh. "We Are Seven," *Modern Music* 1 (June 1924):10-17.

Reply to an article by Emile Vuillermoz attacking Les Six published in the February 1924 issue of *Modern Music* [See B557]. "Post-war youth, in Europe at least, has seen its flower squandered, to salvage with blood and agony the paunchy incapacity of age. It has beheld the exposure of the giant myths of European culture and civilization. It is skeptical, determined to get beneath mere phrases and sentiments, to eschew illusion . . . May not this, at least as much as any blatant desire for publicity, account for what M. Vuillermoz . . . terms the 'blasphemies' of the six?"

While Henry found that there were essential differences between the members of the group, he also noted important similarities: common "impulses and convictions," use of popular melody, assertive tunefulness, and a quality that he compared to the use of flat color in painting. In tracing the fore-runners of the group, Henry mentioned the spiritual relationships with Rabelais, Villon, and Beranger; the poetry of Apollinaire; and Erik Satie.

Finally, Henry questions the derivation of Poulenc's style as understood by Vuillermoz. Henry notes the influence of Debussy in his use of comedy and caricature, especially in the late piano preludes, and the influence of Stravinsky.

B236   Herman, Justin R. "Poulenc: Concerto for (2) Pianos," *New Records* 52 (December 1984):4.

Review of the Angel 38122 recording of the two-piano concerto and *Concert champêtre*. "Tacchino, Ringeissen and Prêtre don't get all they can out of the piece [the two-piano concerto] with their very serious approach. Seraphim's Whittemore and Lowe version with the old Philharmonia under Pierre Deraux [sic] remains more enlightening, even if it is not as well recorded. Brosse and Prêtre are more with it in their light and piquant Concert champêtre." See: D139; D153.

B237   Hill, Edward Burlingame. "Musical Boston in the Gay Nineties: Pursuing a Specialty," *Etude* 47 (April 1949):229.

An essay on Satie and the members of Les Six that concentrates on the historical background of their association, the musical educations of the Six, and Satie's influences on them. Hill, who knew Poulenc and the other members of the group personally, discussed the musical style of each. "In temperament he [Poulenc] was more akin to Satie than the older members of this liberal coterie. At the time of my visit, Francis Poulenc, then slightly over twenty years of age, was at the beginning of his career. . . . As proved by his later works, Poulenc's talent was essentially lyric, and the older members of 'The Group' regarded him as a gifted youngster from whom much was to be expected."

B238   Hinds, James. "Poulenc," *Fanfare* 1 (March 1978):58.

Review of a performance of the organ concerto on RCA AGLI2445. "Munch's interpretation is most appropriate, with forward driving momentum holding one's interest to the final note. Zamkochian . . . together with the Boston Symphony display musicianship which is difficult to fault." See: D174.

B239   Hinton, James, Jr. "Records in Review," *High Fidelity* 2 (January-February 1953):57.

Review of a performance of *Les Biches* on London 11-624. The piece is "charmingly light-hearted" with "eighteenth century elegance spiced by the jazzy idiom of Paris." See: D71.

B240   Hinton, James, Jr.   "Records in Review," *High Fidelity* 9 (May 1959):
        54-56.

Review of the recording of *Dialogues des Carmélites* on Angel 3585 C/L.
A list of productions of this opera and a history of the development of
the libretto is included in the review. "It is on the whole, a very sweet,
pretty score, but not, it seems to me, one that ever really comes to grips
with the dramatic conflict. For this--in any meaningful sense--is all within
the soul of Blanche . . . and the music never really strikes the darker,
more perverse chords that are surly demanded by Bernanos's pon-
derings on the inevitability of dying." See: D217.

B241   ___.   "Very French and Very Funny: Poulenc's *Mamelles de Tirésias*,"
        High Fidelity 4 (August 1954):45.

Review of the Angel 35090 recording of this opera with Denise Duval,
soprano. "In assessing a work like *Les Mamelles de Tirésias* . . . it is
hard to keep from wishing that some magic could be worked whereby
it would become more accessible to listeners on this side of the Atlantic
without becoming a whit less French, or a whit less Poulenc. . . . The
text is not only French but very, very special French. . . . The music
presents Poulenc at his most urbane, at his wittiest and . . . also at his
most maturely sensitive." See: D325.

B242   Hoerée, Arthur.   "Francis Poulenc: Poèmes de Ronsard," *La Revue
        musicale* 7 (February 1926):179-81.

Review of the song cycle. "We must admire without reservation the
profoundly original conception of these five songs where the music takes
the most simple forms to attain the most persuasive eloquence." The
majority of the review is devoted to analysis of the setting of the texts.
See: W95.

B243   Holland, Bernard.   "Great Composers Celebrate the Charms of the
        Clarinet," *New York Times* March 23, 1986, II:26.

Review of the Musical Heritage Society MHS827387 recording entitled
Poulenc: Complete Music for Wind Instruments and Piano.   The
performances are by the Chamber Music Society of Lincoln Center. "The
Élégie for horn and piano . . . and the Oboe Sonata . . . both have a
bleakness bordering depression. The contrast to the Flute Sonata's
enchanting melodiousness . . . is a startling one. There are some
beautiful moments here--especially the finale of the Sextet and in the
slow movement of the Clarinet and Piano Sonata." See: D227; D453;
D474; D487; D502; D523; D529; D605; D649.

B244   Holmberg, Arthur. "Act of Faith: Apollinaire's Humor in 'Les Mamelles de Tirésias'," *Opera News* 50 (December 21, 1985):10-12.

This essay provides a biography of the poet and an assessment of his place in the avant-garde of pre-war Paris. Holmberg discussed the play and the several themes with which it deals--sex, gender and love--and stated that it was the mood of affirmation that attracted Poulenc to Les Mamelles. Poulenc called the score his "happiest work." See: W2.

B245   Holmberg, Arthur. Confrontation With the Self," *Opera News* 43 (January 13, 1979):12-15.

An exhaustive analysis of the libretto for *Dialogues des Carmélites*. The author wrote that this final work of Georges Bernanos "recapitulates the major themes that occupied his interior life--fear of death, faith in God, a deep concern for the honor of France. . . . Anyone unfamiliar with French history and literature and Catholic dogma will have an arduous task trying to penetrate this difficult, complex work." Holmberg explained the allusions to French history and literature and revealed what Poulenc omitted from Bernanos' material and why. The author also defended his idea that each character in the opera represents an idealized class of French society. See: W1.

B246   Hope-Wallace, Philip. "Gérard Souzay," *Gramophone* 42 (March 1965): 440.

Review of the Philips PHM 500 132 recording of songs. "If enunciation, good taste, sense of style and response to the poetic idea were the whole of the art of singing there would be hundreds to acclaim this record as a model. Alas, one element is left out; tonal range and beauty. . . . The near conversational level is good for Poulenc however. The selection of songs and the imaginative rightness pay handsome dividends." See: D17; D285; D350; D398.

B247   ___. "Poulenc," *Gramophone* 45 (November 1967):274.

Review of the Philips 900148 recording of *Calligrammes, Chansons villageoises, La Fraîcheur et le feu,* and *Le Travail du peintre.* "The exemplary performance of these four delightful song cycles should be of great value especially to those embracing the difficult art of French song. The fine nuance, the light clear enunciation, the management of tone colour and phrasing to fit the mood are in abundant example. I can hardly imagine the songs better sung, unless by a voice naturally more beautiful. As for the music itself it is apt to seem slightly monotonous if you play the whole four cycles on end." See: D85; D117; D272; D595.

B248   "Horowitz *Before*," *Saturday Review* 48 (August 28, 1965): 56.

Review of the Angel COLH 300 recording of *Pastourelle* and *Toccata* performed by Vladimir Horowitz. Horowitz's performance of *Pastourelle* is an "instance of more virtuosity than even a virtuoso piece can accommodate, but the Toccata (which is dedicated to him) is a living instance of the competence that made his contemporaries despair." See: D631.

B249   Hughes, Allen. "Also Cited: 'Gloria'," *New York Times* May 7, 1961, X:19.

Review of the Angel S35953 recording of *Gloria* and the organ concerto. "This new composition [*Gloria*] probably ranks with the finest of Poulenc's major creations. . . . The performance here is quite good, with the bulk of the credit going to conductor Prêtre and the orchestra. . . . The recording of the organ concerto is noteworthy in itself, for it makes the work seem considerably more dramatic and tragic than E. Power Biggs' famous recording of many years ago did. Maurice Duruflé is the soloist here, and although his playing is poorly articulated in the rapid passages--damagingly so, in fact--the interpretation is otherwise powerful and vivid." See: D164; D167; D275.

B250   ___. "Bittersweet Poulenc," *New York Times* May 5, 1968, D:28.

Review of recordings of the sonatas for clarinet and for oboe on Lyrichord LLST7193. "There was one instrumental area, however, in which he produced distinctive products that won popularity as soon as they were performed and still are very listenable. These were compositions that combined one or more woodwind instruments with piano. . . . Both sonatas have an intimate eloquence that lingers in the memory after the sound has faded away and the performances of both are excellent." See: D484; D521.

B251   ___. *"Dialogues des Carmélites,"* *American Record Guide* 25 (April 1959):502-03.

Review of the recording of *Dialogues des Carmélites* on Angel 3585 C/L. "His richly colored but essentially simple score supports Bernanos' quietly eloquent speech as though the two had been conceived simultaneously. The words are set with the same faultless clarity that characterizes Poulenc's songs, but lyricism continues to flow unimpeded throughout the work." See: D217.

B252   Hughes, Allen. "Disks: Feast for Francophiles," *New York Times* April 9, 1961, X:18.

Review of the recording of *Sextuor* by the Philadelphia Woodwind Ensemble and Poulenc, piano, on Columbia MS6213. "In Poulenc's Sextet the admirable Philadelphians are joined by none other than the composer himself, who still plays the piano with inimitable vivacity and elan when he puts his mind to it and practices a bit. The music itself is joyous, pungent, impudent at times, and a recommended antidote for sagging spirits." See: D446.

B253   ___. "Francis Poulenc 1899-1963," *Musical America* 83 (February 1963): 20.

Obituary. "He used to like to refer to himself as 'half monk and half bounder,' and both his life and his music gave evidence of the qualities of each. The 'monk' was dismayed by the 'bounder's' excesses, but the 'bounder' would not be tamed. And so they struggled through the years, the man and the boy, the sacred and the profane, the bourgeois and the rebel. And out of their struggle came inimitable music--some of it good, some of it bad, all of it Poulenc." A list of works that the author believed contain "the essence of the composer and the man" completes the obituary.

B254   ___. "Gounod Father of French Art Song," *New York Times* February 19, 1967, D:24.

Review of a recording of songs by Souzay, baritone, and Baldwin, piano, on Philips PHS500-132. "'La Grenouillère' is a particularly happy choice, because it is one of Poulenc's best songs and, not being part of a cycle or collection, has been given little recording attention in the past." The reviewer praised the performers: "Their interpretations may be regarded as definitive in every way." See: D17; D285; D350; D398.

B255   ___. "'Mamelles de Tirésias' Is at Theater Club," *New York Times* April 18, 1974, p. 50.

Review of the Manhattan Theater Club production of the opera. "All right, 'Les Mamelles' is zany. Apollinaire's play has, in fact, been called the first surrealist play, although it antedated surrealism by a generation. What Poulenc did was to make sense of it through a musical score that ricochets beguilingly between gravity and frivolity without losing its sense of unity. . . . The Manhattan Theater Club production, directed by Christopher Alden, gives little nudges here and there that help still further to guide the uninitiated observer and listener through the fun and games, and everything emerges crystal clear." See: W2.

B256   Hughes, Allen.   "Matrimony Mixed With Music," *New York Times* November 9, 1969, D:38.

Review of four cello sonatas performed by Grant Johannesen, piano, and his wife Zara Nelsova, cello, on Golden Crest CRS40899. Hughes liked the performances but found the Poulenc sonata, "of some interest as a seldom-played novelty, but it does not do great things for either the cello or the composer's reputation." See: D466.

B257   ___. "The Most Satisfying Instrument of All," *New York Times* October 18, 1970, II:31.

Review of Leontyne Price's performance of "Mes filles, voila que s'achève" from *Dialogues des Carmélites* on RCA LSC3163, which the reviewer did not like as much as her performance in the "memorable San Francisco Opera production of 1957" when she sang the aria with "moving simplicity." See: D218.

B258   ___. "A New Whiz on Piano," *New York Times* October 26, 1969, D:36.

Review of the Grant Johannesen 25th Anniversary Concert on Golden Crest CR40866, including the *Thème varié*. "It is a credit to the pianist that he does not slight what he must recognize as inferior products in his interpretations." See: D588.

B259   ___. "An Opera and Its Source," *New York Times* December 1, 1972, p. 31.

Review of the double-bill performances at the Cubicula in Manhattan of Poulenc's *La Voix humaine* and the Cocteau play of the same title on which it was based. "When he composed his opera in 1958, Poulenc condensed Cocteau's original and fleshed the whole out with music that underscored the inherent drama and commented on it." Hughes compares the two works and concludes that the opera will outlast the play, "It is at once richer in texture and less repetitious, and the music is quite eloquent at times." See: W4.

B260   ___. "Poulenc's Carmelites," *Saturday Review* 42 (March 28, 1959):56.

Review of the recording of the opera on Angel 3585 C/L characterized as, "a recorded version that is not only definitive, but a source of listening pleasure in every way. . . . The work itself is so deeply rooted in the musical and literary, as well as historical, traditions of France. . . . Poulenc's vibrant score, moreover, has so much in common with the narrative sensitivity of Debussy's *Pelleas et Melisande*, the lyricism of Massenet, and the clarity of the best French composers." See: D217.

B261   Hughes, Allen. "Poulenc's 'Dialogues' at La Scala," *Saturday Review* 40 (February 23, 1957):54-55.

Review of the premiere production of the opera. Hughes believes the opera might well become a familiar repertory item, because, "First of all, the story, which is told clearly, is likely to arouse the sympathy of almost anyone who hears it, for it is the story of ordinary human beings grappling with doubt and fear in believable crises. Secondly, the musical fabric clothing the story offers no listening problems whatsoever. Essentially uncomplicated, the score has a kind of voluptuousness that can exert an immediate effect on even the most unprepared auditor. Finally, there is the splendor of the vocal writing itself, which must inevitably excite the senses of all who hear it." See: W1.

B262   ___. "Poulenc's Music Reflected Man: Works, Like Writer, 'Half Monk, Half Bounder'," *New York Times* February 2, 1963, p. 5.

An essay on the musical career of the composer. "Francis Poulenc liked to describe himself as 'half monk and half bounder,' and the music he composed in the 45-year career that ended with his death Wednesday, tended to verify the description. There is probably no composer of concert music in this century whose secular works have offered more lighthearted, impudent fun to listeners than those of Poulenc, and none whose sacred music is more intensely devout and communicative in expression. . . . Georges Auric, one of 'Poulenc's best friends,' said a few years ago that Poulenc 'found' the technique for the pieces he really wanted to write, and that when he could not find a technique for something it was because the project did not interest him. . . . Probably the most telling proof of Poulenc's greatness as a composer is the fact that he was always able to put his own stamp on his music no matter how many borrowings of other people's styles and ideas it contained."

B263   ___. "Sing It, Don't Meow It," *New York Times* July 28, 1968, D:23.

Review of recordings of songs by Souzay, baritone, and Baldwin, piano, on RCA LSC3018 and Philips PHS900148. Poulenc "was the greatest song composer of his generation and his equal has not yet been discovered among composers of generations later than his. Despite the protests he often made about interpretations of his songs during his lifetime, he was singularly blessed with a group of gifted singers who knew him well and who performed in recitals and on recordings with him as piano accompanist. . . . In addition to knowing Poulenc well, [Souzay] also studied with Bernac." The reviewer compared the singing of teacher and pupil and concluded, "The ultimate accomplishment of Souzay is precisely that of Bernac. The variety and excellence of Poulenc's songs are illuminated in such a way as to focus the listener's attention upon the songs themselves rather than upon the details of interpretation." See: D85; D117; D272; D595.

B264   Hughes, Allen. "Les Six," *Musical America* 74 (February 1954):12.

A Société des Concerts du Conservatoire program devoted to the compositions of Les Six was the occasion that inspired this essay on the group of French musicians. The author discussed the origins and development of the group, the philosophy and influences that bound them together, their association with Cocteau and Satie, their early concerts, the spirit of comradeship that characterized them, how they drifted apart, and what each was doing at the time of this special concert.

B265   Huth, Arno. "News from Paris and Elsewhere in Europe," *Modern Music* 20 (November-December 1942):40-43.

Review of music performances in war-time Europe. "Choreographic spectacles in Paris seem to be having a tremendous almost pre-war vogue. . . . The Opéra has just put on a new work by Francis Poulenc, *Les Animaux modèles* . . . The music, at times gay, at times solemn, is said to be spirited and agreeable--like most scores by Poulenc, whose lack of personality is compensated for by solid workmanship and French charm." See: W5.

B266   Huxsoll, Mark. "Poulenc: Aubade," *New Records* 53/3 (May 1985):6-7.

Review of the Gallo 30.169 recording. "The Camerata of Geneva gives us . . . delightful chamber pieces in very displeasing performances. Francesco Zaza gives an acceptable performance of the solo piano in Poulenc's Aubade, but remains somewhat unnoticeable due to the distractions of the 18 instruments scored in the accompaniment. Marcello Viotti and the Camerata give a sincere and spirited performance, but blatant intonation and missed note problems are frequent." See: D23.

B267   Indcox, J. F. "Records in Review," *High Fidelity* 1 (Fall 1951):57.

Review of the Columbia ML 4399 recording of Poulenc performing the *Suite française* and *Trois mouvements perpétuels*. "Some of these pieces have received more knowing performances. Poulenc . . . doesn't strike me as being any virtuoso." See: D569; D615.

B268   ___. "Records in Review," *High Fidelity* 2 (November-December 1952): 56-57.

Review of a recording of a selection of short pieces suitable for encores, including Poulenc's *Presto in B Flat Major*, on Columbia ML 4534. The performances were described as "distinguished, refined, impeccable in taste." See: D390.

B269   "Italian Academy Names Five," *New York Times* March 6, 1956, p. 27.

Announcement that Poulenc had been named an honorary member of the Academy of St. Cecilia in Rome.

B270   J. H. "The New Releases," *High Fidelity* 20 (March 1970):94.

Review and comparison of two recordings of choral music on Music Guild MS870 and Lyrichord LLST7208. "The penitential motets are closest to the worldly Poulenc, with lesser reliance upon a constant procession of stern chords, more use of independent phrases . . . while in the last two sections, there are decided echoes of the old boulevard languor." Both performances of the Laudes are excellent. The Caillat Vocal Ensemble is "weaker in the tenor voices but more musically sensuous," the Whikehart Chorale "producing a far more vibrant, fresher sound and giving the more exuberant interpretation." See: D96; D309; D311; D414.

B271   Jacobson, Bernard. "The New Releases," *High Fidelity/Musical America* 17 (August 1967):89-90.

Review of the recording of *Concerto for Piano and Orchestra* and *Aubade* on Angel S36426. The reviewer, who prefers this performance by Gabriel Tacchino, compares it to that of Février on Nonesuch. *Aubade* is the more successful piece, because "its structure accepts the sectionalism of Poulenc's mind more completely and more frankly." The concerto "tries harder to achieve large-scale coherence, and fails in the attempt." See: D20; D26; D146.

B272   Jacobson, Bernard. "Records in Review," *High Fidelity* 16 (December 1966):103.

Review of the recording of *L'Histoire de Babar* in the orchestral version by Jean Françaix with Peter Ustinov, narrator, on Angel 36357. "An obvious love of children shines through Poulenc's setting . . . The style is the simplest possible. For the most part, he sets the scene in brief portions of narration, on which the music then comments with short descriptive pieces." See: D290.

B273   Jacobson, Robert. "Recitals," *Musical America* 83 (June 19, 1963):28-29.

Review of the Composers' Showcase concert in memory of Poulenc on April 10,1963, in Carnegie Hall. Benny Goodman and Leonard Bernstein performed the premiere of the *Sonata for Clarinet and Piano*. "This uncomplicated piece is filled with charming ideas, typical of Poulenc's boulevardier side at its most delightful." Also on the program were a group of songs, "*C;*" *Voyage à Paris; Hôtel*; and *Fiançailles pour rire; Sonata for Two Pianos*; the four Christmas Motets, *Vinca mea electa*, and two songs from *Huit chansons françaises*." See: W46; W47; W60; W77; W81; W84; W115; W153.

B274   ___. "Reports: U.S., New York," *Opera News*, (February 24, 1979):50-52.

Review of the January 1, 1979, performance of *Dialogues des Carmélites* by the Metropolitan Opera. "John Dexter's stunning staging seemed even tauter and more brilliant this time, having solved the problems of the final scene at the guillotine with glowing results, while Michel Plasson's effective conducting explored the work's humanity and drama. . . . Carmelites remains an extraordinarily moving, human work of drama and ideas, here played as a study of fear in a black void, its musical idiom more refreshing twenty years later than at its premiere, strengthened by the test of time." See: W1.

B275   Jellinek, George. "Leontyne Price: Prima Donna Vol. 3," *Stereo Review* 26 (January 1971):88.

Review of the recording on RCA LSC3163 of "Mes filles, voila que s'achève" from *Dialogues des Carmélites*. Price and to RCA for having included the Mother Superior's touching exhortation from Les Dialogues, a soothing oasis in the dreary desert of contemporary opera." See: D218.

B276   Jewett, Diana. "Francis Poulenc: The Man and the Composer," *Piano Quarterly*, no. 126 (Summer 1984): 41-44.

Brief biography of the composer with analysis of his compositional style. The author concluded that "although Poulenc constantly tried [to] display a light-heartedness and an unfailing humor in his music and in his personal life, to his close friends he stood revealed as an insecure and troubled man."

B277   Jones, Ralph E. "Poulenc: Sextuor," *New Records* 29/2 (April 1961):3.

Review of the Columbia ML5613 recording. "Place the composer of one of the most delightful chamber works of the twentieth century at the keyboard and add five of the finest woodwind instrumentalists in the world. Having done so, one can easily expect about the finest recording yet of the familiar Poulenc Sextuor, classic in form, Gallic in wit and grace." See: D446.

B278   ___. "Poulenc: Stabat Mater," *New Records* 32/7 (September 1964):8.

Review of the Westminster WEST 9618 recording, "an early presentation of this score, and it is an idiomatic reading, lovingly performed and adequately recorded. Competition comes from the recent Angel stereo release (ANG-S36121) with Régine Crespin which stands to come out on top, both musically and technically." See: D561; D563.

B279   Jourdan-Morhange, Hélène. *Mes amis musiciens*. Paris: Éditeurs français réunis, 1955.

In this personal tribute to musicians the author had known, Chapter 10 was devoted to Poulenc. "I had the joy to have been his first interpreter, at the Vieux- Colombier, in one of those avant-garde concerts which the musical flair of Jane Bathori had put before the public. We presented, not without disquiet, his first piece, the *Rapsodie nègre*. . . . Poulenc had already imprinted there his young signature: charming naiveté, sense of humor, and the instinct of musicality which is found in his so diverse works. 'How gifted he is,' said Ravel, 'provided that he works'."

The author gave a description of Poulenc's appearance at this time: "this young boy who seemed--nose in the air, crew-cut hair, vacant eyes that darted about--a schoolboy grown-up too fast." Some evaluation of compositions by Poulenc was included, especially those that were favorite pieces of the author.

B280   Kaback, Elliott.   "Poulenc: Organ Concerto," *Fanfare* 3 (May 1980): 131-32.

Review and comparison of two performances of the organ concerto on Orion 79346 and Argo ZRG878. The Orion recording "catches much of the intensity, along with some unsettled ensemble and curtailed frequency range. The organ speaks with clarity and immediacy, but the orchestra seems trapped in a hard, echoey acoustic suggestive of a public restroom. . . . The Argo, conversely, suffers from the moist and clinging reverberation of the chapel of St. John's College, Cambridge. . . . Malcolm's playing and his instrument are lacking in color and vigor. Orion's Roger Nyquist is far more authoritative." See: D166; D172.

B281   Kerner, Leighton. *"Parade--*Elle marche," *Village Voice* 26 (March 11-17, 1981):70.

Review of the Metropolitan Opera triple bill performances of Satie's ballet, *Parade*, Poulenc's *Les Mamelles de Tirésias*, and Ravel's *L'Enfant et les sortilèges*. "With Mamelles, entertainment was unfurled like a flag. Satie's plain planks of harmony and tone-color had given way to Poulenc's waltzes, chorales, and 1920s and 1930s pop rhythms." See: W2.

B282   Kingsley, Adrienne. "Chansons d'Acadie et de France," *New Records* 53/1 (March 1985):11.

Review of the Fanfare FL6005 recording containing songs sung by Rosemarie Landry. "Her performance is really outstanding. Her voice is even and beautiful, and her interpretation of the varied styles of songs is satisfying in every way. Pianist Dalton Baldwin . . . is a suitable match for Ms. Landry's voice." See: D4; D121.

B283   ___.   "Poulenc: L'Embarquement pour Cythère," *New Records* 52/6 (August 1984):14.

Review of the recording on Pianissime Magne 2005.   "Danielle and Marielle Renault play so well together it is impossible to distinguish more than one performer, and their interpretation is just right for the music's transparent textures." See: D240.

B284   Kisselgoff, Anna. "The Irreverence of Cocteau Sparkles Once More," *New York Times* April 17, 1988, H:8.

Review of a new production of *Les Mariés de la Tour Eiffel* recreated for the opening of the Florence Gould Hall in New York City. The review included a history of the ballet, and a discussion about its importance to the modernist movement. The production was praised for the excellence of the costumes and sets and for the preservation of the spirit of the original production translated into 1980s humor. See: W9.

B285   Klein, D. Arkus. "Pianists by the Pair," *American Record Guide* 30/9 (May 1964):814-15.

In this favorable review of the performance of the Sonata for two pianos on Command CC11013, the reviewer also gives a brief history of performances on two pianos. See: D549.

B286   Klein, Howard. "From Behind the Scenes to Center Stage," *New York Times* April 24, 1966, X:21.

Review of a recording of songs performed by Bernard Kruysen, baritone, and Jean Charles Richard, piano, on Westminster WST17105. "Almost any grouping of Poulenc songs will be effective. . . . This is one of the finest Poulenc song albums around, including the fine disks by Gérard Souzay." See: D46; D64; D194; D274; D323; D352; D368; D587.

B287   ___. "Sad and Solemn: Serious Side of Poulenc Is Stressed In Recording of 'Stabat Mater'," *New York Times* March 1, 1964, X:18.

Review of the recording of *Stabat Mater* and the four Penitential Motets on Angel S36121. "Nowhere is Poulenc's serious side more apparent than in his Stabat Mater. . . . It is a sad and solemn work but one whose sadness is softened by human warmth and even a comforting sensuousness." The motets, "are not polyphonic motets, but are conceived, like Bach's chorales, harmonically rather than contrapuntally.   The rich washes of harmonic color, the blending of voices to gain the best sonorities for the harmonies and the haunting tunes that float on the surface make them rare modern examples of traditional choral writing." See: D411; D561.

B288   Kolodin, Irving. "The Merit of Poulenc," *Saturday Review* 46 (February 23, 1963):49-50.

In this essay the author assessed the musical career of Poulenc shortly after his death in 1963. Kolodin presented a history of the early years of Les Six, reviewed Poulenc's early reputation as a composer, traced his development as a song writer and as a composer of large-scale compositions. "It is enough to say here that in the works by which he is best known today, the immemorial attributes of melody, harmony, rhythmic zest, and formal balance have been organized by Poulenc into shapes that are at once appealing and distinctive. . . . Taking the amount and diversity of Poulenc's work into full consideration with the high quality of much of it, Francis Poulenc stands, in my view, as the last in a long line of French composers descended from Couperin and Rameau." A photograph and a drawing of Les Six by Cocteau are included.

B289   Kolodin, Irving. "Music to My Ears," *Saturday Review* 4 (March 3, 1977): 47-48.

Review of the New York premiere of *Dialogues des Carmélites* at the Metropolitan Opera. "Poulenc's work takes high rank among the best productions of opera seen in New York in recent times." Kolodin praises the excellence of the production, especially the sets designed by David Reppa and the outstanding cast of singers. There is an analysis of the plot and the music's relation to it. See: W1.

B290   ___. "Music to My Ears: Denise Duval and Poulenc in Town Hall," *Saturday Review* 43 (March 26, 1960):36.

Review of a New York recital. Duval sang, among other selections, Poulenc's *Trois poèmes, Trois poèmes de Louise Lalanne: Hier, Air champêtre*, and *Air de Thérèse* from *Les Mamelles de Tirésias*. "In a time when composers are known by the systems they pursue rather than the results they achieve, it is refreshing to encounter a man who writes from impulse as well as calculation." See: W2; W59; W105; W106.

B291   ___. "Music to My Ears: Poulenc's Carmelites," *Saturday Review* 47 (February 1, 1964):24-25.

Review of the American Opera Society performance of the opera at Carnegie Hall without scenery or costumes. "What in the end emerges is a series of tentacles stretching back to the main source of French composition for the theatre as remote as Rameau and as recent as Ravel. It is a work of mood, passion, and invincible conviction, made into an artistic whole by the embracing craftsmanship of its creator." See: W1.

B292   ___. "Music to My Ears: Poulenc's 'Gloria'," *Saturday Review* 44 (April 22, 1961):30.

Review of the Boston Symphony performance of *Gloria* in New York City. "It is consistently, almost insistently vocal, which should not be in the least surprising for a composer of as many fine songs (and other vocal works) as Poulenc." See: W41.

B293   Kolodin, Irving. "Recordings," *Saturday Review* 31 (June 26, 1948):44.

The Robert Shaw recording of *Petites voix* on RCA Victor 10-1409 is described as "fanciful, delicate settings by Poulenc, finely sung by the Shaw group." See: D384.

B294   ___. "Recordings in Review: A New Voice for Poulenc," *Saturday Review* 49 (May 28, 1966):54.

Review of the Westminster WST17105 recording of songs by Bernard Kruysen, baritone, and Jean Charles Richard, piano. "That Kruysen's effort may be matched by the high standard of any, or all, of them [Bernac, Souzay, Jennie Tourel, Povla Frijsh] is proof that he is, indeed, a new voice for Poulenc. . . . Beyond all question of range and register, quantity and quality of sound, the clear fact is that Kruysen is that real rarity, an interpretative personality." See: D46; D64; D194; D274; D323; D352; D368; D587.

B295   ___. "Recordings in Review: A Pair by Poulenc," *Saturday Review* 50 (August 26, 1967):79.

Review of the recording of *Aubade* and the piano concerto with Gabriel Tacchino, piano, and Georges Prêtre, conductor on Angel S36426. "It may escape recollection that it was as a collaborator with Poulenc himself that Prêtre first came to phonographic attention. What he learned then is the secret of the proper tempo: a little faster than most would consider suitable in the fast movements, definitely slower than others incline to in the slow movements. . . . Certainly it works beautifully in these two scintillating performances with the youngish (thirty-two) pianist Gabriel Tacchino." See: D20; D146.

B296   ___. "Recordings in Review: Poulenc Sonata," *Saturday Review* 47 (December 26, 1964):52.

Review of the recording of *Aubade* and the sonatas for clarinet and piano and oboe and piano on Nonesuch H1033. "Boutard's artistry and the well-balanced participation of Février give an element of interest to this late work of Poulenc which it did not possess when first performed. . . . The matching artistry of Pierlot in the oboe sonata is highly advantageous to the composer's purpose. . . . All the values of the *Aubade* . . . are deftly realized under the direction of Serge Baudo." See: D26; D488; D524.

B297   Kolodin, Irving. "Recordings in Review: Precious Poulenc," *Saturday Review* 39 (February 25, 1956):46.

Review of the Gold and Fizdale recording of the Sonata for Two Pianos (1953) on Columbia ML5068. "Composed specifically for Gold and Fizdale--who, in such literature as this, strike me as the most able exponents of their craft now active--it is best described as an intensely French piece of music. . . . It has gravity, wit, tenderness, and above all a sustaining intellectuality." See: D547.

B298   ___. "Recordings Reports: Classical LPs," *Saturday Review* 36 (November 28, 1953):82.

Review of the MGM E3069 recording of *Aubade* with Fabienne Jacquinot, piano, and Anatole Fistoulari, conducting the Westminster Symphony Orchestra. "Poulenc's quondam ballet score is full of his special brand of ingenuity and musicianship, brightly re-created by Miss Jacquinot. Fistoulari . . . strikes me as a shade overenergetic in an attempt to make the work more dazzling than it inherently is." See: D24.

B299   ___. "Recordings Reports I: Orchestral LPs," *Saturday Review* 46 (April 27, 1963):62.

Review of the Angel 35993 recording of *Concert champêtre*, Aimée van de Wiele, harpsichord, and *Concerto in D minor for Two Pianos*, Poulenc and Jacques Février, pianos. "It is some time since there has been an issue as good as this of the Concerto for Two Pianos . . . For all the fact that they [these two compositions] deal more with style than with substance, their verve, gaiety, and spirit of calculated nonchalance are ingratiating. And whatever the mood of his expression, Poulenc's craftsmanship is unvarying." See: D138; D151.

B300   ___. Recordings Reports II: Miscellaneous LPs," *Saturday Review* 40 (October 26, 1957):56.

Review of a recording of *Stabat Mater* and *Le Bal masqué* on Westminster XWN18422 with Jacqueline Brumaire, soprano, in the former and Bernac and Poulenc in the latter. Stabat Mater "is a deeply conceived, fully accomplished work in which the mature musicality of

Poulenc is shown full force. . . . Bal masqué is moderately entertaining, but a little long." See: D39; D563.

B301   Kolodin, Irving. "Recordings Reports II: Miscellaneous LPs," *Saturday Review* 43 (July 30, 1960):42.

Review of the recording of *Élégie* for horn on Boston BST1009. "Outstanding among all the contents of the record is the Poulenc *Élégie*, an angry (if bereaved) protest at the wastage of precious talent that perished when Dennis Brain smashed his car into a tree." See: D223.

B302   ___. "Recordings Reports II: Miscellaneous LPs," *Saturday Review* 44 (March 25, 1961):50.

Review of the recording of *Sextuor* by the Philadelphia Woodwind Ensemble with Poulenc, piano, on Columbia MS6213. "The happy participation of the composer with the exemplary first-desk men of the Philadelphia Orchestra provides a performance at once authentic and entertaining. In this revised version of 1939, the work looks backward to the audacities of Poulenc's earlier works, and, in the slow movement, ahead to the deepened expressivities of later ones." See: D446.

B303   ___. "Recordings Reports II: Miscellaneous LPs," *Saturday Review* 47 (July 25, 1964):46.

Review of the Westminster 9618 recording of *Le Bal masqué* and *Stabat Mater*. The Bernac performance of *Le Bal masqué* "remains the model for anyone undertaking to reproduce these settings of verses by Max Jacob, while the composer's effort is much more than that of just another pianist." See: D39; D563.

B304   ___. "Recordings Reports II: Miscellaneous LPs," *Saturday Review* 51 (April 27, 1968):76.

Review of the recording of the sonatas for clarinet and for oboe on Lyrichord S7193. "Admirers of late Poulenc will find an abundance of his typical quality--melodic, harmonic, organizational--in these two works of 1962." See: D484; D521.

B305   ___. "Recordings Reports II: Miscellaneous LPs," *Saturday Review* 52 (January 25, 1969):54.

Review of the recording of the Mass and two motets by The Festival Singers of Toronto, conducted by Elmer Iseler, on Seraphim S60085. "The Festival Singers' performance throughout is a powerful endorsement of Iseler's abilities as a choral trainer. Insofar as the musical values of Poulenc are concerned, he could indulge much more of a personalized view than he does." See: D339; D410.

B306 Kolodin, Irving. "Recordings Reports II: Miscellaneous LPs," *Saturday Review* 52 (August 30, 1969):48.

Review of the recording by Gabriel Tacchino of piano music, including *Suite française*, three *Novelettes*, *Mouvements perpétuels*, three *Nocturnes, Presto, Pastourelle, Toccata*, and *Valse* on Angel S 36602. "Those who know the *Mouvements perpétuels* will find that everything else flows forward from that source; those who have not yet encountered these likable works . . . will find themselves with a diverting experience for the asking. Tacchino contributes mightily to both the diversion and the experience." See: D197; D249; D370; D375; D389; D568; D613; D632; D642.

B307 ___. "Reviews of the Month," *Saturday Review* 32 (February 26, 1949):52.

Review of the Bernac-Poulenc recording of *Métamorphoses* and *Le Bestiaire* on RCA Victor 12-0426. "*C'est ainsi que tu es* is a little masterpiece both of suggestive melodic line and subtle exposition of it. Poulenc, of course, is his own insuperable interpreter at the piano." See: D62; D345.

B308 Kresh, Paul. "Poulenc: The Story of Babar," *HiFi/Stereo Review* 17 (December 1966):100.

Review of the Angel S36357 recording. Babar is "one of Poulenc's most irresistible impressionist scores. Ustinov is always winning but never coy." See: D290.

B309 Lange, Art. "Poulenc: Gloria," *American Record Guide* 41 (April 1978): 25.

Review of the Columbia M34551 recording with Judith Blegen, soprano; New York Philharmonic; Leonard Bernstein, conductor. "The use of peculiarly spiky, jazzy rhythms in a sacred work might be considered crass by some, but these passages are balanced by sections of true religious fervor and heartfelt passion. . . . Bernstein presents as strong a case for this music as any previous recording . . . powerful, vibrant, joyful." See: D279.

Laurencin, Marie. Watercolor design for Poulenc's ballet, *Les Biches*. See: B210.

B310   Lazarus, Daniel. "At the Olympic Games," *Modern Music* 1 (November 1924):29-31.

Reviews of performances of new works in Paris. *"Les Biches* by Francis Poulenc, following no precise plot, consists of a group of charming dances accompanied by delicate and subtle music continually striving to please and succeeding." See: W7.

B311   ___. "Study of a Recent French Movement," *Modern Music* 3 (March-April 1926):8-12.

Essay on compositions by young French composers of the avant-garde "which form a singular, bright spot on the international horizon. . . . . Differing in certain details of style they are closely related by a new and distinctive technique." Analysis of the works is intended to reveal the new and distinctive techniques found in them. Included in the discussion are five new ballets, among them *Les Biches*, Poulenc's sonatas for wind instruments, and the piano concerto of Tailleferre. See: W7; W114; W117; W119.

B312   Lee, Carole Ann. *The Piano Toccata in the Twentieth Century: A Selective Investigation of the Keyboard Styles and Performance Techniques*. Ph.D. dissertation, Boston University, 1978.

This study includes Poulenc's "Toccata" from *Trois pièces*. "This is not a history of the twentieth-century toccata, rather a performer's approach to selected toccatas, demonstrating why, despite a gap of seventy years in the nineteenth century, where very few toccatas were written, the form has enjoyed such a great revival in this century." See: W146.

B313   Leonard, Arthur S. "Poulenc: Gloria," *Fanfare* 1 (March 1978):58-59.

Review of the Columbia 34551 recording of this work compared with the Angel recording conducted by Prêtre. "Bernstein['s] . . . Gloria is suavely recorded and played, with more pep in the fast movements and a much greater attention to the details of the scoring. . . . Blegen's singing in the hushed concluding pages of the score is really haunting by comparison, and her vibrato is much more in control." See: D275; D279.

B314   Levinger, Henry W. "Orchestras: Philharmonic Firsts," *Musical America* 83 (June 1963):22.

Review of a performance of the organ concerto, Thomas Schippers, organist and conductor, and the premiere of *Sept répons de Ténèbres* on April 14, 1963, by the New York Philharmonic. The choral work, Poulenc's last major composition, was commissioned by Lincoln Center to celebrate the opening of Philharmonic Hall. "Had Poulenc written his own requiem, he could not have composed a more touching work." See: W30; W52.

B315   Lifar, Sergé. "Fin de saison chorégraphique à l'opéra," *Le Figaro* August 7, 1942.

In this article that appeared the day before the premiere of *Les Animaux modèles* at the Paris Opéra on August 8, 1942, Lifar, who choreographed the work, wrote that the ballet possessed "a lively, alert, frolicsome, sweetly lyric score." See: W5.

B316   Lincoln, Dorothy Ashbacher. *Musical Analysis and Stylistic Interpretation of Five French Choral Works by Francis Poulenc*. Ed.D. dissertation, Arizona State University, 1973.

Analysis of musical style in *Chanson à boire, Quatre petites prières, Petites voix, Huit chansons françaises*, and *Sept chansons*. See: W37; W45; W48; W51; W84.

B317   Linossier, Raymonde. "Autograph letter to Francis Poulenc," *La Revue musicale*, no. 312 (1978):52-54.

Autograph letter in French dated Monday, July 6, 1925. The letter described the death and burial of Erik Satie. Linossier answered several questions that Poulenc had apparently asked in an earlier letter about the disposition of Satie's manuscripts and his receiving last rites.

B318   Linstead, George. "The Charm of Poulenc," *Chesterian* 19 (May-June 1938):134-38.

Essay on musical style in the early works. "As one would expect from a member of 'Les Six,' and from one who was strongly influenced by

Satie's 'Simplicity' movement, the style of Poulenc is more markedly humorous, familiar (and at times delightfully vulgar), than that of the Impressionists." Linstead reviewed musical style in compositions from *Rapsodie nègre* of 1917 through *Suite française* of 1935 and concluded that it "is a real joy now and then to find a composer who prefers to entertain rather than preach. Such a composer is Poulenc, and therein lies much of his charm."

B319   Lockspeiser, Edward. "An Introduction to Poulenc's 'La Voix Humaine'," *Opera* 11 (August 1960):527-34.

Much of this essay is devoted to consideration of Cocteau's play of the same title. "Whatever may be Cocteau's limitations as a dramatist, he has a wonderfully sure touch in the theatre, and I think it will be illuminating to see how he was led to this splendid idea." Lockspeiser traced the history of productions of the play and discussed the plot and characterization. Lines of the dialogue were quoted. He analyzed Poulenc's solutions to the problems of defining in the music the meaning of the text and of underlining the significant ideas while allowing the singer the freest possible scope. See: W4.

B320   ___. "The Irony of Francis Poulenc," *The Listener* (September 19, 1957): 453.

In this essay Lockspeiser traced Poulenc's use of "music-hall" style from Chabrier: "C'est lui mon grand-papa," ("He is my grandfather") acknowledged Poulenc. The author discussed Poulenc's harmonic style in relation to l9th century Romanticism, Poulenc's songs, and his religious choral works.

B321   ___. "Tirésias at Aldeburgh," *Chesterian* 33 (Autumn, 1958):45-47.

Review of the English premiere of *Les Mamelles de Tirésias*. "Poulenc's abundant melodious flow floods the crazy skit with some of the finest lyrical music he has ever written. . . . Poulenc cleverly turns the dramatic defects of his libretto into musical virtues." See: W2.

B322   ___. "The Wit and the Heart: A Study of Francis Poulenc," *High Fidelity* 8 (July 1958):35-37.

Essay on musical style in the works of Poulenc. The ironic elements can be traced back to his Gallic inheritance from Chabrier and Satie, but that was only one side of this composer, as Poulenc was also a melodist. The author heard a remarkable change in the religious works that

Poulenc began to compose around 1938, culminating in the "largest and most consistently inspired of all his works--the three act opera 'The Carmelites'. . . . Since its first performance at La Scala two years ago, 'The Carmelites' has been variously evaluated in several countries. But I am not sure that its peculiar significance has yet been grasped. My conviction is that this work of Francis Poulenc solves the riddle of the enigmatic composer and, in the golden decline of our musical civilization, marks out this thoroughly traditional French figure as an exquisite survival." Two photographs of the composer are included.

B323   Luten, J. C. "Poulenc: Improvisation No. 5 in A Minor," *American Record Guide* 22 (December 1955):62.

Review of the Angel 35261 recording, Jean Casadesus, pianist. "His playing has many of his father's hallmarks--clean outline of phrase, discreet pedaling, attention to composers' indications, and musical spirit. Young Jean does not yet have the finger technique of his father." See: D306.

B324   ___. "Poulenc: Le Bal masqué," *American Record Guide* 16 (May 1950): 310.

Review of the Esoteric 2000 recording. "The execution . . . is first class. Poulenc's music, which fits these poems like a glove, is noteworthy for vocal writing of the utmost elegance and an instrumentation that is as clear as spring water. . . . It is one of the best examples of Poulenc's ability to make use of any melodic material (serious or popular, original or unoriginal) or any harmonic or instrumental device to convey objectively any idea or emotion that is in a poem he wishes to set to music." See: D35.

B325   Lyons, James. "Poulenc: Les Mamelles de Tirésias," *American Record Guide* 20 (June 1954):322-23.

Review of the Angel LP35090 recording. "The sorry decadence underlying the saucy story line is glossed over with infinite skill in Poulenc's ever fresh and delightful music, which is just as felicitous for the voices as it is for the orchestra. . . . All of the singers, from the leads to the least important, are entirely in the spirit of the thing." See: D325.

B326   Macdonald, Malcolm. "Works for Clarinet and Piano," *Gramophone* 56 (September 1978):499.

Review of the Desmar 1014G recording of the clarinet sonata. "I see one of the strongest pieces in the clarinet repertoire, with its share of those melting moments which a Poulenc tune characteristically offers, and with a total understanding of everything the instrument can be expected to do best. Including making a splendid partnership with the piano, not for the composer the easiest of instrumental pairings.   Stoltzman and Vallecillo have the measure of the sonata." See: D480.

B327   ___.   "Works for Wind Orchestra," *Gramophone* 56 (May 1979):1905.

Review of the WEA Enigma Classics K53574 recording of *Suite française* praised for its sharp attack in the playing, good ensemble, and simply splendid balance. "Probably this is the original form of the music now more familiar as a piano suite (it would have been agreeable if the sleeve-note had told us the provenance of this wind version); for that original form was intended for theatrical use as incidental music to Bourdet's play *Le Reine Margot*." See: W18; D565.

B328   "Mme. Duval On the Phone," *Newsweek* 60 (Mar. 7, 1960):65.

Review of the American premiere of *La Voix humaine* sponsored by the American Opera Society with Denise Duval and Georges Prêtre. The opera "is another tribute to the 61-year-old Poulenc's apparently inexhaustible creative resources. Since 1944 he has composed three operas, all successful, all totally different--and all with leading roles created by Mme. Duval." See: W4.

B329   Mann, William. "Bartok; Poulenc," *Gramophone* 46 (October 1968):532.

Review of the Decca LXT6357 recording of the sonata for two pianos. "The Poulenc sonata is enjoyable to play (plenty to keep you occupied, few hair-raising difficulties . . . It's music that brings out all the artistry in the Tamir duo, touch, nuance, sonority, singing tone, impeccable phrasing." See: D550.

B330   ___.   "Opera Diary," *Opera* 9 (March 1958):189-92.

Review of the Covent Garden production of the Carmelites on January 18, 1958. "The effect of the opera is largely the effect of Bernanos's text. It doesn't really need the music at all." Mann points out that melodic ideas are used throughout the opera in association with specific characters. Five photographs of the production accompany the review. See: W1.

Mantelli, Alberto. "Introduzione." See: B210.

B331   Manuel, Roland. "Ravel and the New French School, "*Modern Music* 2 (April 1925):17-23.

Essay treating the relationships between Ravel and the "school" which arose as the French Six under the influences of Satie and Cocteau. "Satie was the high-priest of the little musical chapels which arose in Paris about the end of the war. He was the patron first of the society of the 'Nouveaux Jeunes,' out of which in 1919 came the famous Group of Six." The author did not directly discuss the relationships between Ravel and Poulenc, but rather the influences Satie had on the Group in their evaluation of Ravel as a composer.

B332   Mark, Michael. "Sonates françaises pour clarinette et piano," *American Record Guide* 46 (September 1983):78-79.

Review of the Harmonia Mundi HMB5121 recording of the *Sonata for Clarinet and Piano*. "These five works are engaging trifles but Faucomprez and Raes play them with the kind of care some performers reserve only for so-called masterpieces." See: D483.

B333   Marnold, Jean. "Musique," *Mercure de France*, no. 134 (July-August 1919):128-34.

Review of performances at the Salle des Agricultures organized by Félix Delgrange. The programs included works by Poulenc and other young French composers. "M. Francis Poulenc cultivates with predilection, if not absolutely the form at least the term, classicism. For four hands, for piano and violin, and for two clarinets, he bestows on us no less than three *Sonatas*. Truly, regarding their small size, one would not find it at all extraordinary had M. Poulenc written a dozen. The name *Sonatine*, in like manner, would appear exaggerated, and because of the instantaneous fleeting succession of these [pieces], one would with difficulty resist the vague impression of some mocking practical jokes." See: W119; W150.

B334   ___. "Musique," *Mercure de France*, no. 165 (July-August 1923):200-01.

Review of a performance in Paris by Artur Rubinstein, who played Poulenc's *Promenades*. "It is one of the latest productions of this young composer, so young that he left his regiment only months ago. Not only because of his young age, but also for their intrinsic value, *Promenades* is an extremely remarkable work and one marking a turning in the evolution of the musician. M. Francis Poulenc was welcomed from his debut as an adolescent most rarely gifted. Music, it seems flows from him like a natural river with a delicious ingenuity. . . . The abundance of inspiration, the variety of rhythm, the unselfconscious originality, personal to the maximum degree, all are simply astonishing. In truth, it is a work of a master. One must warmly thank and praise M. Arthur Rubenstein, who interpreted it superbly, and for having adopted it into his repertory." See: W140.

B335   Marnold, Jean. "Musique," *Mercure de France*, no. 175 (October-November 1924):524-31.

Review of the premiere performance of *Les Biches*. "Certain pages of Biches call to mind Moussorgsky, Schubert, Verdi, with brief inspirations from popular songs, one of the most distinctive traits of the author. In the Adagietto, he reaches a Romantic classicism, and, in the Andantino, a Mozartian purity. . . . His orchestration has transparency, clarity, cool sonority, and always entirely spontaneously without searching for effect; *Fâcheux* and *Les Biches* are works by masters and inspired youth--sane and fresh youth which nothing could supply and nothing fill the place of. Our French music can look on without fearing the future." See: W7.

B336   Matz, Charles A. ". . . and Coast-to-Coast," *Opera News* 22 (January 6, 1958):29-30.

Review of a television broadcast of *Dialogues des Carmélites* on December 8, 1957, by the NBC Opera Co. Matz traced the history of the Carmelite order that is the central concern of the libretto and the evolution of their story into the opera libretto. There is a synopsis of the plot and a description of each character's personality and motivation. The reviewer praised the singing, orchestral accompaniment, and the sets, and concluded that the TV close-up technique "permitted vivid affinity with the torments of the protagonists and startling delight in the savor of their triumphs over the flesh." See: W1.

B337   Mayer, Tony. "France: Anniversary 'Carmélites'," *Opera* 43 (October 1983):1133-34.

Review. "There are very rare occasions in the theatre when, during a performance, a state of grace gradually pervades the house, when the performers identify themselves absolutely with the characters they impersonate, when the public is mesmerized, and the show not only comes to life, but is life itself. This happened at Avignon on June 3 at the performance of Dialogues . . . given in honour of the 20th anniversary of Poulenc's death. . . . a superb performance of a great work." See: W1.

B338   McMullen, Roy. "Notes from Abroad: Paris," *High Fidelity* 13 (May 1963):18.

Obituary of the composer. "Francis Poulenc died unexpectedly, in full career, as if he had intended to catch solemnity unprepared. . . . What he liked and did best was to set French words to French music."

B339   McPhee, Colin. "Scores and Records," *Modern Music* 16 (May-June 1939):264-67.

Review of a Columbia recording of the Mass. "The Columbia release of the *G-major Mass* of Poulenc is not so stimulating. The work itself is none too interesting, and the intonation of the Chanteurs de Lyons at times far from certain. The Agnus Dei, however, has a certain acoustic poetry; soprano solo and unison chorus alternate in the continuation of the melodic line (with curious Javanese inflections) during which one can at times distinctly hear the chilly echos in the cathedral at Lyons where it was recorded." See: D335.

B340   Mellers, Wilfrid. "Gramophone Records," *Musical Times* 108 (1967):147.

Review of the HMV ALP2296 recording. *Le Bal masqué* "goes on too long; . . . it is cafe music that finds itself a bit forlorn without a cafe. . . . On this disc the *Chansons Villageoises* are indeed 'popular songs with orchestra'; if all cafe music were equally witty or wistful, and brief, the world would be a happier place." In the *Rapsodie nègre* "something freshly personal survives through the years, in the sheer audacity of the boy Poulenc's rejection of academic pretension." *Le Bestiaire* is "his first miniature masterpiece. Here the model is specifically Satie. One wouldn't expect a boy of 18 to achieve the oddly disturbing reverberation that Satie wrings from apparent banalities, but Poulenc comes pretty close to it." See: D31; D54; D113; D431.

B341   ___. "More Light on the British Case: Berkeley and Rawsthorne," *Modern Music* 22 (March-April 1945):161-64.

Essay on the lack of an English musical tradition, because English music has been dominated since the Tudor period by foreign influences. Mellers contrasted the English situation with the rich musical traditions of France, a tradition inherited by Poulenc. "I was reminded of this point by a broadcast of French music given the other night by Poulenc and

Bernac. No one would claim that Poulenc is a great composer; and yet it seemed to me that these two artists had something which it would be difficult, if not impossible, to parallel in this country. They had behind them a 'continuous tradition,' implying standards of professional artistry, competence and elegance which touch human life at every point."

B342   Menasce, Jacques de. "Poulenc's Les Mamelles de Thirésias [sic]," *Musical Quarterly* 35 (April 1949):315-22.

In his analysis of the plot and its serious and comic intentions, the author described the surrealistic aspects of the libretto and its relationship to the post-Romantic world "which disappeared with the outbreak of World War I." The majority of the article is devoted to analysis of the music with many musical examples included. "Composed in 1944 . . . [the opera] is essentially the work of a musician who has assimilated with care all materials that have come to him by way of a great national tradition and who now is endorsing this tradition with finality, regardless of fads and fashions." Included is a photograph of Poulenc. See: W2.

B343   Michaels, Everette.   "Miscellaneous," *New Records* 53/9 (November 1985):16.

Review of the recording of *L'Histoire de Babar* on Spectrum SR187. "This new Spectrum recording, however, has one strike against it: Robert J. Lurtsema, the narrator. He seems to sound as if he is forcing some aspect of his voice, thereby creating a sound which I find grating. It seems that Mr. Lurtsema took it upon himself to add a cello to Poulenc's score so that 'Poulenc's music might be enhanced by an additonal [sic] instrument . . . I still, after all these years, prefer the Ustinov recording." See: D290; D294.

B344   Michaut, Pierre. "Cocteau et le ballet," *Empreintes*, nos. 7-8 (May-June, July 1950):62-67.

In this review of the premiere of *Les Mariés de la Tour Eiffel* in 1921 by the Ballet Suédois de Rolf de Maré, the author stated his opinion that the ballet "remains the most original and rich spectacle, and the newest." See: W9.

B345   Milhaud, Darius. "Music and Politics," *Modern Music* 22 (November-December 1944):5-6.

Essay on the fates of musicians in Europe during the war. "During these four years I have sometimes had news from Francis Poulenc who managed to reach me by people who escaped from France and sent me a letter from Spain. He wrote about the magnificent activity of the French musicians, writing and performing for the French public. I know now that Poulenc, Louis Durey, Georges Auric and Roger Désormière were active in the Resistance."

B346   Miller, James. "Collections: Vocal," *Fanfare* 6 (September 1982):402-03.

Review of the Spectrum SR147 recording of songs. "The 5 Poulenc songs do not form a cycle . . . and were composed between 1928 and 1939. Oddly, I find them to be among the least interesting morsels on the record. Maybe it's because Poulenc wrote so many better ones, or maybe it's because these are Logios's weakest performances." See: D7; D15; D134; D262.

B347   ___. "Bizet: Te Deum," *Fanfare* 6 (May 1983):112.

Review of the performance of *Gloria* on Argo ZRDL1010. "Both of these works have been well treated on records . . . I would choose this new Argo disc because the more important of the two works, Poulenc's Gloria, receives a more idiomatic performance that rivals the best the piece has received." See: D277.

B348   Miller, Philip L. "A Critic's Choice," *American Record Guide* 22 (September 1955):2.

Review of the RCA Victor LCT1158 recording of "*C.*" "Paul Hume has left the beaten path in making up this program, and has made available again a number of gems that a new collector might otherwise miss. . . . The present performance [of "*C*"] is the more official for the presence of Poulenc himself at the piano, and it brings us the Bernac of some ten years ago when his vocal resources were greater than they are today." See: D214.

B349   ___. "Now That This Definitive Recording Has Been Made, Who Can Hope to Rival It?" *American Record Guide* 26 (May 1960):704-05.

Review of the recording of *La Voix humaine* on RCA Victor Soria Series LS2385 with Denise Duval. The reviewer stressed the circumstances under which the work was composed and addressed the question of who can hope to rival this excellent recording. A photograph of Duval from the original Paris production is included. See: D652.

B350   Miller, Philip L. "Poulenc," *American Record Guide* 35 (September 1968): 10.

Reviews of recordings of songs, Odyssey 32 26 0009 with performances by Bernac and Poulenc, Philips PHS900148 performed by Souzay and Baldwin, and RCA Victor LSC3018 performed by Souzay and Baldwin. The Bernac-Poulenc recording contains songs by Ravel, Chabrier, Debussy, and Satie, in addition to the Poulenc songs. "The generous portion of Poulenc songs (including four cycles) is particularly important, for these must remain the final 'official' interpretations, whatever may be added by imaginative singers present and to come." Much of the remainder of the review was devoted to a comparison of the recordings by Bernac and Souzay, who was a student of Bernac. See: D44; D84; D116; D320; D359; D425.

B351   ___. "Poulenc: Mouvements perpétuels," *American Music Lover* 5 (December 1939):309-10.

The reviewer noted that the Poulenc pieces start where Fauré leaves off, with rebellion against tradition, and that they contain the "elegance and charm of the old French School . . . with just enough harmonic freedom to make them witty and piquant." The reviewer acknowledged that Rubinstein fully realizes these qualities in the performance. See: D620.

B352   ___. "Recorded Music," *Library Journal* 75 (June 15, 1950):1062.

Review of the recording of *Le Bal masqué* on Esoteric 2000. "This amusing surrealist music from AD 1932 begins to sound curiously old-fashioned. Set to an untranslatable Max Jacob text, the work has become something of a period piece. Strange what a lapse of eighteen years can do! The most interesting thing about the performance is the fact that after the passing of time it still sounds authentic . . . This is partly due to the fact that Fendler was the conductor at the world premiere." See: D35.

B353   ___. "Recorded Music," *Library Journal* 76 (February 15, 1951):352.

Review of the Bernac-Poulenc recording of *Banalités* and *Chansons villageoises* on Columbia ML4333. "The singer is not generously gifted with voice, and he sounds better on records than in real life. His long suit is diction, vocally he doesn't much care what he does, and the messages of his songs are carried by his pronouncement of the words without benefit of vocal tone color. Poulenc can play wonderfully, though some of this program is on the heavy side, and he uses a great deal of pedal." See: D41; D114.

B354   Miller, Philip L. "Recorded Music," *Library Journal* 76 (November 1, 1951):1821-22.

Review of Poulenc's recording of his own piano works and those of Satie on Columbia ML4399. "As a pianist Poulenc is always vital and intriguing. He has a way of using almost too much pedal in his own music, but he plays Satie's very cleanly." See: D373; D569; D615.

B355   ___. "Recorded Music," *Library Journal* 83 (March 1, 1958):746.

Review of the recording of *Stabat Mater* and *Le Bal masqué* on Westminster XWN18422. "Poulenc's sacred music is sincere and dignified, simple in expression yet never obvious. . . . Its performance here has, and deserves, the composer's blessing. The Bal masqué . . . has all the high spirits and tomfoolery of which Poulenc is capable." See: D39; D563.

B356   Milnes, Rodney. "British Opera Diary," *Opera* 34 (July 1983):785-88.

Review of a revival of Carmelites at Covent Garden, April 26, 1983. "This worthy revival emphasized again the technical brilliance of Poulenc's score: his tactful handling of hugh orchestral forces, his word setting, and his power of characterization through music are beyond criticism. . . . The musical side here was safe in the hands of Michel Plasson, who made no apologies for the score, lavished carefully shaded 'rubato' and some discreet 'portamento' on the deceptively simple musical paragraphs, and ensured that the all-important text (in a poor English translation) was sufficiently audible . . . Much praise for a well-chosen and carefully integrated cast." Photographs of the production are included. See: W1.

B357   *Miniature Essays: Francis Poulenc*. London: J. and W. Chester, 1922.

This essay was one of the first devoted to the young composer, Poulenc. It includes a biography and analysis of musical style in the early compositions. A photograph of Poulenc and an excerpt from *Promenades*, movement 3, are included with a list of the titles of twelve compositions published by Chester up to 1922. The author noted about the early works, "The curious fact is that in spite of this youthfulness and enthusiasm, in spite of this impetus and this ever ready comic spirit, the music of Poulenc is the clearest, the soberest and the best-ordered imaginable." The essayist concluded, "Poulenc will fulfill the promise of his youth."

B358   Mittag, Erwin von. "Viennese Audience Hails Poulenc Work in Local Premiere," *Musical America* 79 (April 1959):3.

Review of the Vienna premiere of *Dialogues des Carmélites* by the State Opera "under the carefully planned production of Margarete Wallmann and with scenery of matchless beauty by Georges Wakhevitch." The favorable review praised the production, singing, and score. See: W1.

B359   Moore, J. S. "Concerto," *New Records* 47/12 (February 1980):4-5.

Review of the Orion ORS79346 recording of the organ concerto. "The performance . . . is quite clean and rather exciting. Both Nyquist and the unnamed orchestra conducted by Lynn Shurtleff certainly do justice to the work, and judging from most live performances of this work (and many commercial recordings) this one is quite exceptional. There are, however, many good reasons why the orchestra should remain anonymous." See: D172.

B360   Morgan, Robert P. "The New Releases," *High Fidelity* 18 (August 1968): 97.

Review of the Lyrichord LLST7193 recording of the sonatas for clarinet and for oboe. "Poulenc's two sonatas, both dating from 1962, are facilely written and undoubtedly great fun to play, but in recorded form they fail to sustain interest." In a comparison with the recording of these works on Nonesuch, Morgan found the Nonesuch performances, "somewhat preferable and technical aspects are superior." See: D484; D521.

B361   Movshon, George. "The New Releases," *High Fidelity* 19 (June 1969):96.

Review of a recording of songs by Maxine Makas, soprano, and Anthony Makas, piano, on Westminster WST17146. "Most of the twenty-five songs recorded here are miniatures, some no more than half a minute long. They are a jumble of real gems and paste beads. . . . It was both original and commendable of Miss Makas . . . to make what has obviously been a deep study of this music. Her master was Pierre Bernac. . . . Her voice is young, clear, free from mannerisms, and has a fresh, 'American soprano' sound. Her command of French is excellent without being entirely native. . . . There is a great deal more in these songs than she extracts from them: fine shadings of tone, more confident nuances with the words and musical phrase, and greater variety of emotional temperature. These qualities tend to escape her." See: D12; D132; D261; D346; D612; D637; D640.

B362   Myers, Rollo. *Modern French Music: From Fauré to Boulez*. New York: Praeger, 1971.

In this historical survey the author traced the gradual breaking down of resistance to new ideas and new techniques in French music during the first six decades of the twentieth century. A brief summary of Poulenc's career appears in Chapter 7, "Ravel, Satie, 'Les Six,': Closer Links Between Music and Letters."

B363   ___. "A Music Critic in Paris in the Nineteen-Twenties: Some Personal Recollections," *Musical Quarterly* 63 (October 1977):524-44.

A memoir of artistic life in Paris after the first world war. Myers found it a period of "enormous vitality and creativity." He discussed the relationships among Cocteau, Satie, and Les Six, all of whom he knew and with whom he became friends, especially with Cocteau, Milhaud, Auric, and Poulenc. Included is a photograph of Poulenc with Wanda Landowska.

B364   ___. "Opera Forum: Variations of A Theme; Music's Future: Tonal or A-Tonal?" In *Music Today*. London: Dennis Dobson, 1949.

Several eminent composers were invited to express their views on this controversial question. Poulenc replied, "There were one time three great cubist painters: Picasso, Braque, Juan Gris. About the same time there were likewise three great atonal musicians: Schoenberg, Berg and Webern. Cubism and atonality were for them a means of expression as natural as breathing. To make from cubism or atonality a system, is to make the whole world breath with an iron lung. For my part I refuse to submit to it."

B365   Nagley, Judith. "The Carmelites," *Musical Times* 123 (May 1982):348.

Review of the Guildhall School's production of the opera in English translation by Joseph Machlis. "There is careful character delineation and moments of high drama, and the intensity of the score is wholly in sympathy with the story's devotional element. . . . The predominance of female voices soon cloys, however, and one must be a devotee of Poulenc's peculiar Debussy-influenced harmonic idiom to enjoy the piece to the full." See: W1.

B366   Nelson, Jon Ray. *The Piano Music of Francis Poulenc*. Ph.D. dissertation, University of Washington, 1978.

Musical analysis of the forty-five original works and ten transcriptions for piano solo.

B367   "The New Recordings," *Saturday Review* 31 (June 19, 1948):37.

Review of a recording of *Petites voix* by the RCA Victor Chorale, Robert Shaw, conductor, on RCA Victor 10-1409. "Excellent recording of small group voices. Five delightful little chansons about children, beautifully written, ultra-French." See: D384.

B368   Noble, Jeremy. "Nijinska," *Musical Times* 107 (May 1966):422.

A revival of *Les Biches* provided an opportunity for a review of Nijinska's choreography for this ballet. Nijinska was "one of the very great choreographers of our time." See: W7.

B369   O'Conner, John J. "TV: Liv Ullmann in Cocteau Drama," *New York Times* November 28, 1979, C:28.

Preview of Cocteau's drama *La Voix humaine* produced for WNET-TV. The drama, starring Liv Ullmann, was immediately followed by a performance of Poulenc's opera. "One is enough for any normal evening. The repetition of the same story in a different form may be of interest to scholars or buffs, but, in the end, both productions suffer from the pointless overexposure." See: W4.

B370   Oliver, Michael. "Poulenc," *Gramophone* 55 (April 1978): 1756.

Review of the recording of *Gloria* on Columbia M34551 compared with performances conducted by Prêtre and Frémaux. "Bernstein's reading . . . is excellently clear and crisp, but one only has to turn to Frémaux's HMV account to discover what is missing, a deft, Gallic lightness of touch, and economical energy that allows the 'très vif et joyeux' character of the music to emerge effortlessly and unemphatically. . . . George Prêtre . . . occupies a position midway between Bernstein and Frémaux, with attractively French-inflected Latin from his eloquent and committed choir and a touch of grandeur here and there that even Frémaux, for all his precisely calculated subtlety, occasionally misses." See: D275; D276; D279.

B371   ___. "Poulenc: Gloria," *Gramophone* 60 (January 1983): 853.

Review of the Argo ZRDL1010 recording. "Poulenc's Gloria has seldom seemed so tinglingly Stravinskyan, its textures so spare and so tautly articulated by staccatos and sforzandos . . . sung here with cool purity by Sylvia Greenberg." See: D277.

B372   Olsen, William A. "Alleluia," *New Records* 38/7 (September 1970):9.

Review of the Berkshire Boy Choir performance of *Timor et Tremor* on RCA LSC3081. "The singing is angelic, the recording superb and the music ranges from old to contemporary." See: D416.

B373   ___. "Chamber Music," *New Records* 37/5 (July 1969):7-8.

Review of the Angel S36586 recording. "The Angel disc offers, albeit unintentionally, dramatic evidence of the decline in absolute artistic and musical values from 1905 [Ravel's Introduction and Allegro] through the middle and late Thirties [Poulenc] and finally the late Thirties and early Forties [Françaix]. To me it was pitiful. . . . Poulenc's pieces have a certain surface charm, a slickness that might intrigue those who do not want to be bothered. . . . And yet, on all this, the Melos Ensemble lavishes its perfect techniques and understanding." See: D467; D600.

B374   ___. "Opera: Poulenc, La Voix Humaine," *New Records* 28/5 (July 1960):11.

Review of Duval's performance of the opera on RCA Victor LS2385. "It is a sign of the times, and a rather depressing one, that music of this sort is accorded a serious reception. Gone are the men who could write music that would leave one the better for having heard it. . . . We must observe, however, that because of the excellent performance turned in by Mme. Duval (and it is really a *tour-de-force*!), the fine recording, the superior packaging, and the spirited direction offered by George Prêtre, this is most clearly a case of *materiem superabat opus*." See: D652.

B375   ___. "Poulenc: Sinfonietta," *New Records* 36/10 (December 1968):5.

Review of the Angel S36519 recording. "Poulenc's Sinfonietta, for all the care, effort and genuine musical attention it receives, remained, for me, an exercise in platitudes à la the Twenties, even though it dates from 1947. The music for the Wedding on the Eiffel Tower and the (2) Marches and Intermezzo are both watered Satie--and without a spark of the older man's genius. The Suite Française derives what little charm it has from the music of Claude Gervais (1671-1744), which is souped up here in a tasteless manner." See: D183; D327; D459; D566.

B376   "The 'Opera League:'   Sir Thomas Beecham Reports Progress of Movement," *New York Times* March 2, 1930, II:9.

"Francis Poulenc's *Aubade*, a new work for solo piano and an orchestra of eighteen solo instruments (string and wind, excluding violins) had its first London performance recently . . . with the composer at the piano. It is described by the London Telegraph as 'a jolly work, not masterly in the creative sense, but extremely well-wrought." See: W6.

B377   Osborne, Conrad L. "Gérard Souzay: A Century of French Song," *High Fidelity* 16 (April 1967):101.

Review of the Gérard Souzay recording of songs on Philips PHS900132 with Dalton Baldwin, piano. "An interesting grab-bag of items, some of them familiar and recorded by Gérard Souzay before, some of them almost never heard on record or on our recital stages. . . . Souzay's performances are expectably expert, though there is some crooning that borders on the effete and some mannered interpretation that strikes a false note." See: D17; D285; D350; D398.

B378   ___. "Jennie Tourel: A French-Italian Program," *High Fidelity* 9 (August 1959):66.

Review of Tourel's recording of *Violon* on Decca DL10013. "It is with regret that I have to say of this recording that I can summon only sympathy for Tourel's intentions and respect for her ability to make an effect with very little aid from her now frayed voice. . . . I am a bit dumfounded by the programing on the French side, for there is not a significant piece of music presented." See: D263.

B379   ___. "The New Releases," *High Fidelity* 17 (November 1967):108-10.

Review of a recording of songs on Philips 500148 by Souzay and Baldwin. "The distinguishing virtues here are in Souzay's knowledgeable and effective styling . . . in the balance and consistently high level of the program, which presents some of the finest of Poulenc's songs; and not least in the splendid accompanying of Baldwin, fine pianism in its own right and admirably integrated with the singer's work." See: D85; D117; D272; D595.

B380   ___. "Poulenc's *La Voix humaine*, A Monodrama Turned Into Music," *High Fidelity* 10 (June 1960):55-57.

Review of the RCA Victor LSS2385 recording of the opera with a short essay on the relationship between the drama and the music. "I do not think it is correct to say that he [Poulenc] has merely written continuous incidental music to a successful play--the score seems to me to create an entire dimension that could not possibly be present in the spoken drama. In the first place, the musical inflections indicated for the solo voice constitute in themselves a reinterpretation of the woman's role; in the second place, the orchestra adds a point of view on her situation which simply could not be there without the music." The reviewer praised the performances, especially that of Denise Duval: "It is inconceivable that anyone could play the role better." See: D652.

B381   Osborne, Conrad L.   "Records in Review," *High Fidelity* 16 (June 1966):86.

Review of a recording of songs performed by Bernard Kruysen, baritone, and Jean Charles Richard, piano, on Westminster WST17105. "It's about time some serious and comprehensive attention were paid the songs of Poulenc by recording companies, and this is the first LP in the domestic catalogue to be devoted entirely to them . . . . This is a Poulenc who has put banalities and *Banalités* behind him, and who has arrived at full maturity as a great composer of songs and a great setter of modern poetry. . . . [Kruysen] is without doubt a fine artist, but the challenges of these songs expose his vocal weaknesses." See: D46; D64; D194; D274; D323; D352; D368; D587.

B382   ___. "Records in Review," *High Fidelity* 16 (November 1966):120.

Review of four song cycles recorded on Angel S36370 by Jean-Christophe Benoit, baritone, with orchestra conducted by Georges Prêtre. "This collection includes a complete *Le Bestiaire*, with the orchestral accompaniment--one of Poulenc's most successful essays, for all its brevity, and in an excellent performance. The orchestral version does not seem to me really to add much, but neither does it stand in the way of the songs' points. . . . We also have what is really a curiosity, the Op. 1 *Rapsodie nègre*, which is a little chamber orchestra suite with some pidgin-African nonsense for baritone. It's enjoyable in a sophomoric way." The recording also contains *Chansons villageoises* and *Le Bal masqué*. See: D31; D54; D113; D431.

B383   Osborne, Richard. "French Orchestral Works," *Gramophone* 51 (May 1974):2032.

Review of the HMV ASD2989 recording. "*Les Biches* is an irresistible score, witty, elegant, and superbly wrought. I know no melody more haunting--more smilingly, more confidingly beautiful--than that of the 'Adagietto.' It epitomises the bitter-sweet twenties mood, pleasing and saddening at the same time. . . . Frémaux's way with *Les Biches* is smart, exuberant and (in the nostalgically trailing phrase-ends of the 'Adagietto') quietly affecting." See: D70.

B384   Parmenter, Ross. "Denise Duval and Poulenc in Program," *New York Times* March 11, 1960, p. 21.

Review of a recital of music composed by Poulenc and others and performed by Poulenc and Duval, their first joint appearance in New York. "Judging from the applause, the listeners enjoyed themselves. In the last half of the program one could easily see why. . . . This was the part devoted to M. Poulenc's music. In it, of course, both performers were thoroughly at home. . . . In the earlier part of the program, however, both performers were out of their element. The composer is no longer a very accurate or skillful pianist." See: W2; W59; W105; W106.

B385   Passarella, Lee J. "Recital at Wigmore Hall," *New Records* 53/2 (April 1985):12-13.

Review of the Etcetera ETC1029 recording of *Fiançailles pour rire*. "Australian soprano Yvonne Kenny sings a nicely varied program and chooses works well suited to her light, clear, Ameling-like voice. . . . She gives lovely readings of the . . . Poulenc." See: D259.

B386   Peckham, Anson W. "Poulenc: Mass in G," *American Record Guide* 17 (November 1950):106-07.

Review of the RCA Victor LM1088 recording. "This Mass--stark, bare, unadorned as it may be-- . . . is as filled with the distilled essence of devotion, of genuine religious feeling as any of the full-length scores of the classical or baroque periods. I know of no unaccompanied work in the modern idiom that can approach it. The Robert Shaw Chorale sing the difficult score with admirable intonation and fine-textured quality." See: D338.

B387   ___. "Sauguet; Poulenic [sic]; Auric; Preger; Milhaud: Mouvements du Coeur," *American Record Guide* 16 (May 1950):310-11.

Review of the REB Editions REB-2 recording. This suite for bass and piano, commissioned by Doda Conrad, is based on poems by Louise de Vilmorin expressing the various moods of Chopin's life. Each section is based on a dance-form used by Chopin and composed by one of the composers listed in the title of this review. The movement contributed by Poulenc, a *Mazurka*, "is outstanding, but the work as a unit holds together well enough." See: D331.

B388   Pettitt, Stephen. "Choral Proms," *Music and Musicians* 28 (November 1979):53.

Review of a BBC telecast of the Mass. "There seems to be an intensity of introspective religious fervour; and the music which flows from Poulenc's pen conveys, at the same time, a simple honesty, devoid of any attempts at cleverness or wittiness." See: W44.

B389   Peyser, Herbert F. "Concert champêtre," *New York Philharmonic Program Notes*. November 20, 1949. Wanda Landowska, harpsichord.

Much of the material concerns the world premiere of this work in 1929 and the American premiere on November 11, 1948, with Poulenc as pianist. The remainder is devoted to extensive quotes from *Le Guide du Concert* (April 26, 1929) about the piece and Poulenc's work on the composition with Landowska. See: W28.

B390   Pirie, Peter J. "Broadcasting," *Musical Times* 105 (April 1964):283.

Review of the first radio broadcast in England of the *Gloria* with Rosanna Carteri, soprano, and the chorus and orchestra of French Radio conducted by Georges Prêtre. "In sound it was pure Poulenc, that curious attempt to bend the melodic formulae of Les Six and the anti-monumental reaction of the twenties to monumental purposes. This was the paradox of Poulenc. He adopted uncritically the basically frivolous music that was all around him in his early career, and then in his last years tried to write great music with it. The result is pungent and personal." See: W41.

B391   ___. "20th Century Vocal," *Musical Times* 166 (1975): 1076.

Review of recently published scores of "Margoton va t'a l'iau" from *Chansons françaises* and *Un Soir de neige*, "a substantial work of great imagination, matching Eluard's lovely words." See: W38; W53.

B392   Pittaluga, Gustavo. "Francis Poulenc and the Praise of the Paradox in Art," *Chesterian* 17, no. 124 (November-December 1935):37-40.

A rather involved and convoluted discussion of Poulenc's aesthetic approach to composition. The author concluded that Poulenc rejected the forms of expression current in his day and found within himself new means of expression that more fully expressed his own personality.

B393 Plaistow, Stephen. "Artur Rubinstein," *Gramophone* 42 (March 1965):434.

Review of the RCA Victor recording. "There is nothing to temper enthusiasm for this record . . . Rubinstein is at his best and is a superb exponent of French music." See: D308.

B394 ___. "Bracha Eden and Alexander Tamir: Recital for Two Pianos," *Gramophone* 42 (May 1965):535.

Review of the Decca LXT6158 recording. The performers "attained an excellence which rivals in technical command that of the world's best, and which in musical feeling is perhaps on the way to supremacy. They are thoughtful players, not at all addicted to that mechanized domestic brilliance which propels some teams round the world." See: D537.

B395 ___. "Music for Two Pianos," *Gramophone* 50 (July 1972):197-98.

Review of the Decca SXL6551 recording and comparison with the Poulenc-Février recording on HMV ASD517. The performances of Eden and Tamir are "lively, in a garrulous sort of way, with some highly polished piano playing decently but not impeccably supported by the orchestra." Of the older HMV recording the reviewer found "rather to my surprise I enjoyed the Concerto more than I've ever done. . . . The Concerto hung together better and seemed a much stronger piece. In the HMV performance the bustling gaiety, the *gaminerie*, are less forced, as is the expression as a whole. And thereby the character of the piece, for me, seemed to gain a lot, to be not just less bizarre but altogether more unified, subtle and interesting. One could say that the composer and Jacques Février in the HMV underplay, whereas Eden and Tamir in the new version tend to underline." See: D151; D156.

B396 Potter, Stephen. "The Story of Babar," *American Record Guide* 33 (December 1966):347.

Review of the Angel 36357 recording. "Pure joy, especially the fortuitous amalgam of de Brunhoff's neoclassic creation with the jaunty Poulenc inventions. . . . The Poulenc score is a masterpiece in its own right." See: D290.

B397   "Poulenc and Bernac to Come to U. S. for Joint Recital Tour," *Artist's Life* (April 1948):1.

Announcement of the first joint concert tour to America with their New York debut planned to take place November 7, 1948, in Town Hall.

B398   "Poulenc: Le Bal masqué," *New Records* 18/9 (November 1950):12.

Review of the Esoteric 2000 recording. "The poems are quite outrageous and sophisticated nonsense . . . Poulenc has written catchy and witty music as a setting to these poems, but the whole thing savors slightly of a naughty boy trying to shock you. . . . Edvard Fendler is the conductor of this performance, and both he and the soloist give an amazingly able account of themselves." See: D35.

B399   "Poulenc of Les Six," *Newsweek* 32 (November 15, 1948):84-85.

Review of the American debut of Poulenc and Bernac at Dumbarton Oaks in Washington, D.C., on November 4, 1948. "The standing and acceptance of Poulenc outside of France have increased immeasurably since the second world war. Often previously dismissed as an extraordinarily talented young man who substituted cleverness for substance, he has now emerged as a solid citizen with a large and devoted following."

B400   "Poulenc: Sextette for Piano and Wind Instruments," *New Records* 22/7 (September 1954):10.

Review of the Capitol P8258 recording. "The Frenchman's compositions for a small orchestra of wind instruments are very singular in that they give the impression of vulgarity without ever descending to it . . . The Fine Arts Wind Players exhibit here an understanding of the works and a fine rapport." See: D445.

B401   Poulenc, Francis. "A propos d'une lettre d'Arthur Honegger," *Schweizerische Musikzeitung* 102/3 (May-June 1962):160-61.

Poulenc relates his first meeting with Honegger at the home of Jeanne Bathori where a group of musicians gathered to sight read Ravel's *Trois chansons*. Charles Koechlin, Honegger, and Poulenc sang bass. After Poulenc made several errors, Honegger nudged him and smilingly said, "et le solfège?" Poulenc relates: "I colored to my ears and before long I applied this witticism to my first works."

In the last years of Honegger's life the two composers became good friends. The text of a letter from Honegger to Poulenc concludes the article. "We are I believe in temperament very different, but I believe I have this in common with you: the love of music more than the love of success. On opposing points we express ourselves similarly. . . . All these differences, far from separating us seem to me on the contrary to bring us closer together. Truth, isn't that the most beautiful thing in life and in art? Will you find me too presumptuous if I place myself at your side in order to say: We are two honest men?"

B402   Poulenc, Francis. Autograph. Inscribed to [Mrs.] Otonita Urchs [Pope]. Paris: May 27, 1925.

This autograph is included in a volume of autographs located in the Performing Arts Division, Library of Congress, Washington, D.C. Two measures of the "Rondeau" from *Les Biches* appear in Poulenc's hand with the date, 1923, underneath. The inscription reads, "à mademoiselle Otonita Urchs avec la trés respecteuse sympathie de Francis Poulenc. Chez Madame Wanda Landowska's le 27 Mai 1925 Paris."

B403   ___. "D'Autriche," *Contrepoints*, no. 4 (May-June 1946):60-62.

A brief article describing a recent visit Poulenc made to Vienna, where he encountered for the first time the compositions of Anton Heiller. Poulenc described the experience as being much like that of his first encounter with the works of Bartok in 1921, also in Vienna. "It may be that Heiller will bring again to Vienna the fallen flame from the dead hands of the marvelous Webern or the great Berg. . . . It is with impatience that I await the new works of Heiller. From today, I will hail him in the same way I was happy from 1937 to recognize Dallapiccola as the best young Italian musician."

B404   ___. "Centenaire de Chabrier," *La Nouvelle revue française* 55 (July-December 1941):110-14.

Poulenc wrote this essay following a series of concerts in Paris to celebrate the centennial of the birth of Chabrier. The article is devoted to analysis of Chabrier's musical style and his development as a composer.

B405   ___. "Le Coeur de Maurice Ravel," *La Nouvelle revue française*, no. 323 (December 1940-June 1941):237-40.

This essay was inspired by a Mozart-Ravel festival conducted by Charles Münch at the Conservatoire. It is a personal guide to Ravel's compositions with analysis of individual pieces that Poulenc liked and admired. For example, Poulenc appraised the concerto for the left hand: "This work is without contest one of the summits of his art." Poulenc also included anecdotes about the composer whom he admired very much as an individual.

B406   Poulenc, Francis. "Comment j'ai composé les 'Dialogues des Carmé-lites'," *L'Opéra de Paris* 14 (1957):15-17.

Poulenc related that he had wanted to write an opera since he began composing. Mr. Valcaranghi, director of Ricordi, suggested Dialogues to him. As Poulenc was in Rome at the time, he immediately bought the book and went to the cafe, Tre Scallini, on the Piazza Navone, where he remained from ten in the morning until two reading. He then sent Valcarenghi a telegram accepting a commission to write the opera. Three photographs are included: Poulenc as a child beside his first piano, as a young man dressed in his army uniform, and on the veranda of the Hotel Majestic where he composed the opera. See: W1.

B407   ___. *Correspondance, 1915-1963*. Compiled by Hélène Wendel. Preface by Darius Milhaud. Paris: Éditions du Seuil, 1967.

This publication includes letters from Poulenc and those addressed to him by others. Letters selected for inclusion in the volume were chosen from the many surviving documents "to permit us to follow not only the elaboration and the evolution of all he wrote, but like the detached leaves of an intimate journal, awaken to us the heart of Francis, his goodness, his solicitude and also the anguish of the creator." Illustrations include photographs, programs, and facsimile pages of scores.

___. *Dialogues des Carmélites*: "La fin des adieux de la prieure." See: B576.

B408   ___. *Emmanuel Chabrier*. Paris: La Palatine, 1961.

Poulenc's personal tribute to the man he called his "musical grandfather." The work includes a brief biography and Poulenc's comments on many of Chabrier's compositions. Section two is devoted to contributions in the form of letters and poetry from those who had known the composer. There are also several unedited letters written by Chabrier. Finally, there is a list of paintings collected by Chabrier with the prices he paid for them. The list, including works by Cezanne, Manet, Renoir, Sisley, and Monet, is in the hand of Mme. Chabrier.

B409   Poulenc, Francis. *Entretiens avec Claude Rostand*. Paris: René Julliard, 1954.

This work, published in French, was compiled from a series of conversations taped for live-radio broadcasts for Radiodiffusion Française from October 1953 to April 1954. Poulenc revealed in the conversations much of his biography and musical development as a pianist and as a composer. He discussed types of compositions that interested him and specific works in each category.   In addition, he discussed his relationships with other members of Les Six and many of his friends, such as Raymonde Linossier, Jane Bathori, Satie, and Cocteau.

B410   ___. "Feuilles américaines," *La Table ronde*, no. 30 (June 1950):66-75.

Extracts from a journal that Poulenc decided to keep during his 1949-50 tour in America in order "to occupy himself during the long waits in American hotels." In the entries, each with date and place, Poulenc wrote about the works performed, the rehearsals, the musicians, the reactions of public and critics, his observations of and reactions to the American scene, and anecdotes about people he knew or met in America.

B411   ___. "Francis Poulenc, ou les prestes pirouettes, "*Contrepoints*, no. 1 (January 1946):49.

Poulenc's response to a question about what is new in his compositions. The question was asked of eighteen contemporary composers. Poulenc's succinct reply: "I understand nothing of the inquiry. When I will have said to your readers:
1. that my counterpoint is instinctive 2. that I don't have principles and that I brag about it 3. that, God have mercy! I have no system of composition (systems are the equivalent of 'tricks') 4. that inspiration is a thing so mysterious that it is better not to explain it
Do you think that they will be transported with interest? I doubt it. Don't count, therefore, on a speech from me."

B412   ___. "Francis Poulenc, ou les prestes pirouettes," *La Revue musicale*, nos. 306-307 (1977):33-34.

Reprint of B411.

B413   Poulenc, Francis. "Homage à Béla Bartok." In *Béla Bartok: L'Homme et l'oeuvre 1881-1945*. Special issue of *La Revue musicale* 29 (1955): 18-19.

Poulenc did not know Bartok personally but heard him play several times. He recalls the first Paris performance of the *Allegro Barbaro*, and the effect that the piece had on the audience. Poulenc believed that the genius of Bartok was not fully recognized because of everyone's great devotion to Stravinsky. The last time Poulenc saw Bartok was at a concert, where he played the two piano sonata with his wife shortly before the war. Poulenc concluded this essay with a physical description of the composer as he looked at that time.

B414   ___. "Igor Strawinsky," *Information musicale*, no. 195 (January 3, 1941): 195.

Essay on Stravinsky's important influence in the development of Poulenc's own works and the development of music in this century. "At the age of twenty, I loved the music of Stravinsky to distraction. Numbers of my first works testify to this passionate veneration, a natural influence, since in a single day, it came to me at this time, to play more than twenty times the overture from Mavra or the finale from Pulcinella. . . . Now that I have passed forty and must become more balanced in my sentiments, I have kept my fervor for the works of Stravinsky intact, and it is always in this master that I find some of my greatest musical joys."

B415   ___. "Inventur der modern französischen Musik," *Melos* 23 (February 1956):35.

An extract from Poulenc's *Entretiens avec Claude Rostand*, in which he discussed contemporary music. (See: B409)

B416   ___. *Journal de mes mélodies*. Translated by Winifred Radford. London: Victor Gollancz, 1985.

Poulenc's diary was originally published in French, in a limited edition in Paris by Éditions Bernard Grosset in 1964. The comments about the songs from the composer's viewpoint are invaluable. Included are remarks about interpretation, the poets and the poetry set to music, influences on the songs, circumstances surrounding the composition of individual pieces and song cycles, and Poulenc's insights into the compositions of other composers, especially Debussy, Ravel, and Fauré. Poulenc also writes about the people and places important to him.

Important people, places, and compositions mentioned in the text are identified in the "Notes and Discographical Appendix" by Patrick Saul. Fifteen photographs of Poulenc, his friends, and places associated with him are included.

Poulenc, Francis. Letter to R. P. Carré. See: B576.

B417   ___. "Lorsque je suis mélancolique," *Mercure de France*, no. 1109 (January 1, 1956):72-73.

A touching tribute to Poulenc's friend, Adrienne Monnier, who was introduced to him by Raymonde Linossier in 1916. When he was melancholy, Poulenc could smile again by thinking about the period in his life when he saw Monnier almost daily. "In her *Gazette* Adrienne Monnier wrote about *Animaux modèles* some of the most pertinent phrases that had ever been written on my music. She always understood me with her heart." See: W5.

B418   ___. *Ma musique est mon portrait*. Sound recording. Paris: Dunod, [197-?]. 13 FT62. 1 disc.

The composer talks about his childhood, his piano training, and his special pleasure in composing religious music.

B419   ___. "Mes mélodies et leurs poètes," *Conferencia* 36 (December 15, 1947):507-13.

This is the text of a lecture-recital performed by Bernac and Poulenc on March 20, 1947. Included on the program were songs by Poulenc and Schubert's *Soleil d'hiver*. Poulenc comments upon when and under what influences his songs were composed. In a discussion of the poets Apollinaire, Eluard, and Aragon, Poulenc relates, "For 25 years the poetic work of Apollinaire has not ceased to inspire me." Included is a photograph of Poulenc as a young man.

B420   ___. "La Musique de piano d'Erik Satie." In *Erik Satie: Son temps et ses amis*. Edited by Rollo Myers as a special issue of *La Revue musicale* 26 (June 1952):23-26.

An essay on Satie and the piano. Poulenc affirmed that Satie rarely played the piano and traced Satie's early study and feelings about the piano as a musical instrument. There is some analysis of Satie's piano music with remarks about style and influences on the works.

B421   Poulenc, Francis. *My Friends and Myself*. Conversations assembled by Stéphane Audel. Translated by James Harding. London: Dennis Dobson, 1978. (Originally published as *Moi et mes amies*. Paris, 1963)

The conversations published in this book were originally broadcast by Suisse-Romande Radio. The first six were aired in 1953 and were devoted to Poulenc's life and compositions. The remaining eight were broadcast in 1955 and 1962 and deal with Poulenc's friends--Satie, Jacob, de Falla, Eluard, Honegger, Prokofiev, Ravel, and Stravinsky. These were to be followed by four additional conversations, but Poulenc died before the recording sessions began.

Audel, who conducted the interviews with Poulenc, introduced the conversations in a Preface that is a personal remembrance of the composer, especially of Poulenc's personality and of his country house at Noizay. This work is important for revealing in Poulenc's own words his thoughts and feelings about so many things and people that touched his life and music. Included are twelve photographs of Poulenc and others.

B422   ___. "Oeuvres récentes de Darius Milhaud," *Contrepoints*, no. 1 (January 1946):59-61.

The receipt of a packet of manuscripts from Milhaud, who was at that time living in America, inspired Poulenc to write this essay about his friend's recent compositions and "to salute in the first issue of *Contrepoints* this great musician of whom I am proud to be the friend." The compositions are listed by title with brief remarks about each piece.

B423   ___. "Opera in the Cinema Era." As told to Elliott Stein. *Opera* 12 (January 1961):11-12.

A conversation in which Poulenc discussed ideas about opera in the twentieth century, especially at a time when audiences have been conditioned by movies. "The cinema has modified our point of view, and the public has come to expect a great variety of scene-changes. Debussy sensed this in *Pelléas*; and Berg, in his operatic version of *Wozzeck*, made a successful innovation in keeping the drama in many short fragmentary scenes, with changes of sets and atmosphere corresponding to the varying 'states of soul' of the central character. It was exactly this sort of problem that interested me in the dramatic structure of *Dialogues des Carmélites*." See: W1.

B424   ___. "Tributes to Christian Bérard," *Ballet* (April 1949):30-31.

A tribute to the painter, Christian Bérard to whom Poulenc dedicated the *Stabat Mater*. The brief tribute recounts several memories Poulenc had of his friend, who lived near, ("a few doors away," in Poulenc's words) so that they met often. See: W54.

Poulenc, Francis. *Tu vois le feu du soir*. See: B576.

B425   Prêtre, Georges. "Recherche du Francis Poulenc," *Music Journal* 23 (January 1965):58.

A memoir of the five years of friendship and professional association shared by the author and Poulenc. Prêtre's assessment of Poulenc's compositions was that while he was known at the time of this article for the songs and droll, humorous pieces, in future the music that will remain in the repertory are works like the *Gloria* and *Stabat Mater*--the religious works.

B426   "Promenades (Chester)," *Musical Times* 64 (1923):709.

Review of the newly published score of this work. "There are ten of them, and it is hard to say which is the most uncomfortable way of getting anywhere. . . . It is like a progress over broken bottles, with an occasional banana skin for a change. . . . There are plenty of the now conventional strings of consecutive discords--especially minor ninths . . . There is a lot of good fun in the pieces, though the player will joke *wi' deeficulty*." See: W140.

B427   Prunières, Henri. "Les Fâcheux de Georges Auric et Les Biches de Francis Poulenc aux Ballets Russes," *La Revue musicale* 5 (July 1924):61-64.

Review of the premieres of the two ballets and a comparison of the works. "The two works are very different and opposites in their qualities, if not in their like faults." Descriptions of the settings and plots are given for each work with some analysis of the music. See: W7.

B428   ___. "Francis Poulenc," *Cahiers d'art* 3 (1928):125-29.

An essay on French music during the 1920s with a critical review of the early works of Poulenc. In tracing the state of French music during this era, Prunières discussed Satie's influences on young musicians after the war, and the influence of Cocteau and Stravinsky on Poulenc. The author's assessment of Poulenc's future as a composer: "It is evidently premature to pass a definitive judgement on so young an artist who has before him so many years of creation, but one must consider the author of Biches, Bestiaire, the Trio, the Chansons Gaillardes and the Concerto as one of the most gifted most interesting musicians of the new French school." Included is a rare photograph of Poulenc as a young man, wearing a checked suit and neck scarf, holding a cockatoo, and leaning nonchalantly on a table.

B429   R. A. E. "American Opera Society Offers Poulenc Premiere," *Musical America* 80 (March 1960):32.

Review of the semi-staged performances of *Les Mamelles de Tirésias* and *La Voix humaine* with Denise Duval and Georges Prêtre sponsored by the American Opera Society. Poulenc was in the audience. The reviewer stated of this New York premiere of *La Voix humaine*, "What great sensitivity it took to create a kind of endless aria, in which the voice rises and falls naturally, yet never grows monotonous nor seems to repeat a pattern. . . . One wonders if the opera would have the success it did without Miss Duval in it." Her performance was described as "superb and haunting." See: W2; W4.

B430   ___. "Fauré Ballade," *Musical America* 74 (November 1954):20.

Review of the Concert Hall Society CHS-1181 recording of the eight *Nocturnes* and *Trois mouvements perpétuels* performed by Grant Johannesen. Poulenc's pieces are described as, "engaging, insouciant pieces, in spite of the slightness of their content." The performances by Johannesen are, "remarkably lucid and beautifully poised pianism." See: D371; D616.

B431   R. E. "Recitals in New York," *Musical America* 80 (April 1960):34.

Review of the March 10, 1960, Town Hall recital with Denise Duval, in her New York debut, and Poulenc. "Poulenc is not as good a pianist as he used to be, except in his own music, and Mlle. Duval tends to be uncomfortable and shrill in music which does not suit her temperament exactly." See: W2; W59; W105; W106.

B432   Rabinowitz, Peter J. "Pál Kadosa At the Piano," *Fanfare* 3 (November 1979):164-65.

Review of the Hungaroton LPX12009-10 recording of *Suite in C*. "Pál Kadosa is a Hungarian pianist, composer, and pedagogue. . . . [The recording] is an offbeat collection of early 20th-century snippets, recorded between 1950 and 1958, apparently after Kadosa had retired from regular concertizing. . . . The overdriven Vif of the Poulenc lacks not only Gallic grace, but also the intensity that Kadosa is aiming at, because it's imprecise." See: D577.

B433   Rabinowitz, Peter J. "Vocal," *New Records* 54/3 (May 1986):20.

Review of the performance of *A sa guitare* on Calliope CAL1885. "Herbillon is stylistically comfortable with the wide range of music he presents, but his voice is threadbare and unsteady, and is recorded with a metallic edge. The production is mediocre in other ways as well: the jacket and label are a maze of mistakes, the notes (in French only) are poor, and the texts (also in French only) are confusingly presented." See: D1.

Radiguet, Raymond. *Les Mariés de la Tour Eiffel.* See: B210.

B434   Ramsey, Basil. "Gramophone Records," *Musical Times* 106 (1965):690.

In the Argo ZRG5430 recording of *Quatre motets pour un temps de pénitence* and *Laudes de Saint-Antoine de Padoue*, Ramsey heard "unexpected riches from an unpredictable talent." See: D404; D412.

B435   Rasin, Vera. "Les Six and Jean Cocteau," *Music and Letters* 38 (April 1957):164-69.

Essay on the development of a new artistic aesthetic during the 1920s by Les Six and the influence Cocteau had on the members of this group. The members of the group met frequently to discuss the latest trends in the arts, including in their gatherings performers, painters and writers. "The young musicians of the time found inspiration in the music of Erik Satie, and in 1918 Jean Cocteau provided them with their Bible, in the form of *Le Coq et l'Arlequin.* . . . The book certainly expresses many of the young composers' aims and ideals." The author found that on the purely musical side the members of the group were linked by technique and inspiration from their Saturday evening visits to the music-halls and circus. A list of compositions that were collaborations between Jean Cocteau and members of the group of six concluded the article.

B436   Rasponi, Lanfranco. "The Voice of Poulenc: Lanfranco Rasponi Talks With Denise Duval," *Opera News* 41 (February 5, 1977):17-19.

A conversation with Duval about her years of association with Poulenc and the roles that she created in his opera. A short biography of Duval introduced the conversation. "Musically speaking, in my opinion Les Mamelles is the most imaginative of Poulenc's operas, Dialogues the most touching and La Voix humaine the most compelling. . . . Poulenc in my estimation was the last of the great modern opera composers, and I'm proud my name will always be connected with his. I owe a lot to him, and for that I am grateful."

B437   Rauhut, Franz.   "Les Motifs musicaux de l'opéra Dialogues des Carmélites de Francis Poulenc," La Revue des lettres modernes, nos. 340-45 (1973):211-49.

Extensive analysis of the musical motives of the opera in relationship to the drama. Analysis of melodic and harmonic motives and of style in the recitatives is included with musical examples and a table of musical motives. See: W1.

B438   Rich, Alan. "Records in Review," High Fidelity 14 (April 1964):86.

Review of recordings of Stabat Mater and the Penitential Motets on Angel S36121. "The deep and somber Stabat Mater . . . is put together out of short, jagged fragments, setting the Latin poem verse by verse in remarkably concise fashion. . . . The music is spare, reticent, and immensely poignant. . . . The Motets . . . are a cappella and extremely austere in texture, somewhat beholden in style to medieval French music. They lack the immediate beauty of the Stabat Mater." The performances are "beautifully detailed and stylish." See: D411; D561.

B439   ___. "San Francisco," Musical Quarterly 44 (January 1958):92-95.

Review of the American premiere of Dialogues des Carmélites by the San Francisco Opera Company. Rich concluded that the major weakness of the opera lies in the fact that "the music fails the drama. The central character, Blanche, undergoes in the text a considerable growth. . . . Poulenc's music does not supply a convincing motivation for this action, because among his many skills there is lacking that of development, of working to a climax." See: W1.

B440   Robertson, Alec. "Bernac and Poulenc," Gramophone 23 (April 1946): 132.

Review of the HMV Gramophone DB6267 recording with performances of Métamorphoses and Deux poèmes (Aragon). "Poulenc's setting of

Louis Aragon's "C" is the loveliest song that has lately reached us from France and also, I think, the loveliest song Poulenc has written. . . . Full of the most heart-felt but restrained emotion, Poulenc's music fits the poem like a glove and it has a 'burden' in it, an exquisite sequence, that long haunts the memory." See: D207; D343.

B441   Robertson, Alec. "Bernac and Poulenc," *Gramophone* 23 (August 1946): 34.

Review of the HMV Gramophone DB6299 recording. In *Le Bestiaire* "the piano parts are suggestively descriptive and particularly successful in the third, fifth and sixth numbers of the charming little songs. . . . Montparnasse is a much more important affair and, indeed it is one of Poulenc's most beautiful songs. . . . The vocal line of the song is exceptionally lovely and the final cadence quite exquisite. Needless to say the singing and accompanying of Bernac and Poulenc is of the finest quality." See: D58; D362.

B442   ___. "Poulenc; Scarlatti," *Gramophone* 30 (October 1952):107-08.

Review of the Decca LXT2720 recorded performance of *Les Biches*. "Poulenc re-orchestrated the music in 1939-40. . . . This record shows not only how much more effective it is in orchestral dress [than the piano version] but also how the sudden discordant passage, so harsh on the piano, blends into its context in a natural way. . . . It would be foolish to take this pastiche of styles seriously and it is enough that it is ingenious, amusing, and tuneful. The music is played expertly, in exactly the right style, by Désormière and the orchestra." See: D68.

B443   Rockwell, John. "A Risky Venture at the Met," *New York Times* February 15, 1981, D:17.

"This Friday, the company will present the premiere of as risky a venture as it has yet assayed, a triple bill of three 20th-century French works: Erik Satie's ballet *Parade*, Francis Poulenc's farce *Les Mamelles de Tirésias* and Maurice Ravel's *L'Enfant et les sortilèges*. The overall title of the evening is *Parade*. The combination has whetted appetites because of the panache and rarity of all three works." See: W2.

Rognoni, Luigi. *Due colloqui con Arthur Honegger*. See: B210.

B444   Rorem, Ned. "Afterthoughts on Francis," *American Record Guide* 41 (September 1968):11.

A portrait of the composer as a man and musician written by a personal friend. See: B445.

B445   Rorem, Ned. "Bernac and Poulenc." In *Music and People*. New York: George Braziller, 1968.

A review of two recordings, Odyssey 32-26-0009 and Pathé FALP50036, that is a virtual reprint of the review published in *High Fidelity* [See: B450]. Here there is more material on musical style in general. In the conclusion, entitled "Afterthoughts on Francis," Rorem told several stories that reveal the personality of Poulenc. For example, he related that he and Poulenc made a trip on the train by second class to the com- poser's country home at Noizay, because Poulenc thought "the people are more fun to watch." Rorem also repeated the story that Poulenc wept openly at Duval's performance of his *La Voix humaine*. See: W4; D44; D84; D116; D204; D320; D359; D365; D425.

B446   ___. "Francis Poulenc: A Souvenir." In *Music from Inside Out*. New York: George Braziller, 1967.

This personal tribute to Poulenc originally appeared in *Village Voice*, February 21, 1963.   Rorem described the composer as a man of contradictions--dapper and ungainly, unpressed clothes from Lanvin, scrubbed hands with bitten fingernails, his physiognomy a cross between weasel and trumpet, "with a large nose through which he wittily spoke." The author concluded, "Not since Ravel's death in 1937 . . . can I recall being so disturbed as by the news of Poulenc last week. For Poulenc had inherited Ravel's mantle, and today in leaving us he has taken with him the best of what remained in musical France."

B447   ___. "Monologue and Dialogues," *Opera News* 41 (February 5, 1977): 10-16.

In this assessment of Poulenc's compositional style, Rorem wrote, "In the purely Puccinian sense of soaring sweep, Poulenc was no melodist at all. His tunes--usually they are true tunes, not recitations--stem from speech. . . . Take Chopin's dominant sevenths, Ravel's major sevenths, Faurés straight triads, Debussy's minor ninths, Mussorgsky's augmented fourths. Filter them, as Satie did, through the added-sixth chords of vaudeville . . . blending a pint of Couperin with a quart of Stravinsky, and you get the harmony of Poulenc." The author told about his many visits with Poulenc in the composer's Paris apartment. Included are several photographs of Poulenc, his home at Noizay, and a scene from a production of *Dialogues des Carmélites*.

B448   Rorem, Ned. "Notes on Parade: Theater Works of Ravel, Poulenc, Satie," *Opera News* 45 (February 28, 1981):8-18.

This essay is a very personal view of Poulenc as composer and man by a fellow composer who knew Poulenc personally, has a vast knowledge of twentieth-century music, and does not mind expressing his opinions. The essay was inspired by a Metropolitan Opera triple-bill performance of stage works by the three composers named in the title of the article. Poulenc's *Les Mamelles de Tirésias* was one of the three: "It's the one real opera on the Met's triple bill, and eminently stageworthy . . . Though Poulenc never penned an original note, every note became pure Poulenc through some witty alchemy. I learned too that Poulenc's so-called profane and sacred styles are really the same. . . . Poulenc composed duds and hits in equal measure. The utter duds are among his piano solos. Because he was a glib, natural keyboard technician, he was inclined to pass off as finished compositions what in fact were passing improvisations. . . . Poulenc the man, finally, like his music, was a sum of his obvious parts: dapper and ungainly, wicked and pious, a slipshod perfectionist. As a performer he led a very public life; as a citizen, as a denizen of both salon and bistro, he was outspoken about his private life. But his private life was not, unlike Cocteau's, his public life." The essay also includes much information about the influences and relationships between Satie, Ravel, and Poulenc. See: W2.

B449   ___. *The Paris Diary of Ned Rorem*. With a Portrait of the Diarist by Robert Phelps. New York: George Braziller, 1966.

Rorem's diary of the years he passed in Paris includes important information about Poulenc, whom Rorem knew socially and professional-ly. His observations about the man are revealing. Rorem wrote (page 129) that he "spent the afternoon . . . at Poulenc's in that sunny high apartment on the Luxembourg, with chairs of orange plush and squeaking floors." Rorem described (page 109) a "cool and languid lobster lunch" at Marie Laure's [Vicomtesse de Noailles] with Poulenc, "who is witty and bright and religious and knows it." Rorem wrote about his own reactions to the compositions of Poulenc but recorded those of the composer as well: Page 141, "Poulenc's music is adroit, clean and powdered, dépouillée [reduced to essentials] yet expressive, economic and religious, careful, witty uninhibited and schmaltzy;" Page 227 (quoting Poulenc), "La pire chose, c'est de vouloir être à la mode si cette mode ne vous va pas." ["The worst thing is to want to be fashionable if this mode does not suit you."]

B450   ___. "Poulenc and Bernac--French Song, With Pleasure the Aim," *High Fidelity/Musical America* 17 (November 1967):85-86.

Reviews of recordings of songs composed by Poulenc and others and recorded by Poulenc and Bernac. Pathé FALP 50036 includes works by Gounod, Duparc, Chabrier, Chausson, Fauré, Roussel, Ravel, Milhaud, Auric, and Poulenc's *Montparnasse* and *Dans le jardin d'Anna*. All are reissues of recordings made in the early years of their affiliation. Rorem concluded that the "approach to this non-Poulenc repertory shines with both responsibility and love . . . Bernac's voice was never to sound fresher and Poulenc's pianism was exemplary, if occasionally too toned down." See: D204; D365.

The two discs of Odyssey 32 26 0009 contain Poulenc's songs *Banalités, Chansons villageoises, Quatre poèmes* (Apollinaire), *Tu vois le feu du soir, Main dominée par le coeur,* and *Calligrammes,* with works by Ravel, Chabrier, Debussy, and Satie. "The performance represents the peak of the team's expressive powers in 1950 during the American successes." See: D44; D84; D116; D320; D359; D425.

B451   Rorem, Ned. *Setting the Tone: Essays and a Diary.* New York: Coward--McCann, 1983.

There is much valuable information about Poulenc in this volume, although most of the essays were published previously. Sources of the originals are listed in the front of the book. Rorem commented about Poulenc, the man and his music; quoted Poulenc concerning his own compositions and those of others; gave an analysis of Poulenc's compositional style; and discussed his relationships to others, especially to Cocteau, Esty, Honegger, Ravel, Satie, and Stravinsky.

B452   ___. *Settling the Score: Essays on Music.* New York: Harcourt Brace Jovanovich, 1988.

In the Preface to this anthology of essays previously published elsewhere, Rorem pointed out that none of the material published in this volume duplicates any material still in print. The five essays about Poulenc are "Francis Poulenc: A Souvenir" (see B446); "Afterthoughts on Francis" (see B444); "Poulenc's *Dialogues*" (see B447); "Bernac and Poulenc" (see B445); and "Poulenc's Chamber Music" originally published in 1984 as liner notes for a recording on Erato STU 71539.

B453   Rostand, Claude. "Festival de Strasbourg: De Lalande à Poulenc," *Carrefour* (June 26, 1957):7.

Review of the world premiere of the *Sonata for Flute and Piano* at the nineteenth international Festival of Strasbourg. "The new work by Francis Poulenc sounded like the young Poulenc. It rediscovers the gracious, elegant but always incisive Les Biches. The legendary melodic invention of the composer is given free rein in the poetic climax with this inventive originality which belonged only to the person of Francis Poulenc. . . . The composer at the piano, Jean-Pierre Rampal on flute, we were given an exemplary performance." See: W116.

B454   Rostand, Claude. "France: Two from Les Six," *Musical America* 84 (March 1964):19.

Essay about *Sept Répons des Ténèbres*, commissioned by the New York Philharmonic for the opening of Lincoln Center. "Poulenc has treated the texts with great simplicity, returning to the style of his early church music. Nevertheless, he retains an expressive intensity which underscores the instrumental and choral material." See: W52.

B455   ___. "La Musique: Poulenc, musicien des coeurs attentifs," *Carrefour* (May 5, 1945):5.

Review of the first Paris concert devoted entirely to the music of Poulenc. The program included new works on poems of Apollinaire and Aragon, *Litanies à la vierge noire*, and *Motets pour un temps de pénitence*. "This evening confirms for those who were still in doubt that his place is well assured in the first rank of great modern French composers."

B456   ___. "Poulenc's La Voix Humaine Acclaimed in Paris Premiere," *Musical America* 79 (March 1959):5.

Review. The world premiere of the opera "was a brilliant success with the critics and the public." The staging by Cocteau was "a masterpiece of tact, nuance, and profound psychological truth. . . . Duval deserves highest praise for her singing." Rostand provided a history of Cocteau's drama and relates that the same subject had already attracted other composers, including Hans Werner Hans, but that Poulenc's opera was the first to be produced. See: W4.

B457   ___. "Premiere mondiale à la Scala de Milan 'Dialogues des Carmélites' de Georges Bernanos et Francis Poulenc," *Carrefour* (February 6, 1957):10.

Review of the world premiere of the opera praised by Rostand for the exceptional quality of the production. Much of the review is devoted to analysis of the plot. "It [the text] is comprised of only two truly spectacular episodes--the death of the first Prioress and the scene at the scaffold. The rest is only inner action, elusive movements of feelings.

All written in a language set in stone, refusing all metric concession, all anecdotal suggestions, all easy attraction. In brief, at first hearing, this dramatic text is in defiance to the opera." A photograph of Poulenc and Georges Wakhevitch, the production's designer, is included. See: W1.

B458   Roussel, Albert. "Young French Composers," *Chesterian* 2 (October 1919):33-37.

An article about the youngest generation of composers just then making reputations for themselves in Paris. "M. Francis Poulenc . . . [who] is only nineteen and who owes nearly everything to his very remarkable natural gifts, has a predilection for the classical sonata form, but his sonata is a different kind of developed composition from that usually found under this head. The sonatas for violin and piano, for piano duet and for two clarinets . . . are very short pieces of a charming musicality which often makes one regret their brevity. . . . Apart from a *Rapsodie nègre* for voice and chamber orchestra and three *Mouvements perpétuels* for piano, deliciously young and fresh, M. Poulenc has written a ballet entitled *Jongleur*, which one hopes to see staged soon."

B459   Roy, Jean. *Francis Poulenc*. Paris: Éditions Seghers, 1964.

A biography, in French, based on *Entretiens avec Claude Rostand* and other works with extensive quotes from the Rostand conversations and from books and articles about Poulenc by many who knew him, including Cocteau and Bernac as well as critics such as Fred Goldbeck. A chronological list of works, a discography, photographs, and facsimiles of manuscripts are included.

B460   ___. *Présences contemporaines musique française*. Paris: Nouvelles Éditions Debresse, 1962.

A book of essays on several twentieth-century French composers, including Poulenc. Remarks about musical style are general; most of the information is easily obtainable elsewhere. There are lists of works about Poulenc, an incomplete bibliography of writings by Poulenc, a list of pieces by Poulenc with dates of composition and publisher, a discography, and a chronology of the composers life.

B461   Roy, Klaus George. "Six Indivisible, Who Helped Make Modernism Respectable," *High Fidelity* 4 (December 1954):76.

A review of the Angel ANG3515B recording of the music of Les Six, in which the author evaluated the position of the "Group" in music history.

Roy narrated again the forming, naming, and association of Les Six and concluded, "'Modernism' has become more stable with their help; maturity which is not static has been attained, the promise largely fulfilled." Poulenc's *Sécheresses*, included on this recording, is described as "powerful stuff by one of the great eclectics of our time. . . . macabre wit (no clowning here), intense lyrical impulse, a sure hand for choral and instrumental sound infuse this work." A photograph of Les Six with Jean Cocteau was included. See: D440.

B462   S. "Concerto," *New Records* 16/7 (September 1948):4-5.

Review of the RCA Victor Set DM-1235 recording of *Concerto in D minor for Two Pianos*. "Whittemore and Lowe find this work congenial material and do a splendid job with it. Their performance is enthusiastic and entirely convincing. Mitropoulos companions them perfectly; he obviously feels the music, too, and is not just tagging along. The rapport between all three is quite remarkable." See: D161.

B463   S. "Le Groupe des Six," New Records 23/1 (March 1955):2-3.

Review of Angel 3515B, a recording of the November 1953 gala concert in honor of Les Six. The program included *Sécheresses*. "Angel has supplied a deluxe package, with an eight page booklet . . . that is full of fascinating information and pictures, although the program notes are on the sketchy side, with texts (of sung music) missing. . . . Performances, under Georges Tzipine, are uniformly excellent, as is the reproduction." See: D440.

B464   Sabin, Robert. "Poulenc: 'The Essence is Simplicity'," *Musical America* 69 (November 1949):27.

In this interview Poulenc discussed his understanding of French art and his own work: "the essence of French art is simplicity." He also evaluated the compositions of other composers, including Sauguet, Jolivet, Messiaen, Martinet, and Milhaud. There is a copy of a photograph of Poulenc with Wanda Landowska and extensive quotes from a letter from the composer to Landowska about their work together on his *Concert champêtre* in 1928.

B465   ___. "Poulenc Gloria in New York Premiere," *Musical America* 81 (May 1961):44.

Review of the New York premiere of *Gloria* performed at Carnegie Hall by the Boston Symphony Orchestra, Charles Münch, conductor, on April

8, 1961. An "enchanting piece of music. Never have his melodic spontaneity, marvelous color sense, economy of style and wit been more felicitously combined." See: W41.

B466   Sabin, Robert. "Poulenc Honorary Concert Museum of Modern Art, December 11," *Musical America* 69 (January 1, 1949):10.

Review of a concert sponsored by the League of Composers honoring Poulenc with performances of his works and a reception. Poulenc participated in the program with Bernac and others in performances of *Le Bestiaire; Banalités; Trio for Oboe, Bassoon, and Piano*; and a group of songs. The reviewer also mentioned that *Le Bal masqué* was performed at the festival of contemporary French music at the Julliard school on December 1, 1948, by Warren Galjour, Poulenc, and Bernac. See: W55; W60; W61; W122.

B467   ___. "Poulenc Performs New Piano Concerto," *Musical   America* 70 (January 1950):59.

Review of the New York premiere of the Piano Concerto at Carnegie Hall on January 14, 1950, with Poulenc, pianist, and the Boston Symphony conducted by Charles Münch. The concerto is "a work of considerable length, and rich, sometimes massive, sonority, but it is essentially blithe in spirit . . . It is a witty and beautiful musical discourse, enhanced by piquant orchestration. . . . Poulenc played his concerto with delightful nonchalance and refinement of accent." See: W31.

B468   ___. "Recitals," *Musical America* 72 (February 1952): 224.

Review of the February 10, 1952, Town Hall recital by Pierre Bernac and Poulenc characterized as "a feast for musical epicures . . . They have the added advantage of being able to give definitive interpretations of Poulenc's songs."

B469   ___. "Records," *Musical America* 70 (August 1950):31.

Review of the Esoteric 2000 recording of *Le Bal masqué*, a piece filled with "copious melody, witty harmony, fascinating instrumental color and bumptious humor . . . The recording is an engineering triumph." See: D35.

B470   ___. "Unashamed Beauty," *Musical America* 81 (August 1961):47-48.

Review of the Angel S35953 recording of *Gloria* and the organ concerto. "There is nothing to quarrel with in this performance. But one misses the exquisite voice and ease of Adele Addison in the solo and the finesse of the Boston Symphony. . . . Actually, the recording of the *Organ Concerto in G minor* is the more completely satisfying of the two. . . . Duruflé plays the solo part with baroque sumptuousness." See: D164; D275.

B471   Sabin, Robert. "Witty Winds," *Musical America* 74 (November 1954): 16.

Review of the Capital P8258 recording. "The *Sextette* represents Poulenc at his second-best, but it is irresistible for all its banality of material." See: D445.

B472   Salter, Lionel. "French Ballet Music of the 1920s," *Gramophone* 62 (April 1985):1233.

Review of the Chandos ABRD1119 recording of *L'Éventail de Jeanne* and *Les Marié de le Tour Eiffel*. "All this music, Gallic in its unsentimental clarity, demands the cleanest and crispest playing, and this the Philharmonia Orchestra admirably supplies. The fidelity of the sound quality, brilliantly vivid in the Eiffel Tower ballet, is even heightened on CD." See: D248; D328.

B473   ___. "O Sacrum Convivium," *Gramophone* 48 (February 1971):1338.

Review of the recording by the choir of St. John's College, Cambridge, of *Litanies à la Vierge Noire* on Argo AZG662. "It is the musical content which first attracts notice . . . But in fact what quickly absorbs a great deal of one's attention and calls forth unqualified admiration is the performance. I have frankly not heard a better choir . . . they phrase with unfailing flexibility and musicality, and their intonation and enunciation alike are impeccable." See: D313.

B474   ___. "Opera," *Gramophone* 62 (June 1984):67.

Review of the Andante AD72405 recording of *La Voix humaine*. "Carole Farley makes a brave attempt, but her French is unconvincing (vowels and stresses often not quite right, liaisons not made, syllables often slurred over), her tonal nuances are much less varied, and she consistently projects her voice . . . too much for what should be an intimate *tête à tête*." See: D650.

B475   Salter, Lionel. "Poulenc," *Gramophone* 41 (April 1964):470.

Review of the HMV ALP2034 recording of *Stabat Mater* and *Quatre motets pour un temps de pénitence*. "The *Stabat Mater* is a typically light-textured and luminous Poulenc score, with a mixture of simple directness and, post-Massenet sugariness, so intent on avoiding portentousness that it comes in places perilously near the casual. . . . The performance is a tolerably good one, though the chorus needs greater precision in *Concta Mater* and shows some signs of unease when left a cappella . . . The joy of the performance is Crespin, who despite one or two scoops delights with her beautifully floated tone." See: D411; D561.

B476   ___. "Poulenc," *Gramophone* 57 (July 1979):209.

Review of the Argo ZRG878 recording of the organ concerto and *Concert champêtre*. Comparing the performance of the organ concerto by Preston on Angel 3744I and that by Malcolm on Argo, the Preston recording "has the more impressive and incisive declamation and the greater sense of forward drive and cohesion." Malcolm's performance of the *Concert champêtre*, "for all that the orchestral tone is very clean and light, makes the harpsichord sound even more puny." See: D141; D165; D166.

B477   ___. "Poulenc," *Gramophone* 63 (August 1985):163.

Review of the Harmonia Mundi HMC5149 recording of *Stabat Mater, Salve Regina*, and *Litanies à le vierge noire*. Compared with the 21-year old performance of *Stabat Mater* by Prêtre, the reviewer said of this performance, "Now that the work is available with a chorus of more polished technique and far more reliable chording, one which uses its words expressively and whose dynamic range is well served by the engineers, it makes an infinitely more telling effect. . . . Apart from an insufficiently soft final line from the chorus, this [Litanies] too is well sung and played. The mellifluous unaccompanied and largely homophonic *Salve Regina*, though emotionally charged, sounds less assured." See: D314; D435; D561; D562.

B478   ___. "Poulenc," *Gramophone* 63 (February 1986):1032.

Review of the Erato NUM75203 recording of *Concerto in D minor for Two Pianos and Orchestra, Piano Concerto*, and *Aubade*. "As in some earlier Duchable recordings, the piano is placed much too forward, in a different aural perspective from the orchestra--which, except in the last two movements of the piano concerto, seems to be banished to the background. The result is that in the *Aubade* piano figures or chords are far louder than melodic lines they are meant to accompany . . . even the first orchestral statement of the initial theme of the single-piano concerto is buried under the soloist's passage-work. A disappointment." See: D22; D149; D157.

B479   Salter, Lionel. "Poulenc: Chamber Music," *Gramophone* 58 (February 1981):1098.

Review of the latest recordings of the complete chamber works on EMI 2C12519-22, a continuation of a two-record set begun in 1976, now expanded to four discs. "The standard of performance throughout is of the highest . . . It should be added that the well-written presentation booklet (in French only) contains many unfamiliar photos of Poulenc and his friends." See: D90; D226; D230; D237; D451; D465; D468; D481; D496; D512; D519; D528; D530; D539; D551; D603.

B480   ___. "Poulenc: Chamber and Vocal Works," *Gramophone* 64 (October 1986):608.

Review of the CRD 3437 recording. "A hugely enjoyable disc, its appeal heightened by superlatively clean and lifelike recording. . . . The delicacy and crisp staccato it brings to the first movement, and the buoyant bounce to the finale, of the 1926 Trio . . . are delightful. . . . Both in this and the Sextet (and indeed in *Le bal masqué* too) the piano--Poulenc's own instrument, of course--is allotted the lion's share, and Ian Brown deserves great credit for giving his part the requisite sparkle without submerging his excellent partners. . . . The earlier Stravinsky of *The soldier's tale* is evoked in one of the purely instrumental movements of *Le bal masqué* . . . Once again the Nash Ensemble capture its *gamin* frolics with delicious lightness, and Thomas Allen, admirably clear in his enunciation and faithful to the composer's every dynamic nuance, invests Max Jacob's surrealist poems with character . . . *Le bestiaire* [is] here performed in the original version for seven instruments . . . This is the one disappointment of this disc." See: D33; D56; D450; D602.

B481   ___. "Poulenc: Concerto in D minor for 2 Pianos; Concert champêtre," *Gramophone* 40 (April 1963):468.

Review of the HMV ALP1967 recording. "The new issue, despite a more modern recording, strikes me as slightly less engaging on several counts . . . One forgives a good deal of rather casual playing because of the infectious high spirits of the composer and his partner." See: D138; D151.

B482   Salter, Lionel. "Poulenc: Mélodies," *Gramophone* 63 (October 1985):534.

Review of recordings of songs on Hyperion A66147 and The Friends of Pierre Bernac PB1/3. "A comparison of the songs common to both releases is . . . of particular interest. Bernac, whose impeccable clarity of enunciation has become legendary and who was unrivalled in verbal nuance and coloration, might well have been proud of these disciples of his. Felicity Lott knows how to spin a fine line . . . and has a beauty of vocal quality that enables her to outdo her mentor.

To return to the Bernac records, what is particularly striking is the evidence of his ability to extend his compass and to switch from one style to another . . . The voice as such was not a God-given glory, . . . but he used it with consummate artistry and taste, bringing everything he touched to vivid life, employing a surprising diversity of timbres." See: D5; D49; D78; D88; D123; D208; D299; D344; D358; D363; D396; D403; D583; D639; D656.

B483   ___. "Poulenc: Orchestral Works," *Gramophone* 59 (September 1981): 388.

Review of the HMV ASD4067 recording. The reviewer stated about *Les Biches*, "the vocal items in the ballet are very rarely heard and have not been recorded before. . . . The exceptionally vivid recording here matches the ebullience of the performance, which the Philharmonia sounds as if it were thoroughly enjoying . . . and the Ambrosians are lusty in their apparently inconsequential but subtly barbed folk-song-based choruses." See: D66; D80; D247; D329.

B484   ___. "Poulenc: Vocal Works," *Gramophone* 64 (March 1987):1314.

Review of the EMI EL270296-1 recording of songs, an "excellent selection, covering more than 30 years of his output . . . Mady Mesplé's light, bright voice may be somewhat limited in variety of timbre, but her subtlety of shading, exemplary enunciation and responsiveness to verbal nuances, flexibility and purity of intonation are outstanding." The accompanist, Gabriel Tacchino, is "an idiomatic Poulenc interpreter." See: D3; D9; D94; D120; D178; D180; D211; D258; D342; D402; D636.

B485   ___. "Records from Abroad: International Piano Archives," *Gramophone* 54 (March 1977):1453.

Review of Landowska's performance of *Concert champêtre* on IPA. "It is indifferently balanced, with the recording engineer conspicuously experimenting with his levels, and the harpsichord (not at all well in tune) sounds distinctly tinny in places; but it does show how to link the awkwardly disparate tempi of this piece." See: D144.

B486   Salter, Lionel. "Records from America," *Gramophone* 28 (February 1951): 204.

Review of Columbia ML4329, a recording of the organ concerto. "It is something of a surprise to see so urbane a composer as Poulenc toying with this potentially dangerous combination, (organ and orchestra), and even more (recalling some of the embarrassingly trivial stuff he has produced) bringing off a lengthy work of coherence and serious purpose. . . . The performance is a good one, though the ear becomes a little fatigued with the prevailing high level of dynamics in the greater part of the work." See: D167.

B487   Salzman, Eric. "The Many Paradoxes of Monsieur Poulenc," *New York Times* February 28, 1960, II:9.

Essay and report on a conversation with the composer who was on tour in America. "Best known as the witty and iconoclastic member of *Les Six* who revels in banal music-hall tunes, he has nonetheless written one of the most successful operas of recent years, *Les Dialogues des Carmélites* . . . Poulenc is staying in New York until the middle of next month. . . .'If I had to name my favorite work,' he confided, speaking in French, 'I would say *Les Mamelles*. It sums up all my youth and my youthful experience; in spite of its *bouffe* appearance, it is a poetic work. Behind the irony and farce of Apollinaire . . . there is a real poetic melancholy.' This then would be a link that might connect the irreverent, surrealist music with the lyric and religious works. . . . astonishingly enough, he is not only au courant with the European avant-garde, but he admires its music enormously." See: W2.

B488   ___. "Records in Review," *High Fidelity* 13 (June 1963):68-69.

Review of the Poulenc-Février recording of *Concerto for Two Pianos* and *Concert champêtre* with van de Wiele, harpsichord, on Angel S35993. The performance of the Two-Piano Concerto is "amiable, with a kind of delightful, sentimental refinement and elegance--one might almost say casualness and even indifference. . . . The *Concert champêtre* is, like the Two-Piano Concerto, one of a number of concerted pieces that Poulenc wrote in his mixed classical-pops vein. The gestures are those of a great *commedia dell'arte* mime; a compendium of classical motion and mimic comedy." See: D138; D151.

B489   Salzman, Eric. "Recordings in Review," *High Fidelity* 13 (August 1963): 86-87.

Review of the Music Guild S39 recording of *Suite française* performed by the Paris Ensemble conducted by Poulenc. "All of the performances are good and they are well recorded. One should point in particular to the excellent wind playing; it is charming, elegant, and stylish." See: D567.

B490   ___. "Recordings in Review," *High Fidelity* 13 (December 1963):78-80.

Review of the Everest S3081 recording of *Sextuor*. The performance is "successful, expert, and idiomatic. The work is of the vintage of the popular and hilarious Two-Piano Concerto, and both pieces are cut from the same brightly colored cloth." See: D452.

B491   ___. "Records in Review," *High Fidelity* 14 (February 1964):75-76.

Review of the Columbia MS6518 recording of *Sextuor*, with Poulenc, piano, and the Philadelphia Wind Quintet; three songs performed by Jennie Tourel and Leonard Bernstein; and *Sonata for Two Pianos* with Gold and Fizdale. The high point of the disc is the Two-Piano Sonata, "a work that might possibly turn out to be the composer's most important instrumental composition. This is serious, even weighty music, which betrays a good deal more thoughtfulness than one sometimes credits Poulenc with having possessed." See: D48; D210; D447; D548.

B492   Sams, Jeremy. "Poulenc's *Carmelites*: the Background," Opera 34 (April 1983):375-79.

This essay traced the history of the story from its beginnings on July 17, 1794, when sixteen Carmelite nuns from Compiègne were tried, convicted, and sent to the guillotine, through Poulenc's setting of the tale as an opera. The author does more than state the facts of the story and how those facts were treated through several different accounts, including a biography, a novel, a screen-play, and the opera. He discussed also the significance of each of those different treatments and how Poulenc set the text to music. See: W1.

B493   Sandow, Gregory. "Song Albums: Strings of Pearls," *Saturday Review* 9 (March 1983):55-56.

Review of the EMI 2C 165-16231/5 recording of Poulenc songs by various artists and Dalton Baldwin, pianist. These five disks are intended as a complete recording of all the songs. [But see B533 for omissions.] "Poulenc's development . . . is disappointing. . . . It's a bad omen, though, that his best known and in some ways most inventive songs are his first, the Bestiaire cycle, which he wrote when he was 20. When he settles into his maturity somewhere on the third side of this collection, his songs start sounding too much alike." See: D2; D8; D42; D57; D77; D83; D93; D98; D107; D115; D128; D131; D135; D136; D177; D181; D188; D200; D206; D220; D244; D255; D257; D269; D283; D295; D300; D318; D324; D330; D341; D353; D378; D381; D385; D387; D395; D401; D424; D432; D580; D590; D594; D610; D635; D638.

B494   Sargeant, Winthrop. "Musical Events," *New Yorker* 33 (14 December 1957):213-17.

Review of the televised production of *Dialogues des Carmélites* presented by the NBC Opera Company. Poulenc "has, to my mind, succeeded in creating the strongest French opera to appear in a generation . . . Poulenc's score . . . is poetic, evocative, emotional, and even *romantic* . . . Because of the intimacy of its setting, Dialogues . . . lends itself admirably to the television screen." See: W1.

B495   ___. "Musical Events," *New Yorker* 36 (5 March, 1960):166-67.

Review of the American Opera Society presentation of *La Voix humaine* and *Les Mamelles de Tirésias*. Concerning Poulenc's score for the former, Sargeant wrote, "M. Poulenc's music was deftly put together and pleasant enough to listen to, but it never became anything more than a mildly evocative background for the words." He liked Les Mamelles better: "On second hearing, it still seemed to me a delightful and sophisticated spoof, full of antic incongruities, with music that, though satirical in intention, is actually quite expressive." See: W2; W4.

B496   ___. "Musical Events," *New Yorker* 37 (October 28, 1961):161-64.

A performance of Poulenc's *Concerto for Two Pianos* by the New York Philharmonic, conducted by Leonard Bernstein, was the occasion for Sargeant to re-affirm his belief that "Poulenc is by far the finest French composer of his era. . . . His pre-eminence lies in what, for want of a better term, I must describe as his unfailing musicality." He stated that the concerto "is not a pretentious work. It plays delightfully and affectionately with the grand traditions of keyboard music."See: W29.

B497   ___. "Musical Events," *New Yorker* 39 (April 20, 1963):107-10.

Review of an all-Poulenc concert given by the Composers' Showcase, conducted by Thomas Schippers, as a memorial to the composer. "I venture to place Poulenc in what I consider his proper niche--that of a true genius and certainly one of the greatest of all twentieth-century composers. The conservatism of his style was simply a matter of preference." In assessing Poulenc's reputation as a member of the avant-garde, Sargeant stated, "It is surprising, in retrospect, that it could ever have been applied to him."

B498   Sartori, Claudio. "Italy," *Opera* 8 (March 1957):170-71.

Review of the world premiere of *Dialogues des Carmélites* at La Scala, January 26, 1957. "It was a considerable disappointment. . . . The musician's sincerity--which is affirmed by his religious conversion--is not sufficient to give life to a score which is pervaded by monotony. The text, in fact, is too rich in its own sense of theatre and literary vitality to be fulfilled by this rather indifferent musical portrayal. This work will probably be staged by many other opera houses, but it is doubtful whether it will outlive its initial attraction." See: W1.

B499   Schaeffner, André. "Le Concert champêtre pour clavecin et orchestre de Francis Poulenc," *La Revue musicale* 9 (May-June 1929):75-77.

Review of the premiere performance, May 31, 1929. "The *Concert champêtre* is the first work where the renowned music of pleasure has found in our time a continuity of expression, a breadth of form, an architectural complexity worthy of making it the rank of other music. It is thanks to Poulenc, because of his recent progress (*Poèmes de Ronsard, Trio, Chansons gaillardes*) that this work was created. It is also thanks to Wanda Landowska, great interpreter of the music of the 17th and 18th centuries, that this modern concerto for an instrument which, because of her had ceased to be ancient, was played. While listening to her interpret the work of Poulenc, it had never appeared more true to me that she has made Mozart and Bach our contemporaries." See: W28.

B500   ___. "Francis Poulenc: Musicien français," *Contrepoints*, no. 1 (January 1946):50-58.

Essay on Poulenc's musical and stylistic development. Schaeffner proposes that if he were to write a history of French music between the two wars, that two chapters would be devoted to Poulenc--the first and the last. "In my opinion, of all musicians, there is no one who, at one and the same time as interpreter and as creator, can, as well as Poulenc, pretend to have safeguarded the purity of the [French] tradition."

B501   Schaeffner, André. "Stravinsky's *Capriccio*," *Modern Music* 7 (December-January 1929-30):31-34.

Review of performances of new music in Paris, including a concert of music by members of Les Six. "The jubilee of the Six emphasized both their non-existence as a group and the incredible manner with which they lend themselves to poor performances and pseudo-technics imposed by ideologists. A festival of this kind should have been organized with more care and critical sense. It was apparently easy for Poulenc, represented by his new *Aubade* for eighteen instruments and his *Trio*, to rise above his comrades; less expert than Honegger, he nevertheless has youth, a naive sense of play, of melodic rhythmic expression and a spontaneous harmonic grace." See: W6; W122.

B502   ___. "Stravinsky's Two Piano Concerto and Other Parisian Novelties," *Modern Music* 13 (May-June 1936):33-39.

Among the other Parisian novelties mentioned in this article are two works by Poulenc, who as "composer of the *Concert Champêtre* for harpsichord with orchestra--a milestone in his career--has remained faithful to this instrument. He has just used it anew in two pieces of stage music, one for a play by Bourdet, *Margot*, with scenes laid in the sixteenth century, and the other for an animated cartoon in colors, a fairy tale to advertise Vins Nicolas. In both cases he has managed to achieve a sonority, now sad now gay, which is characteristic of the harpsichord and also of Poulenc." See: W18.

B503   Schloezer, B. de. "Francis Poulenc: Chansons gaillardes," *La Revue musicale* 8 (February 1927):169.

The reviewer ranked these songs as "the masterpiece of his vocal music. For the force and originality of the musical thought, for the richness of expression, these short character pieces, surpass by far the *Poèmes de Ronsard* by the same author." See: W66; W95.

B504   Schonberg, Harold C. "From Jester to Master," *New York Times* March 13, 1966, II:17.

A review of the New York City Opera's new production of *Dialogues des Carmélites* was the occasion for an essay on Poulenc's growth from "an enfant terrible" into "a skilled composer. . . . He was one of those modern composers . . . who could remain unmistakably modern without losing contact with the past." In conclusion, there is a comparison of the musical style of Poulenc with those of the other members of the French Six. See: W1.

B505   Schonberg, Harold C.   "Modern French: Concerto by Poulenc Is Typically Irreverent," *New York Times* January 25, 1953, X:10.

Review of the Period 563 recording of the Piano Concerto and three pieces for piano, *Improvisation, Humoresque,* and *Valse,* performed by Annette Haas-Hamburger. "One of Poulenc's typically irreverent pieces is his Piano Concerto, which pokes fun at a good many sacred musical cows. It is, indeed, a type of smart-aleckism that some serious-minded listeners deplore." See: D150; D303; D298; D645.

B506   ___. "Music: A Tribute to Francis Poulenc," *New York Times* April 11, 1963, p. 29.

Review of a recital presented by the Composers' Showcase in Carnegie Hall on April 10, 1963, as a tribute to the composer. "Poulenc was not a 'big' composer, for his emotional range was too restricted. But what he did, he did perfectly, and his music shows remarkable finish, style and refinement. . . . Poulenc ended where he began--broader and more secure, to be sure, and a thorough technician." A photograph of the composer and a program of the concert are included. See: W30; W52.

B507   ___. "Music: Philharmonic Honors Poulenc: Organ Work Played by Conductor Schippers," *New York Times* April 12, 1963, p. 31.

Review of a memorial concert in Carnegie Hall given on April 10, 1963, by the New York Philharmonic. The program included the organ concerto, performed by Schippers, and the world premiere of *Sept répons des Ténèbres,* commissioned by the Philharmonic in celebration of its opening season in Lincoln Center. Comparing *Gloria* with this new work, the reviewer found that "in the *Ténèbre* there is greater depth, passion and mystery." See: W30; W52.

B508   ___. "Opera: *Carmelites* Makes it to the Met," *New York Times* February 6, 1977, p. 49.

Review of a production of the opera in English at the Metropolitan Opera. "It is a beautiful, sensitive, moving work, patterned to a large degree after Debussy's *Pelleas et Melisande.* There are many scene changes, and the fast-moving music does not admit arias in the Verdian sense. Poulenc, used the kind of declamation that Debussy carried off so brilliantly in his one opera. Recurrent snatches of melody, acting almost as leit-motifs, cement the opera. . . . This is a stark, austere, low-priced production. It works, however." A photograph of Shirley Verrett in her role as Madame Lidoine and a list of members of the cast is included. See: W1.

B509   Schonberg, Harold C. "Records: On Stage," *New York Times* March 13, 1955, X:11.

Review of the first recorded performance of *Les Soirées de Nazelles* played by John Ranck on Zodiac 1002. "Poulenc has composed a work consisting of a preamble, eight variations and a finale. It is a graceful salon score, melodious, full of Poulenc's familiar mannerisms, even to thematic suggestions from other works. . . . Ranck plays this collection with skill." See: D464.

B510   ___. "Records: An Opera That Uses Only One Singer," *New York Times* April 24, 1960, X:13.

Review of the RCA Victor LSS2385 recording of *La Voix humaine* performed by Denise Duval. In this opera "we have a play with music. The music, true, does underline the mood, and the opera is cannily constructed, with thematic threads running through the entire structure and holding it together. . . . La Voix humaine has the drama; but does it have the song? Poulenc, who can spin a melody with the best of them, takes sparing advantage of his gift. . . . The performance on this disk is flawless." See: D652.

B511   ___. "Records: Quartets," *New York Times* July 11, 1954, X:6.

Review of the Capital P8258 recording of *Sextuor*. "The music has nothing to say that Poulenc has not said before; all his favorite cliches are present, and all of his struggles with *sonata form*. But while the music may be schmalz, it is positively transcendental schmalz." See: D445.

B512   ___. "Records: Two-Piano: Gold and Fizdale Play Contemporary Music in Comprehensive Survey," *New York Times* May 2, 1954, X:9.

Review of the Columbia ML4854 recording, including the Sonata (four hands). "Poulenc, in his sonata, is grinding the same old tune. . . . Gold and Fizdale play beautifully and have been given wonderful recording. Seldom has two-piano sound and balance been more successfully solved on records." See: D536.

B513   ___. "Saint-Saëns Septet," *New York Times* December 16, 1951, X:10.

Review of a recording of *Sonata for Horn, Trumpet and Trombone* on Stradivari 605. "Poulenc draws upon French music hall material, the circus, jazz--everything that would be a shock to those brought up in the classical or romantic tradition.   The performance here is excellent--properly rowdy, yet with the basic order inherent in the music."   See: D516.

B514   Schonberg, Harold C.   "'Les Six' Once More: Famous French Group Reunited in Album," *New York Times* January 23, 1955, X:11.

Review of a recording devoted to the music of the members of the French Six, including Poulenc's *Sécheresses*. "They were smart-alecky, outrageous, chip-on-shoulder-ish. They were Dada, when it suited them; and they all revered papa Satie. In their day they made a big commotion; and today some of them are ranking composers. . . . Poulenc writes best in small forms and turns out very possibly the finest songs written today. Especially interesting are Poulenc's imaginative *Sécheresses*." See: D440.

B515   ___. "The Smart-Aleck Composer of a Religious Opera," *New York Times* January 30, 1977, II:19.

Essay treating *Dialogues des Carmélites* preceding a Metropolitan Opera production in an English translation by Joseph Machlis. Schonberg quotes Poulenc's statements to Machlis about translation: "Opera should be sung in the language of the country in which it was being staged. . . . the dialogues must be understood or the meaning of the opera is lost. . . . the melody must be connected with the word. . . . the translation should not be by rhythm but by word. The key word of any particular sentence has to float on the top of the phrase. That means the audience will get the drift of the action no matter how bad the diction of the singers." See: W1.

B516   ___. "The Wheel Spins, Poulenc Wins," *New York Times* October 31, 1971, II:15.

Essay on Poulenc's success as one of the most steadily performed composers of the twentieth century. "His music may be considered lightweight, and certainly nobody in the avant-garde pays much attention to it." In comparing the music of Honegger, Milhaud, and Poulenc, Schonberg believes that "while the wheel [of fortune] was spinning, nobody would have placed many bets on Poulenc's number. . . . Poulenc matured as he grew older. He never lost his sophisticated outlook and he never tried to go outside his particular view of life, but his later music has a depth and compassion never encountered in his earlier works. . . . Francis Poulenc could end up as the most important minor master of the century. And his music probably will continue to give more pleasure than the music of many of his contemporaries who are considered major."

B517   Selfridge, Cecil Blanchard. "French Song Since Ravel," *NATS Bulletin* 12 (September 1955):17-18.

The majority of this article is devoted to the songs of Poulenc, because he is the "most prolific of those who have achieved fame outside of their own land." The author discussed musical character and style in the songs and vocal problems encountered in performing them.

B518   Shattuck, Roger. "Surrealism at the Opéra-Comique," *Theatre Arts* 32 (January 1948):51-52.

Review of Opéra-Comique production of *Les Mamelles de Tirésias*. "The cast is young and good-looking and Denise Duval sings the part of Thérèse brilliantly if somewhat coldly." Examined in light of the question "is it opera? The answer is yes, but it has severe faults of unevenness. . . . Opera is song, it is theatre, and it is dance. *Les Mamelles* is weakest as theatre; it makes up for much of this weakness by its excellent use of dance movements; and it is strongest as song." See: W2.

B519   Shead, Richard. *Music In the 1920s*. New York: St. Martin's Press, 1977.

In this study of a formative decade in the history of twentieth century music the author discussed compositions by Poulenc composed during that era, as well as many works composed later. The compositions are related to movements and ideas that prevailed in the 1920s, and Poulenc's pieces are compared to those of his contemporaries.

Shead attempted in this work to connect Poulenc's homosexuality to his "musical ambiguity and capriciousness." He chose *Aubade* as an example to prove this novel idea. "The concept that he began as a *gamin* and turned into a religious mystic is a false one. He was both from the beginning." The author stated that Poulenc was in a state of depression at the time of the composition of the piece. Shead interpreted Diana's "erotic restlessness" as a reflection of Poulenc's own state of thought at the time. See: W6.

B520   Shupp, Enos E., Jr. "Chamber Music," *New Records* 37/3 (May 1969):5.

Review of the London CS6583 recording of the Sonata for two pianos. "Eden and Tamir find a most congenial vehicle in the Poulenc sonata, which they play with the utmost subtlety and refinement. If the substance of this work is not great, the craft is, and it results in a pleasant enough piece to hear." See: D554.

B521   Shupp, Enos E., Jr. "Chamber Music," *New Records* 40/10 (December 1972):8.

Review of the Orion ORS7292 recording of the *Sonata for Violin and Piano*. "Kaufman's tone is edgy; his attack, rather slashing. After getting used to the sound, one is aware that Kaufman's familiarity with the Poulenc is complete and born of long association with it, for he premiered it in New York in 1948." See: D533.

B522   ___. "Miscellaneous," *New Records* 44/9 (November 1975):15-16.

Review of the Orion ORS76231 recording with an arrangement for harp of the *Suite française*. "Pearl Chertok is a seasoned artist of long experience . . . [and] plays superbly, including such clean and twang free playing that Orion's very, very close microphones bring us a harp sound that is supercritical, bright and realistic." See: D575.

B523   ___. "Piano Music of Francis Poulenc," *New Records* 37/7 (September 1969):11-12.

Review of the Angel S36602 recording of piano music. "Poulenc was a miniaturist in his piano writing, none of which gets too far beneath the surface of the subject. His *Suite française* lacks well-defined pictorial music and the wit and lightness of Milhaud. The rest of the pieces are facile works, rather light and charming affairs, nice for encores maybe, or to read by." See: D197; D249; D370; D375; D389; D568; D613; D632; D642.

B524   ___. "Poulenc: Concerto in Gm," *New Records* 46/8 (October 1978):4-5.

Review of the Angel 3744I recording. In his review of the organ concerto Shupp expressed his opinion that "this is its best recording so far, incontestably so as far as clear, close reproduction is concerned. Simon Preston is a fine player whose work here is marked by his usual crispness and adroitness. . . . Previn and the London Symphony strings give pinpoint collaboration." He found the harpsichord used for this performance of *Concert champêtre* "too anemic in sound, but the performance bristles with contrast and animation under Previn's direction." See: D140; D615.

B525   Shupp, Enos E., Jr. "Poulenc: The Model Animals," *New Records* 35/7 (September 1967):4.

Review of the Angel 36421 recording. "What Poulenc's ballet sounds like, at least as music without benefit of stage action, is rather ordinary movie music, and definitely second-rate Poulenc. . . . In all, a dismal disc." See: D18.

B526   ___. "Poulenc: Sextuor for Piano and Woodwind Quintet," *New Records* 41/7 (September 1973):9-10.

Review of the Turnabout TV34507 recording. "For program, excellence of performance, and good recorded sound, the Turnabout disc of French music . . . is a blue ribbon winner in the chamber music category. I do not recall a better such disc in a long time, for every single moment is jewel-like. The Dorians are incomparable in this prevailingly light-hearted music; the sound is simply perfect for them." See: D456.

B527   ___. "Poulenc: Sonata for Oboe and Piano," *New Records* 36/4 (June 1968):9.

Review of the Lyrichord LL193 recording. "Well tailored, often brilliant, playing and vivid reproduction characterize the . . . disc of clarinet and oboe music.   Both performers are immaculate technicians on their instruments, evenly balanced between solo instrument and piano." See: D521.

B528   ___. "Poulenc: Stabat Mater," *New Records* 32/1 (March 1964):9.

Review of the Angel 36121 recording of *Stabat Mater*, "a work of enormous power and depth and one that projects the anguish of the text with remarkable realism. . . . This is certainly a major religious work of our time. Prêtre is aware of every dramatic effect built into the *Stabat Mater* and elicits a superb performance . . . The chorus, *a capella*, is a marvel of expressiveness in the four motets [*Quatre motets pour un temps de pénitence*]." See: D411; D561.

B529   ___. "The Spanish Guitar," *New Records* 40/10 (December 1972):16.

Review of the Angel S36849 recording of the *Sarabande*. "Oscar Ghiglia has among the most gentle of ways with the guitar, with a subtlety that yields a consistently finer quality of sound than nearly any of the other stellar classical guitarists. . . . Technique he has to match any of them; it is the lyric sound that he consistently gets that is so unusual." See: D437.

B530   Slonimsky, Nicolas. "Concerto," *Disques* 1/12 (1931):515.

Review of the Columbia C LF33-35 recording of *Aubade*. "Born into this unprincipled century, [Poulenc] cares little where he gets his inspiration, and his compositions are rich in reminiscences and direct quotations. . . . Altogether a pleasurable affair." See: D21.

B531   Smith, Patrick J. "New York," *Opera* 30 (April 1979):370-71.

Review of the Metropolitan Opera revival of Dialogues in an English translation by Joseph Machlis. "It is certainly one of John Dexter's strongest efforts with the company, and benefits from ideal casting in several of the roles," among them Betsy Norden, Régine Crespin, Leona Mitchell, Maria Ewing, and Mignon Dunn. "Dexter's production is notable for its unity and force, but this time I was more disturbed by the conscious departures from the score: notable in the playing of the opera with the curtain up so that action continues during the orchestral interludes." See: W1.

B532   ___. "Our Critics Abroad: America," *Opera* 28 (August 1977):747-49.

Review of New York's City Opera production of Mozart's *Der Schauspieldirektor*, Stravinsky's *L'Histoire du soldat*, and Poulenc's *La Voix humaine* on a triple bill. While Poulenc's opera was too intimate for the State Theatre, "the strength of Maralin Niska's performance (the role lies well for her voice. . .), the fluidity of Corsaro's production, and the Art Deco set by Lloyd Evans mitigated the problems." A photograph of Niska in the role is included. See: W4.

B533   ___. "Schubert's Successor," *High Fidelity/Musical America* 31 (May 1981):51-52.

Review of the EMI 2C 165-16231/5 recording of Poulenc songs by Elly Ameling, Nicolai Gedda, Michel Sénéchal, Gérard Souzay, and William Parker, with Dalton Baldwin, piano. This is intended as a complete recording on five disks, but the reviewer notes the absence of *Les Chemins de l'amour* and songs for chorus or those with orchestral settings. The reviewer analyzed the spirit of the songs and what they mean and discussed performance difficulties for the singer and for the pianist. In listening to these five records, Smith was surprised by "the range, not the limitations of Poulenc's talents. . . . These performances throb with life and zest and bring in strongly the music-hall ambience that hovers in the wings of many Poulenc songs." See: D2; D8; D42; D57; D77; D83; D93; D98; D107; D115; D128; D131; D135; D136; D177; D181; D188; D200; D206; D220; D244; D255; D257; D269; D283; D295; D300; D318; D324; D330; D341; D353; D378; D381; D385; D387; D395; D401; D424; D432; D580; D590; D594; D610; D635; D638.

B534   Smith, Patrick J. "Soirée Française," *New Records* 20/5 (July 1952):14.

Review of the Columbia C-ML4484 recording of songs. "To put it briefly, this is too 'much of a muchness' as Alice once said. There is not enough variety in Poulenc's muse to make fourteen songs interesting . . . It is unfortunate that neither Pierre Bernac nor Francis Poulenc is able to realize the humor inherent in the music." See: D82; D357.

B535   Spence, Keith. "Television," *Musical Times* 115 (January 1974):64.

Review of a BBC-2 program to mark the tenth anniversary of Poulenc's death. Guests included pianist Jacques Février, the singer Pierre Bernac, and Milhaud and Auric. Compositions by Poulenc that were performed include *Concert champêtre; Trio for Oboe, Bassoon, and Piano*; extracts from *Litanies à la vierge noire; Carmelites*; and *Les Biches*. Bernac coached a young singer in *Voyage à Paris*. See: W7; W28; W43; W60; W122.

B536   Stadlen, Peter. "Aix Festival," *Musical Times* 101 (September 1960): 549-50.

Review of a performance of *La Voix humaine* at the music festival at Aix-en-Provence. "Poulenc's music not only manages to sustain it [the drama], he convinces us that it is a singer rather than an actress who will most compellingly portray the lonely woman. . . . Admittedly he sometimes lacks the stature that is required by the big climaxes and his power of invention are not always sufficient to hold our attention throughout those forty minutes of recitation." See: W4.

B537   Steane, John. "French Songs," *Gramophone* 55 (March 1978):1606.

Review of the Philips 9500-356 recording of songs. "There is in this singing a mellow flame but no spark. . . . [Jessye Norman] can sing 'Ah, la charmante chose' in *Voyage à Paris* without a smile, and in *Montparnasse* the manner is so non-committal that the 'bearded angel' arouses no feeling, no curiosity even, and the expression changes very little for *La Grenouillère*, though the lovely voice suggests the idyll so pleasantly that perhaps it hardly matters." See: D52; D124; D286; D366.

B538   Straus, Noel. "2 French Artists Make Bows Here: Francis Poulenc, Composer, Pierre Bernac, Baritone, Heard at Town Hall," *New York Times* November 8, 1948, p. 24.

The program for the first Poulenc-Bernac concert in New York included Poulenc's song cycles *Tel jour, telle nuit* and *Chansons villageoises*. "The two visitors from France, fervently received by a large audience, provided an evening of music-making not often equaled for artistry and perfection of ensemble. . . . Poulenc was not only to be admired as composer at this concert, but also as an unusually talented accompanist. His technical proficiency made it possible for him to take some of his own songs at an exceedingly high rate of speed and yet keep his playing expertly clean and transparent. . . . there was an uncommonly sympathetic merging of every detail of the interpretations on the part of the two artists." See: W67; W101.

B539   Strongin, Theodore. "Poulenc Tribute Given at Museum: Gold-Fizdale, Pianists, and Souzay, Baritone, Perform," *New York Times* January 27, 1964, p. 20.

Review of a performance in New York of the music of Poulenc. The program included the *Élégie* and *Capriccio* for two pianos (both played for the first time in New York), the *Sonata* (two pianos), and a group of songs.   The reviewer stated about the pianists: "Their technical perfection was complete, their nuances were apt, their approach was intelligent.   Everything was easy, airy, sophisticated and extremely well-bred." See: W55B; W151; W153.

B540   Stutzenberger, Linda Pruitt. "Poulenc's Tempo Indications: To Follow or Not To Follow," *American Music Teacher* 31 (January 1982):26.

Evidence is cited for Poulenc's conflicting opinions concerning tempi for his compositions.   Poulenc himself stated, "If pianists would have confidence in my metronomic indications, very carefully determined, many evils would be avoided." But Stutzenberger pointed out occasions on which Poulenc himself changed the tempo from that indicated on the score or critized performances of others as too slow or fast when given at the tempi written. The author concluded that the evidence suggests that "the performer should exercise some degree of freedom" in choosing tempi.

B541   Surchamp, Dom Angelico. "A propos de Poulenc," *Zodiaque,* no. 42 (July 1959):33-41.

Essay on musical style in the works of Poulenc. The author pointed to Poulenc's melodic gift as the stylistic characteristic that dominates the compositions. He also mentioned that Poulenc's use of harmony is "rare and inventive" and no less rich than that of his melodic usage. There is a list of works with dates of composition and a discography with brief reviews of each recording.

B542   Taubman, Howard. "Opera of the Spirit: Poulenc's 'Carmelites' in San Francisco Is a Story of Nuns and Sacred Love," *New York Times* September 29, 1957, II:9.

Review of the American premiere of the opera in English by the San Francisco Opera Company. "For the most part the opera is written in a style of nearly continuous arioso . . . The arioso style, fortified by a sensitive but not overbearing orchestral tissue, works admirably for the most part. For Poulenc is the possessor of a flowing lyric vein, and he has the grace to manipulate it easily and naturally. The composer's determination not to let his lyricism flag leads him into some difficulties . . . The expository scene at the start seems awkward and halting . . . But when he is dealing with emotion, particularly with the spiritual feelings of the nuns, Poulenc is a rare artist." Photographs of the production are included. See: W1.

B543   "Ten Works Are Commissioned By the Philharmonic for 1962-63," *New York Times* January 25, 1962, p. 24.

Announcement that the Philharmonic's board of directors commissioned ten major new works for the opening season in the orchestra's new home in Lincoln Center. Works by Poulenc and Milhaud were among those commissions.

B544   Terpander. "Poulenc's Aubade (1929): Concerto choréographique for Piano and 18 Instruments," *Gramophone* 13 (July 1935):58; (August 1935):100.

Essay on musical style in Poulenc's compositions as represented in this work. "Poulenc stands alone as a representative of a school which is now extinct. His 'forte' is light music. . . . Poulenc's music revives the old traditions of light entertainment for an audience incapable of recognizing them. . . . I commend this *Aubade* to those who delight to have their affections trifled with!

The opening 'toccata' is a noble piece of work, of classical proportions, and the final 'adagio' a successful 'perpetuum mobile'--long drawn-out and making a virtue of monotony--by one who is a master of that form. In between come movements informed with the 'buffa' spirit referred to in the July section of this article." See: W6.

B545   Thoresby, Christina.   "Carmelite Dialogues: New Opera by Poulenc Staged at La Scala," *New York Times* February 10, 1957, II:9.

This review of the world premiere of the opera at La Scala in Milan, Italy, on January 26 includes the history of the libretto for the opera which was originally written as a film script based on a novel by Gertrude von Le Fort. The film script served as the basis for a play produced in Paris. Poulenc used the play as his libretto for the opera. "This is magnificent material for music, and Poulenc has made full use of the possibilities . . . He has written a score of rare lyrical beauty, which is clear, flexible and brilliantly manipulated. It is also frankly tonal and utterly sincere. . . . So far as the Scala production is concerned, there can be nothing but the highest praise for all concerned." See: W1.

B546   ___. "International Festival in Paris: State-Subsidized Series Offers Wide Panorama From Many Countries," *New York Times* July 28, 1957, II:7.

Review of the first Paris performance of the Carmelites. "Enormous trouble was taken to do this production in the French way, with the costumes and movements of the nuns, as well as decors, based on the authentic customs and setting of the Carmel de Compiègne. Unfortunately, this led to a very static production and settings that entailed interminable waits between the many scenes. Denise Duval failed to put across the drama inherent in the role of Soeur Blanche, and Liliane Berton, who sang well as Soeur Constance, was unfortunate in having as a precedent the exquisite performance of Eugenia Ratti at La Scala. . . . It is now reported that Poulenc, who apparently approves the devout and sober realism of the Paris version of his opera, will compose some interludes to fill in the waits entailed by this production." See: W1.

B547   Thornton, H. Frank. "Poulenc: (4) Song Cycles," *New Records* 34/9 (November 1966):11.

Review of the Angel 36370 recording. "The Poulenc disc is superb. The four song cycles, ranging from his Op. 1, Rapsodie Nègre (1917), through Le Bestiaire and Le Bal Masqué to the Chansons Villageoises (composed in 1942), are among Poulenc's freshest and most typical works.   One could hardly overestimate the tremendous vitality and energy of the music, the riot of colorful orchestrations, or the pleasing tones and alert artistry of baritone Jean-Christophe Benoit.   Georges Prêtre, who can be an inexplicably erratic and willful conductor, is in his most convincing element here." See: D31; D54; D113; D431.

B548   Thornton, H. Frank. "Prima Donna," *New Records* 38/8 (October 1970): 11.

Review of the RCA Victor LSC3163 recording. "Price concludes with a sympathetic account of the New Prioress' prayer . . . Her admirable performance should bring this beautiful and intense scene to many listeners who would not otherwise be attracted to it." See: D218.

B549   ___. "Vocal," *New Records* 37/4 (June 1969):13-14.

Review of the Westminster WST17146 recording of songs. "The Poulenc disc gave me unexpected pleasure. Her [Maxine Makas'] voice is steady and of good quality, and she sings with color and dramatic awareness; her husband is a good collaborator. These artists project all the relish contained in the songs." See: D12; D132; D261; D346; D612; D637; D640.

B550   ___. "Vocal," *New Records* 43/10 (December 1975):12.

Review of the 1750 ARCH S1754 recording of songs. "Martial Singher's recital, marking his 70th birthday, is an impressive achievement. Limited to French selections . . . it is a model of polished style and an unusually well preserved voice. Singher can be justifiably proud of his efforts. Alden Gilchrist assists ably at the . . . piano." See: D111; D215; D399; D427.

B551   Tours. Bibliothèque municipale. *Exposition Georges Bernanos-Francis Poulenc et les Dialogues des Carmélites: Catalogue*. Tours: Musée des Beaux-Arts, 1970.

Exhibition catalogue for an exhibit held at the museum October 11 through November 15, 1970. The exhibit included 136 photographs, books and items of memorabilia associated with productions of the opera. The catalogue also includes a list of items related to the subject but not included in the exhibit. See: W1.

B552   Turok, Paul. "Poulenc: Figure humaine," *Fanfare* 6 (September 1982): 301.

Review of the Proprius PROP7839 recording.   "The performances are very good, although French as it emerges from these Swedish tongues is totally unintelligible.   There is also a rather unidiomatic doggedness in the Poulenc which comes across because of the very serious nature of the music." See: D266.

B553   Valante, Harry Robert. *A Survey of French Choral Music of the 20th Century With a Performance and Interpretive Analysis of Selected Works*. Ed.D. dissertation, Columbia University, 1968.

This study included the *Gloria*.   "Survey and analysis is designed to encourage the consideration of these works in the programs of college and university choruses. . . . Interpretive suggestions relate to text setting and compositional techniques used by the composer." See: W41.

B554   Vantine, Bruce Lynn. *Four Twentieth-Century Masses: An Analytical Comparison of Style and Compositional Technique*. DMA dissertation, University of Illinois, 1982.

Poulenc's *Mass in G Major* is included in this study.   Historical background for each mass is given with detailed analysis. There is some comparison with the other works discussed. See: W44.

B555   Vein, Irving. "Francis Poulenc," *Chesterian* 29 (July 1954):1-9.

A clear, thoughtful, but personally biased analysis of Poulenc's musical style and the influences on the development of his style.   The author approached his subject out of conviction that the music of young French composers was being ignored on concert programs and that "Poulenc is one of the most prolific composers of our time." The opinions of the author were personal and unsubstantiated. He stated, for example, that Poulenc admired neither the man, Ravel, nor his work, and that for Debussy he displayed ambivalence.   Vein said that Poulenc loved to listen to the music of Debussy, but there are no traces of Debussy in Poulenc's music.

Concerning the compositions of Poulenc, Vein believed the music is "sun-drenched." His works "have the exquisite loveliness of a canvas of Watteau. . . . The most significant, and least appreciated, facet of Poulenc's genius is his work as a song-writer." Poulenc as a performer "is not a pianist of the grand manner given to emotional excesses; but neither is he one of those keyboard masochists whose function seems to be that of drying up all the romance in music."

B556   "La Voix humaine," *Music and Musicians* 25 (June 1977):26-28.

Review of Glyndebourne's production of the opera, designed by Martin Battersby. The majority of the review was devoted to discussion of the plot and the circumstances surrounding Cocteau's writing the play of the same title. The author related the story that Cocteau wrote the play after ending his affair with Raymond Radiquet. See: W4.

B557   Vuillermoz, Emile. "The Legend of the Six," *Modern Music* 1 (February 1924):15-19.

Essay. "These six companions, determined to strike boldly at public opinion, began, therefore, to indulge in some noisy demonstrations. They proclaimed loud blasphemies against the masters of the preceding generation. They affected a profound disdain for a certain Debussy and a certain Ravel, at the same time claiming as patron saints the most unexpected people, such as Ambroise Thomas (!) and Erik Satie. Then with the co-operation of several cubist painters, a few poets of a small coterie and some amateurs, they gave a series of concerts and performances definitely staged for charlatanism and scandal.

They were six composers of very diverse tendencies, and contrary temperaments. No two of them had similar musical convictions. . . . Durey has an amiable and gracious talent full of ingenuity and charm, but extremely timid and as removed as possible from any revolutionary spirit. This is equally true of Poulenc, who makes vain efforts to divert his frankly Debussyan inspiration by caricature and triviality." For a rebuttal of many of the opinions expressed in this essay, see B234.

B558   W.   "Songs of Poulenc, Debussy and Roussel," *New Records* 23/12 (February 1956):13.

Review of the Haydn Society HSL154 recording of songs. The reviewer found the texts of the cycle *Fiançailles pour rire* based on "extremely odd poems . . . They are morbid and difficult of access . . . Nevertheless, Poulenc has set this and the other poems in typically ironic fashion. . . . The music is pungent, somewhat dissonant and generally matches the texts. . . . Mlle. Touraine, who is Gérard Souzay's sister, . . . sings with ease, purity of tone, and expression." See: D260; D611.

B559   Wallmann, Margarita. Translated as "Wallmann Remembers" by Harold
        Rosenthal. *Opera* 28 (August 1977):724-30.

        Anecdotal excerpts from Wallmann's autobiography, *Les Balcons du ciel*
        (Paris, 1976), that relate to Poulenc's composition of *Dialogues des
        Carmélites* and the productions of the opera produced by Wallmann.
        Her first production was for the Vienna State Opera, followed by others
        in several European opera houses. Wallmann claimed that Poulenc
        attended every production. Photographs of Wallmann, Poulenc, and
        others taken at the time of the Covent Garden production in 1958 are
        included. See: W1.

B560   Wechsler, Bert. "New York," *Music Journal* 39 (March/ April 1981):43.

        Review of the Metropolitan Opera's production of *Dialogues des
        Carmélites*. "The poor girls died even before the guillotine could do its
        grisly business. Julius Rudel's conducting was so respectful as to be
        stultifying. . . . Nothing can keep Régine Crespin down, though, and she
        repeated her hair-raising impersonation of the Prioress." See: W1.

B561   Weerth, Ernest de. "The Carmelites Fire La Scala," *Opera News* 21
        (March 11, 1957):10-12.

        Review of the world premiere performance of *Dialogues des Carmélites*.
        "Poulenc is a literary composer par excellence; his musical accompani-
        ment shows profound understanding and culture, at times moments of
        deep feeling and a certain grandeur. . . . The last scene was naturally
        the most impressive. It had a strange 'Cinerama' quality, as did many
        of the twelve effective tableaux. . . . After each act the house cheered
        and at the final curtain there was a miracle in Milan: no one left his seat
        before the curtain calls! Fifteen of these acclaimed the huge cast . . .
        and finally Francis Poulenc alone, tears streaming down his face as he
        bowed in abject humility." See: W1.

B562   Werner, Warren Kent. *The Harmonic Style of Francis Poulenc*. Ph.D.
        dissertation, University of Iowa, 1966.

        Detailed harmonic analysis of fourteen large-scale works.

B563   Whittall, Arnold. "Bartok; Poulenc," *Gramophone* 56 (July 1978):182.

        Review of the Supraphon 110-2074 recording of *Concerto in D minor for
        Two Pianos*. "The Czechs seem more comfortable with Poulenc's blend
        of sugar and sparkle than with Bartok's more monumental concerns:

insofar as they can be said to underplay rather than underline, they come closer to Poulenc and Février than to Eden and Tamir." See: D163.

B564   Whittall, Arnold. "Poulenc," *Gramophone* 59 (June 1981):50.

Review of the Merlin MRF80701 recording of the sonatas for clarinet and piano and for clarinet and bassoon. "The little sonata for clarinet and bassoon by Poulenc is distinctly heavy and charmless, only the finale having the appropriate bite: here a drier, lighter interpretation (and sound) would have been preferable. . . . I found most to enjoy in the Poulenc sonata for clarinet and piano. Kelly and Pearson seem more confident with the work's rather mordant lyricism." See: D472; D486.

B565   Whitwell, David. "'Les Six'--Their Music for Winds," *Instrumentalist* 23 (October 1968):54-56.

This article is devoted to a superficial study of the "significant body of literature for wind instruments" by Milhaud, Poulenc, and Honegger. Basically it is a list of works with instrumentation. Dates of composition and premieres were given for some but not for all works listed.

B566   Wilkins, Nigel. "Erik Satie's Letters to Milhaud and Others," *Musical Quarterly* 66 (July 1980):404-28.

Wilkins selected and translated into English a variety of Satie's letters to various people. Among these were several either addressed to Poulenc or that mention the activities of Poulenc. Annotations provide information about the people and activities discussed in each of the letters. The letters are important for their revelations of details concerning the early compositions of Poulenc, the premieres of his works, and the relation-ships that existed among the members of Les Six.

B567   Wiser, John D. "Carol Wincenc: Solo Recording Debut," *Fanfare* 4 (November 1980):212-13.

Review of the Musical Heritage Society MHS4180 recording of music for flute. "The only solid piece on the disc is the Poulenc Sonata [for Flute and Piano], and here Wincenc maintains her slightly withdrawn manner to the detriment of a near-great piece of music. It still works, but the emotional nuances essential to move the listener . . . are not present." See: D500.

B568   Wiser, John D. "French Sonatas for Clarinet and Piano," *Fanfare* 6 (May 1983):284.

Review of the Harmonia Mundi HMB5121 recording. "Poulenc sonatas are neck-and-neck favorites with recitalists, with attractive and memorable subject matter worked out to the maximum benefit of the clarinet. . . . Faucomprez and Raes play very well in the French manner, but the competition is overwhelming in performance and sound values." See: D483.

B569   ___. "Martin," *Fanfare* 8 (September 1984):256-57.

Review of the Gallo 30-157 recording of *Quatre motets pour un temps le Noël*. "La Psallette de Géneve is an amateur chorus of more than 20 years' experience under one director.   They indeed make up in enthusiasm for what they lack in polish, and the performance of their fellow Genevan's [Martin's] early work is energetic and wholeheartedly committed. They do as much for Poulenc's fine Christmas motets." See: D405.

B570   ___. "Poulenc," *Fanfare* 8 (September 1984):283.

Review of the RBM Records RBM3069 recording of *Élégie, L'Embarquement pour Cythère, Sonata* (four hands), and *Sonata* (two pianos). "Henrici and Schwarz possess crucial advantages of good pacing and aural imagination over dull-to-inept performances by various pairs of American players on the Musical Heritage Society, Orion, and Pantheon labels.   This West German team does not have overmuch energy or finesse, however, and they are recorded distantly and incorporeally." See: D232; D242; D544; D560.

B571   ___. "Poulenc: L'Embarquement pour Cythère; Valse-Musette," *Fanfare* 7 (November 1983):282.

Review of the Pierre Verany PV83011 recording. "The players are well in control of everything, but in particular they provide a clean, spacious, and comprehending reading of the late sonata, which has been severely mauled in various recent small-label American recordings." The pieces included are the same as those on the recent EMI recording by Février and Tacchino, who "provide performances of unparalleled life and buoyancy." See: D92; D231; D241; D543; D559.

B572   ___. "Rhapsodie," *Fanfare* 8 (March 1985):353.

Review of the Chandos ABRD1100 recording of the *Sonata for Clarinet and Piano*. "Hilton has a big, penetrating, rather hard sound. Her pitch is securely focused, her tone always firmly centered. She prefers to cover register breaks, and is not inclined to indulge in much variability of tone in quest of coloration." See: D476.

B573   Wiser, John D. "Satie: Socrate--Drame symphonique," *Fanfare* 9 (May 1986):235-36.

Review of the Nimbus NIM5027 recording, including "*C*" and *A sa guitare*. "Newcomers are warned the Cuenod is 'triple sec,' definitely an acquired taste, but a taste worth acquiring." See: D6; D79; D213; D284; D397.

B574   ___. "Voyage à Paris: The Mélodies of Francis Poulenc," *Fanfare* 9 (January 1986):201.

Review of the Hyperion A66147 recording of songs. "Here, the soprano takes over for the bulk of a program devoted to mostly familiar songs by Poulenc . . . fewer songs are concerned with the Parisian carnival aspect of Poulenc's art, the biggest and best segment being devoted to the harrowing Eluard cycle. . . . Certainly this is one of the most attractive Poulenc song collections to come along in years." See: D5; D49; D78; D88; D123; D208; D299; D344; D358; D363; D396; D403; D583; D639.

B575   Wood, Vivian Lee Poates. *Poulenc's Songs: An Analysis of Style*. Jackson, Miss.: Mississippi University Press, 1979.

The author presented a brief history of French song and a biography of Poulenc. Brief biographies of the poets whose texts were set by Poulenc were given along with explanations of the aesthetic of the poetry of each. Melody, harmony, form, and piano accompaniments in each song were analyzed. Appendices included a catalogue of the published songs and an index to the songs of Poulenc and to the poets.

B576   Wright, Peter. "Radio," *Music and Musicians* 26 (January 1978):37-39.

Review of a thirteen-part portrait of Poulenc in words and music presented on radio by Elaine Padmore under the title "Journal de mes mélodies." Poulenc "appears to have been something of a manic depressive, a characteristic which is often suggested by the wide emotional range of his songs. Musically he is a kind of tragi-comic figure, who is able 'to face the sacred and profane with equal ease' and in an instant can switch from the profound and deeply felt to the comic and burlesque."

B577   *Zodiaque*, no. 99 (January 1974):1-52.

This special issue in commemoration of the tenth anniversary of the death of Poulenc not only recalled the composer, but also his special attachment to Rocamadour. The contents are:

"Introduction de l'Atelier." Page 1. The idea for this special issue originated with Yvonne Gouverné. Those who contributed to the commemorative services held at Rocamadour and who contributed to this issue are listed along with Jean Seringe, Poulenc's niece and god-child, who gave her permission to reproduce family souvenirs and photographs in this issue.

Poulenc, Francis. "Tu vois le feu du soir." Page 2. Facsimile of page 1 of the autograph score of the song cycle. See: W91.

Bernac, Pierre. "En guise d'introduction." Pages 3-4. Bernac, who knew Poulenc well over a long period of time, wrote that ten years after the death of Poulenc the spirit of the composer was still very real to him. Commenting on Poulenc's sacred compositions, Bernac quoted Claude Rostand: "Poulenc continues to speak Poulenc, even when addressing himself to God." Poulenc said of his sacred pieces, "My conception of religious music is essentially direct and often familiar."

Poulenc, Francis. "Dialogues des Carmélites: 'La fin des adieux de la prieure'." Pages 5-6. Facsimile of the autograph score. See: W1.

Gouverné, Yvonne. "Hommage à Francis Poulenc." Pages 7- 26. This address, delivered at Rocamadour on July 8, 1973, was a personal remembrance of Poulenc, the man, by one of his life-long friends. Gouverné explored the personality of Poulenc and the important influences that shaped his spirit. There was some discussion of his music, especially of the sacred works composed after a religious conversion that occurred at Rocamadour in 1936. Gouverné and Bernac accompanied Poulenc on the trip to the shrine in August of that year, and she related the event and its importance to Poulenc's later musical life.

Poulenc, Francis. Letter from Poulenc to R. P. Carré. Page 27. Facsimile reprint of a letter asking Père Carré to come to visit to hear some of the score of Dialogues that Poulenc was composing at that time. He also mentioned that he wished to compose a vocal piece on the Latin hymn, *Adoration of the Cross*, and asked Carré to recommend a Latin scholar capable of stating precisely the accents of the words of the text.

Index of photographs included in this issue. Page 28.

Photographs. Pages 29-44.

Ferrand, Mon. Louis. "En guise de conclusion." Pages 45-48. Text of the sermon delivered on August 4, 1973, at Rocamadour by Mon. Louis Ferrand, Archbishop of Tours, recalling the conversion of Poulenc at Rocamadour and the meaning of that conversion to Poulenc's life.

"Discographie de Poulenc." Pages 49-52. This was conceived as a complete discography of recordings of the composer's works. The project was, however, abandoned. Recordings included in this list are those that appeared since a discography was printed in *Zodiaque* no. 42 (See: B541) that were still available at the time of publication of this issue.

In addition to the obituaries annotated in the Bibliography section of this work, the reader is referred to the following obituaries and miscellaneous references. The reader should be aware that Poulenc is listed in all dictionaries of composers, dictionaries of twentieth-century music, and dictionaries of national biography.

OBITUARIES

ARG 29:510
Arte Musical (Portugal) 29/20-22:463
BAM 18/288:1
Clavier 2/2:48
Diapason 54/3:26; 54/3:34
HF 13/May:18
Hudebni Rozhledy (Czech) 16/4:156
Instrumentalist 17/3:18
Melos 30/Apr:125
MensM 18/Mar:67; 18/Mar:70; 18/Mar:72
Musikhandel 14/Mar:37
MusM 11/Mar:8
Musique et Radio 53/Mar:83; 53/May:146; 53/July:238
Mu(Ch) n109/Apr:13; n109/Apr:36
MA 83/Feb:20; 83/Sept:47
MusE 18/3:28; 18/6:29
MusM 11/Mar; 11/June:44
MT 104:205
NZM 124/3:115
NY 20 Apr '63:107
Nouvelles littéraires 4 May '61

OpN 27/24:30
RMSM 30 Apr '63:9
SR 23 Feb '63:49
SchM 103/2:109; 103/6:352
Show 3/June:29
Slovenska Hubda (Czech) 7/1:18
Sonorum Speculum (Holland) n15/June:39
Sovetskaya Muzka 27/Apr:132
Tempo n64/Spring:28
TLS January 31, 1963:16a
Variety 13 Feb '63:71

MISCELLANEOUS REFERENCES   SUBJECTS

ACR 24/1	entire issue devoted to choral works
AMT 17/5:36 & 17/6:20	songs
Arte Mus 29/20-22:469	biography
Clavier 9/3:17	piano music
Christian Sc Mon	
14 Oct '50:10	compositional style
ChJ 17/6:19; 17/7:16	
17/8:11; 17/9:9	choral works
Disques n105/1:42	songs
JMF June '67:40	compositions
JMF Apr '68:12	hommage
JMF May '68:45	biography
JMF June '70:194	Les Six
London Music Jan '58:18	impressions of
Melos 21:2; 34:3	Les Six
Melos 69:417	translation from letters
MensM Feb '70:40	Les Six
MensM Feb '73:56	early compositions
MensM Jan '78:31	biography
MensM 10:205	conversation with
MensM 10:291	as composer
MEJ 53/4:49	vocal works
MEJ 53/4:51	songs
MM 1:1, 6; 19:47	influenced by Stravinsky
MM 1:2, 20	and polytonality
MM 2:2, 4; 3:1, 4; 13:4, 7	members of Les Six
MM 7:3, 12	general
MM 10:98	and popular music
MM 10:141	and M. Jacob
MM 11:43	and Françaix
MM 13:2, 35	compared with Shostakovich
MM 15:78	and Boulanger

MM 17:174	and Howe
MM 18:45	work (not identified) unwritten because of WWII
MM 19:235	and *L'Information musicale*
MM 22:59	influence on Bowles
MM 23:56	and Menotti
MM 23:186	Rosenfeld on
Music (AGO) 8/7:20	tribute
MR 33/3:194	piano music of
Music News Apr '71:12	piano music of
MusC 15 Feb '50:45	general
MusC Apr '60:35	and Duval
Muzyka 16/4:3	operas
NATS 14/1:6; 36/2:14	songs
NZM 124/3:115	photograph of Poulenc and Bernac
NYT 4 Apr '48,II:7	first tour in America
NYT 22 Jan '50	second tour in America
NYT 20 Jan '59:27	named to American Academy of Arts and Letters
NYT 21 May '59:28	named to Academy of Arts and Letters
NYT 5 Nov '71:95	obituary of Gertrude von La Fort
Piano Quarterly 32/126:41	biography
Recorded Sound 18:315	songs
RMSM 18/4:6	souvenir
Ruch Muzyczny (Poland) 6/16:8	Poulenc on Debussy
St. Cecilia 10/5:100	and Duval
TLS 14 Jan '58:16	photograph
TLS 17 Jan '58:3e	essay on compositions
TLS 26 June '58:6F	Oxford honorary degree
TLS 26 June '58:18	photograph
TLS 22 Nov '85:1317a	review of *Journal de mes mélodies*

GENERAL REFERENCES

Brown, Royal S. "Poulenc," *Dictionary of Contemporary Music*. New York: Dutton, 1971, pp. 586-88.

Burbank, Richard. *Twentieth Century Music*. New York: Facts on File, 1984.

Carner, Mosco. "Music in the Mainland of Europe: 1918-1939," *The Modern Age, 1890-1960* as vol. 10 of *The New Oxford History of Music*. 10 vols. London: Oxford University Press, 1974.

Cobbett, Walter Willson, ed. *Cobbett's Cyclopedic Survey of Chamber Music*, 2nd ed. London: Oxford University Press, 1963.

Espina, Noni. *Repertoire for the Solo Voice*. 2 vols. Metuchen, N. J.: Scarecrow Press, 1977.

Gilder, Eric. *The Dictionary of Composers and Their Music: A Listener's Companion.* New, rev. ed. New York: Holt, Rinehart and Winston, 1986.

Hughes, Allen. "Francis Poulenc," *The International Cyclopedia of Music and Musicians,* ed. by Bruce Bohle. 10thed ed. New York: Dodd, Mead, 1975, pp. 1705-11.

Martin, George. *The Opera Companion to Twentieth-Century Opera.* New York: Dodd, Mead, 1979.

Nardone, Thomas R., *et al* eds. *Choral Music in Print.* 2 vols. Philadelphia: Musicdata, 1974. Suppl. 1976.

Thompson, Kenneth. *A Dictionary of Twentieth-Century Composers.* New York: St. Martin's Press, 1973.

Appendix I:
Alphabetical List
of Compositions

This list includes both collective titles and titles of individual pieces within larger works or song cycles. Numbers following each title, for example, W80, refer to the "Works and Performances" section of this volume.

A peine défigurée, W51
A sa guitare, W18; W58
A son page, W95
A toutes brides, W101
Adelina à la promenade, W104
L'Adieu, W84
Ah! Mon beau laboureur, W38
Air champêtre, W59
Air grave, W59
Air romantique, W59
Air vif, W59
Airs chantés, W59
Allons plus vite, W76
Amoureuses, W70
Amphitryon, W10
Les Anges musiciens, W72
L'Anguille, W99
Les Animaux modèles, W5
Attributs, W95
Aubade, W6
Au-delà, W105
Aussi bien que les cigales, W63
Aux officiers de la garde blanche, W105
Avant le cinéma, W99
Ave Verum Corpus, W36

Ba, be, bi, bo, bu, W72
Badinage, W124
La Baigneuse de Tourville from *Les Mariés de la Tour Eiffel,* W9
Le Bal masqué, W55
Ballet, W95
Banalités, W60
La Belle au bois dormant, W22
Belle et ressemblante, W51
La Belle jeunesse, W66
La Belle se siet au pied de la tour, W38
La Belle si nous étions, W38
Berceuse, W69
Le Bestiaire, W61
Les Biches, W7
Blanche neige, W51
Bleuet, W62
Bonne d'enfant, W71
Bonne journée, W101
Bourrée au Pavillon d'Auvergne, W125
Bucolique, W27

"C," W77
Calligrammes, W63
Capriccio: d'aprés Le Bal masqué, W55B
Caprice: d'aprés le final du Bal masqué, W55A
Le Carafon, W72
Carte postale, W99
Ce doux petit visage, W64
Ce siécle a 50 ans, W23
C'est ainsi que tu es, W90
C'est la petit'fill' du prince, W38
C'est le joli printemps, W67
Chanson (Jacob), W69
Chanson (Louise Lalanne), W106
Chanson à boire (for male choir), W37
Chanson à boire (from *Chansons gaillardes*), W66
Chanson de la fille frivole, W67
Chanson d'Orkenise, W60
Une Chanson de porcelaine, W65
Chansons de F. Garcia Lorca, Trois, W104
Chansons de l'organger sec, W104
Chansons du clair tamis, W67
Chansons françaises, W38
Chansons gaillardes, W66
Chansons polonaises, Huit, W84
Chansons pour enfant, Quatre, W98
Chansons villageoises, W67
Les Chemins de l'amour, W16; W68

La Chien perdu, W45
Cimetière, W69
Cinq poèmes (Eluard), W70
Cinq poèmes (Jacob), W69
Clic, clac, dansez sabots, W38
Cocardes, W71
Colloque, W108
La Colombe, W3
Concert champêtre, W28
Concerto for Piano and Orchestra, W31
Concerto in D Minor for Two Pianos and Orchestra, W29
Concerto in G Minor for Organ, Strings, and Timpani, W30
Couplets bachiques, W66
La Couronne, W84
La Courte paille, W72

La Dame d'André, W81
La Dame de Monte Carlo, W56
Dans l'herbe, W81
Dans le jardin d'Anna, W76
Dans les ténèbres du jardin, W82
Le Départ, W84
Le Dernier mazour, W84
Dernier poème, W73
Deux marches et un interméde, W32
Deux mélodies, W74
Deux mélodies 1956, W75
Deux novelettes, W126
Deux poèmes (Apollinaire), W76
Deux poèmes (Aragon), W77
Deux préludes posthumes et une Gnossienne, W33
Dialogues des Carmélites, W1
Discours du général from *Les Mariés de la Tour Eiffel*, W9
Le Disparu, W78
Le Drapeau blanc, W84
La Duchesse de Langeais, W24

Élégie (Horn and Piano), W110
Élégie (Two Pianos), W151
L'Embarquement pour Cythère, W152
En rentrant de l'école, W45
Enfant de troupe, W71
L'Enfant muet, W104
Epitaphe, W79
L'Espionne, W63
Esquisse d'un fanfare, W11
L'Éventail de Jeanne: Pastourelle, W8
Exultate Deo, W39

Fagnes de Wallonie, W60
Fancy, W80
Le Faux avenir, W50
Fête donnée par des chevaliers normands, W33
Fêtes galantes, W77
Feuillets d'album, W127
Fiançailles pour rire, W81
Figure de force brûlante et farouche, W101
Figure humaine, W40
La Fille du jardinier, W12
Fleurs, W81
La Fraîcheur et le feu, W82
Le Front comme un drapeau perdu, W101

Le Garçon de Liége, W105
Les Gars polonais, W84
Les Gars qui vont à la fête, W67
Le Gendarme incompris, W13
Gloria, W41
Gnossienne, W33
La Grace exilée, W63
La Grande rivière qui va, W82
La Grenouillère, W83
La Guirlande de Campra, W34

Une Herbe pauvre, W101
Le Hérisson, W45
Hier, W106
L'Histoire de Babar, W109
Hodie Christus natus est, W46
Homme au sourir tendre, W82
Hôtel, W60
Huit chansons polonaises, W84
Humoresque, W128
Hyde Park, W85
Hymne (from *Trois pièce*), W146
Hymne (voice and piano), W86

Il pleut, W63
Il la prend dans ses bras, W70
Il vole, W81
Impromptus, W129
Improvisations, W130
Intermezzi, W131
Intermezzo (Incidental music), W14
Intermezzo in A Flat Major, W132
L'Invitation au château, W15
Invocation aux Parques, W66

Je n'ai envie que de t'aimer, W101
Je n'ai plus que les os, W95
Je nominerai ton front, W91
Jouer du bugle, W93

Le Lac, W84
Laudes de Saint Antoine de Padoue, W42
Léocadia, W16
Litanies à la vierge noire, W43
Luire, W51
Lune d'avril, W72

Madrigal, W66
Main dominée par le coeur, W87
. . . mais mourir, W88
La Maîtresse volage, W66
Les Mamelles de Tirésias, W2
Marches, Deux, et un interméde, W32
Margoton va t'a l'iau, W38
Marie, W51
Les Mariés de la Tour Eiffel, W9
Matelote provençale, W34
Le Matin les branches attisent, W82
Mazurka, W89
Mélancolie, W133
Le Mendiant, W67
Messe en sol majeur, W44
Métamorphoses, W90
Miel de Narbonne, W71
Miroirs brûlants, W91
Mon cadavre est doux comme un gant, W81
Monsieur sans souci, W98
Montparnasse, W92
Motets pour le temps de Noël, W46
Motets pour un temps de pénitence, W47
Mouvements du coeur, W89
Mouvements perpétuels, W144
Mutation, W63

Napoli: Suite for Piano, W134
"1904," W99
Nocturnes, W135
Nous avons fait la nuit, W101
Nous voulons une petite soeur, W98
Novelette sur un thème de Manuel de Falla, W136
Novelettes, W126
Nuage, W75
La Nuit de la Saint-Jean, W17

L'Offrande, W66
O magnum mysterium, W46
O mes très chers frères, W48

Paganini, W90
Parisiana, W93
Pastorale (from *Trois pièces*), W146
Pastorales, W145
Pastourelle from *L'Éventail de Jeanne*, W8
Paul et Virginie, W94
Le Petit garçon malade, W45
Le Petit garçon trop bien portant, W98
La Petite fille sage, W45
La Petite servante, W69
Petites voix, W45
Peut-il se reposer?, W70
Pièce brève sur le nom d'Albert Roussel, W137
Pilons l'orge, W38
Plume d'eau claire, W70
Un Poème, W74
Poèmes de Ronsard, W95
Le Pont, W74
Le Portrait, W96
Pour une nuit nouvelle, W51
Prélude du Nazaréen, W33
Préludes, W138
Préludes posthumes, Deux, W33
Le Présent, W106
Presto, W139
Priez pour paix, W97
Promenades, W140

Quatre chansons pour enfants, W98
Quatre motets pour le temps de Noël, W46
Quatre motets pour un temps de pénitence, W47
Quatre poèmes, W99
Quatre petites prières de Saint François d'Assise, W48
Quelle aventure!, W72
Quem vidistis pastores, W46

Rapsodie nègre, W57
Rayon des yeux, W82
Recits for Gounod: La Colombe, W3
La Reine de coeur, W72
La Reine Margot, W18
Reine des mouettes, W90
La Reine de Saba, W51
Renaud et Armide, W19

Le Retour du sergent, W67
Rôdeuse au front de verre, W70
Rosemonde, W100
Une Roulotte couverte en tuiles, W101
Une Ruine coquille vide, W101

Salut, dame sainte, W48
Salve Regina, W49
Sanglots, W60
Sarabande, W111
Les Sauterelles, W50
Sécheresses, W50
Seigneur, je vous en prie, W48
Sept chansons, W51
Sept répons des ténèbres, W52
Sérénade, W66
Sextuor, W112
Sinfonietta, W35
Un Soir de neige, W53
Les Soirées de Nazelles, W141
Le Soldat et la sorcière, W20
Le Sommeil, W72
Sonata (Four hands), W150
Sonata (Two pianos), W153
Sonata: For Cello and Piano, W113
Sonata: For Clarinet and Bassoon, W114
Sonata: For Clarinet and Piano, W115
Sonata: For Flute and Piano, W116
Sonata: For Horn, Trumpet and Trombone, W117
Sonata: For Oboe and Piano, W118
Sonata: For Two Clarinets, W119
Sonata: For Violin and Piano, W120
Souric et Mouric, W69
La Souris, W75
Le Squelette de la mer, W50
Stabat Mater, W54
Suite française, W121
Suite in C, W142

Tel jour, telle nuit, W101
Tenebrae factae sunt, W47
Thème varié, W143
Timor et tremor, W47
Les Tisserands, W38
Toccata (from *Trois pièces*), W146
Le Tombeau, W95
Toréador, W102
Tous les droits, W51

Tout disparut, W82
Tout puissant, très saint, W48
Le Tragique histoire du petit René, W98
Le Travail du peintre, W103
Trio: For Oboe, Bassoon and Piano, W122
Tristis est anima mea, W47
Trois chansons de F. Garcia Lorca, W104
Trois mouvements perpétuels, W144
Trois pastorales, W145
Trois pièces, W146
Trois poèmes, W105
Trois poèmes de Louise Lalanne, W106
Tu vois le feu du soir, W91

Unis la fraîcheur et le feu, W82

Valse, W147
Valse-improvisation sur le nom de Bach, W148
Variations sur le nom de Marguerite Long, W27
Vers le sud, W63
Videntes stellam, W46
Le Village abandonné, W50
Villageoises, W149
Villanelle, W123
Vinea mea electa, W47
Violon, W81
La Vistule, W84
Vocalise, W107
La Voix humaine, W4
Vous n'écrivez plus?, W93
Voyage, W63
Voyage à Paris, W60
Le Voyage en Amérique, W25
Le Voyageur sans bagages (Film), W26
Le Voyageur sans bagages (Incidental music), W21

Appendix II:
Chronological List
of Compositions

Numbers following each title, for example, W80, refer to the "Works and Performances" section of this volume.

1916   *Préludes*, W138

1917   *Rapsodie nègre* (revised 1933), W57

1918   *Sonata: For Two Clarinets* (revised 1945), W119
        Sonata (four hands; revised 1939), W150
        Toréador (revised 1932), W102
        Trois mouvements perpétuels (revised 1962), W144
        Trois pastorales, W145

1919   *Le Bestiaire*, W61
        Cocardes, W71
        Valse, W147

1920   *Impromptus* (revised 1939), W129
        Suite in C, W142

1921   *Esquisse d'un fanfare*, W11
        Le Gendarme incompris, W13
        Les Mariés de la Tour Eiffel, W9
        Promenades (revised 1952), W140

1922   *Chanson à boire*, W37
        Napoli: Suite for Piano (completed 1925), W134
        Sonata: For Clarinet and Bassoon (revised 1945), W114
        Sonata: For Horn,Trumpet and Trombone (revised 1945), W117

1923   *Les Biches*, W7
       Les Biches (transcription for piano solo), W7A
       Recits for Gounod: La Colombe, W3

1924   *Poèmes de Ronsard* (completed 1925), W95

1925   *Chansons gaillardes* (completed 1926), W66
       Sonata (reduction for piano solo of the *Sonata for Clarinet and Bassoon*),
       W114A
       Sonata (reduction for piano solo of the *Sonata for Horn, Trumpet, and
       Trombone*), W117A

1926   *Trio: For Oboe, Bassoon and Piano*, W122

1927   *Airs chantés* (completed 1928), W59
       Concert champêtre (completed 1928), W28
       Deux novelettes (completed 1928), W126
       L'Éventail de Jeanne: Pastourelle, W8
       Vocalise, W107

1928   *Trois pièces*, W146

1929   *Aubade*, W6
       L'Éventail de Jeanne: Pastourelle (version for piano solo), W8A
       Nocturne No. 1, W135
       Pièce brève sur le nom d'Albert Roussel, W137

1930   *Epitaphe*, W79
       Les Soirées de Nazelles (completed 1936), W141

1931   *Cinq poèmes* (Jacob), W69
       Quatre poèmes, W99
       Trois poèmes de Louise Lalanne, W106

1932   *Le Bal masqué*, W55
       Caprice: d'aprés le final du Bal masqué, W55A
       Concerto in D minor for Two Pianos and Orchestra, W29
       Improvisations Nos. 1-6, W130
       Sextuor (completed 1939), W112
       Valse-improvisation sur le nom de Bach, W148

1933   *Feuillets d'album*, W127
       Improvisation No. 7, W130
       Intermezzo, W14
       Nocturne No. 2, W135
       Villageoises, W149

1934   *Badinage*, W124

Huit chansons polonaises, W84
Humoresque, W128
Improvisations Nos. 8-10, W130
Intermezzi, W131
Nocturnes Nos. 3-6, W135
Presto, W139
Quatre chansons pour enfants, W98
Villanelle, W123

1935   *A sa guitare*, W58
La Belle au bois dormant, W22
Cinq poèmes (Eluard), W70
Nocturne No. 7, W135
La Reine Margot, W18
Suite française, W121

1936   *Litanies à la vierge noire*, W43
Petites voix, W45
Sept chansons, W51
Tel jour, telle nuit (completed 1937), W101

1937   *Bourrée au Pavillon d'Auvergne*, W125
Deux marches et un interméde, W32
Messe en sol majeur, W44
Sécheresses, W50
Trois poèmes, W105

1938   *Concerto in G minor for Organ, Strings, and Timpani*, W30
Deux poèmes (Apollinaire), W76
La Grenouillère, W83
Miroirs brûlants (completed 1939), W91
Nocturne No. 8, W135
Le Portrait, W96
Priez pour paix, W97
Quatre motets pour un temps de pénitence (completed 1939), W47

1939   *Les Biches: Suite* (completed 1940), W7B
Bleuet, W62
Ce doux petit visage, W64
Deux préludes posthumes et une Gnossienne, W33
Fiançailles pour rire, W81

1940   *Les Animaux modèles* (completed 1941), W5
Banalités, W60
Les Chemins de l'amour, W68
Colloque, W108
L'Histoire de Babar (completed 1945), W109
Léocadia, W16

Mélancolie, W133

1941   *Exultate Deo*, W39
      La Fille du jardinier, W12
      Improvisations Nos. 11 and 12, W130
      Montparnasse (completed 1945), W92
      Salve Regina, W49

1942   *Les Animaux modèles: Ballet Suite*, W5A
      Chansons villageoises, W67
      La Duchesse de Langeais, W24
      Sonata: For Violin and Piano (completed 1943; revised 1949), W120

1943   *Chansons villageoises* (version for voice and chamber orchestra), W67A
      Deux poèmes (Aragon), W77
      Figure humaine, W40
      Intermezzo in A flat major, W132
      Métamorphoses, W90

1944   *Les Mamelles de Tirésias*, W2
      La Nuit de la Saint-Jean, W17
      Un Soir de neige, W53
      Le Voyageur sans bagages (film), W26
      Le Voyageur sans bagages (incidental music), W21

1945   *Chansons françaises* (completed 1946), W38
      Hyde Park, W85
      Le Soldat et la sorcière, W20

1946   *Deux mélodies*, W74
      Paul et Virginie, W94

1947   *Amphitryon*, W10
      Le Disparu, W78
      Hymne, W86
      Main dominée par le coeur, W87
      . . . mais mourir, W88
      Sinfonietta, W35
      Trois chansons de F. Garcia Lorca, W104

1948   *Calligrammes*, W63
      Quatre petites prières de Saint François d'Assise, W48
      Sonata: For Cello and Piano, W113

1949   *Mazurka*, W89
      Concerto for Piano and Orchestra, W31

1950   *Ce siécle a 50 ans*, W23

La Fraîcheur et le feu, W82
Stabat Mater, W54

1951   *L'Embarquement pour Cythère*, W152
        Quatre motets pour le temps de Noël (completed 1952), W46
        Thème varié, W143
        Le Voyage en Amérique, W25

1952   *Ave Verum Corpus*, W36
        Capriccio: d'aprés Le Bal masqué, W55B
        Matelote provençale, W34
        Sonata (two pianos; completed 1953), W153

1953   *Dialogues des Carmélites* (completed 1956), W1

1954   *Bucolique*, W27
        Parisiana, W93
        Rosemonde, W100

1956   *Dernier poème*, W73
        Deux mélodies 1956, W75
        Sonata: For Flute and Piano, W116
        Le Travail du peintre, W103

1957   *Élégie* (horn and piano), W110
        Laudes de Saint Antoine de Padoue (completed 1959), W42

1958   *Une Chanson de porcelaine*, W65
        Improvisations Nos. 13 and 14, W130
        La Voix humaine, W4

1959   *Élégie* (two pianos), W151
        Gloria, W41
        Improvisation No. 15, W130
        Novelette sur un thème de Manuel de Falla, W136

1960   *La Courte paille*, W72
        Sarabande, W111

1961   *La Dame de Monte Carlo*, W56
        Sept répons des ténèbres, W52

1962   *Fancy*, W80
        Renaud et Armide, W19
        Sonata: For Clarinet and Piano, W115
        Sonata: For Oboe and Piano, W118

Index

About the Compiler

GEORGE R. KECK is Professor of Music at Ouachita University in Arkadelphia, Arkansas. He is co-editor of *Feel the Spirit: Studies in Nineteenth-Century Afro-American Music* (Greenwood Press, 1988), and a former editor of the *Arkansas State Music Teacher.*

**Recent Titles in
Bio-Bibliographies in Music**

Robert Ward: A Bio-Bibliography
Kenneth Kreitner

William Walton: A Bio-Bibliography
Carolyn J. Smith

Albert Roussel: A Bio-Bibliography
Robert Follet

Anthony Milner: A Bio-Bibliography
James Siddons

Edward Burlingame Hill: A Bio-Bibliography
Linda L. Tyler

Alexander Tcherepnin: A Bio-Bibliography
Enrique Alberto Arias

Ernst Krenek: A Bio-Bibliography
Garrett H. Bowles, compiler

Ned Rorem: A Bio-Bibliography
Arlys L. McDonald

Richard Rodney Bennett: A Bio-Bibliography
Stewart R. Craggs, compiler

Radie Britain: A Bio-Bibliography
Walter B. Bailey and Nancy Gisbrecht Bailey

Frank Martin: A Bio-Bibliography
Charles W. King, compiler

Peggy Glanville-Hicks: A Bio-Bibliography
Deborah Hayes